The Folk Art of Japanese Country Cooking

A Traditional Diet for Today's World

The Folk Art of Japanese Country Cooking

A Traditional Diet for Today's World

By Gaku Homma

Translated by Emily Busch

North Atlantic Books
Berkley, California

Domo Productions
Denver, Colorado

The Folk Art of Japanese Country Cooking
A Traditional Diet for Today's World

Published by

North Atlantic Books
P.O. Box 12327
Berkeley, California 94712

and

Domo Productions
988 Cherokee Street
Denver, Colorado 80204

Book design by Domo Productions
Cover photo by Tracy Livingston
Cover design by Paula Morrison
Printed in the United States of America by Malloy Lithographing

The Folk Art of Japanese Country Cooking: A Traditional Diet for Today's World is sponsored by the Society for the Study of Native Arts and Sciences, a nonprofit educational corporation whose goals are to develop an educational and crosscultural perspective linking various scientific, social, and artistic fields; to nurture a holistic view of arts, sciences, humanities, and healing; and to publish and distribute literature on the relationship of mind, body, and nature.

Library of Congress Cataloging-in-Publication Data

Homma, Gaku, 1950–
    The folk art of Japanese country cooking: a traditional diet for today's
world / Gaku Homma.
        p. cm.
    Includes index.
    ISBN 1–55643–098–1 (paper)
    1. Cookery—Japanese.   2. Japan—Social life and customs.
I. Title.
TX724.5.J3H66   1990
641.5952—dc20   90–20733
                                                                        CIP

Preface

Japanese culture wears two faces. One of the faces is well known in the United States. This serene side of Japanese culture has given us the tea ceremony, flower arranging, *Bonsai,* and the theatrical arts of *Noh* and *Kabuki* dance. All of these art forms are products of the imperial courts, or the *samurai* and nobility classes. All of these forms were developed over centuries because of the leisure time the nobles had to devote to their development.

There is another face, another culture that has co-existed with the calm, artful face Americans are most familiar with. This powerful culture, the culture of the common people of Japan, has served as a base on which the arts of the elite have developed and flourished.

This culture, the folk art culture of Japan, is called *jomin bunka,* and it is a culture based on survival.

I am pleased at this time to introduce *jomin bunka* to you by way of understanding its foods.

Many Americans have had a chance to get "off the beaten track" and live in the Japanese countryside. These visitors bring home stories of their experiences with *jomin bunka* that open up for the American people another angle from which to view life in Japan. I welcome and relish this sharing and understanding of another side of Japan's story.

Until recently knowledge of Japanese foods was limited in the United States. The only foods commonly known were *sushi, shabu shabu, tempura,* and *sukiyaki.* I am happy that there is now a wider exposure and understanding in this country of the other foods belonging in the daily Japanese diet.

I, the author of this book, was born and raised in the Japanese countryside. My challenge is to share with you this other side of the Japanese culture by sharing the lives of the country people and the foods they eat.

In this book I have included many childhood memories and opinions. My opinions grow from the opportunity I have had to see my native country and another country from each other's points of view. Please be patient with one person's thoughts and opinions. They are never meant to offend.

If reading this book brings back your own happy memories of childhood, family, and home town, then I have been successful. In order to enjoy the foods we eat it is important to also have and maintain a healthy mind set. If this book brings you enjoyment and happy reflection on your own lives, this alone will help you enjoy not only the foods written about within but all the foods we eat.

The publishing of this book has been supported by the Lake Ogawara Folk Art Museum (Misawa City, Aomori Ken, Japan), where I worked as a curator for four years.

I wish to offer thanks for the support of this foundation to Yukio Sugimoto, founder of the Museum, and chief curator Toshimi Sakuraba for all their help in the creation of this book.

More information concerning the Lake Ogawara Folk Art Museum can be found on the last page.

Thank you,

Gaku Homma

Foreword

It's been said that the way to a person's heart is through the stomach. The implication is that what a person eats tells a lot about who that person is. Similarly, you can learn a lot about a country by examining the foods the people eat, which is one of the major reasons this cookbook was written.

In America, we have largely lost touch with the historical and cultural roots associated with gathering, storing, and preparing foods. Ask an American where last night's dinner came from, and the response will likely be the name of a fast food chain or the local supermarket. The traditional Japanese approach to food is quite different. Preparing and eating food is the final step in a process that begins at the source: the fields where grains are harvested; the sea where fish are caught and sea vegetables are harvested; the mountains where animals are hunted and all sorts of plants are gathered.

The difference between the American and Japanese approach to food is also reflected in the typical American cookbook, which usually begins abruptly with breakfast recipes and ends with desserts. You seldom find information about the historical and cultural background of the ingredients and the recipes. Gaku Homma, the author of this book, was born and raised in Akita prefecture, a rural area in northeast Japan. And he gives this book a uniquely Japanese perspective. Before jumping into recipes, he explains the historical and cultural aspects of the ingredients, the traditional Japanese approach to diet, and how the preparation of authentic Japanese dishes is the result of customs and techniques that have evolved over thousands of years. In this context, the recipes become more than merely formulas for food preparation; they tell us much about Japan and its people.

As students of Aikido we have been very fortunate to study under Sensei Gaku Homma, one of the foremost Aikido instructors in the world. Even luckier, our association with Nippon Kan has given us opportunities to sample the extraordinary fare of Chef Gaku Homma, former owner of Domo, one of Denver's finest restaurants.

This cookbook is a unique piece of Japanese culture. Anyone interested in understanding more about Japan will find it an invaluable source of information. And for those of you who enjoy Japanese foods, well, you're in for a treat — or more accurately, hundreds of treats.

John Cruise
Jeff Gregory,
Editors

Table of Contents

Table of Contents

Table of Contents

Table of Contents

Chapter

1

INTRODUCTION

Mother's Package

Ejiko — cold wintertime baby's crib.

When I first moved to Denver, Colorado, 12 years ago I had many different experiences. Some were happy, others were painful. With the help of friends I survived those first few years, but what helped me the most were packages from my home so far away.

These packages drove the customs officials crazy. Every item was meticulously wrapped

Mother's package from Japan.

tightly with newspaper. The contents of the box — dried, preserved foods, fish, and vegetables — rarely exceeded the value of the postage. I never asked for these boxes, but believe me that even being over 30 years old, it brought real joy to see my favorite foods. Somewhere my mother always hid a few yen and a letter. "Are you eating enough? Please take these yen and buy some Japanese food! If you want you can come back home anytime ...." Each letter said the same thing, each written in beautiful brush calligraphy by a strong woman over 70 years old.

I was born in 1950, five years after the end of World War II. During the war, my father was highly ranked in the military, and my family lived in Manchuria with a household staff of 10 personal soldiers. Just before the war ended, with two sons dead of natural causes, my mother fled Manchuria with my brother and sister and returned to Japan. My father became a prisoner of war in Indonesia. He returned to my mother a few years later with only a backpack of clothes.

Although my father and mother were well-bred and educated, my father was not allowed to hold a government position after his return from the prison camp in Indochina. Financially life was very hard. Part of our family heritage is based on Shintoism and the duties of maintaining the Shinto shrine. When the war was first beginning, the entire country prayed for victory before the Shinto gods. With the ending of the war, Shintoism's popularity was shattered and shrines were left to ruin. Emperor Hirohito, the living incarnation of god, had let the people down, too many had died. The belief in Shintoism died as well.

It was during this period following World War II that my family endured the hardest times. When my mother was told by her doctor that she was pregnant with me he advised her that she was getting too old and the health risks were too great. I was born against the odds.

The change in lifestyle from the wife of a high-ranking army officer to the life of near-poverty was hard on my mother. She became ill much of the time. I remember her strength and devotion to her family even when in pain. As a child of five, I remember kneeling at her bedside and crying together in a determined embrace.

My father and older brothers and sisters were working, so as the child still at home (in school) I took over many of my mother's duties. Not having much choice, I picked up a cooking knife at an early age.

Shortly after my mother's first illness, I left home to live with other families. The purpose they said was to start my Shinto training, but as I reflect now, it may have only been because there was not enough to feed us all. I lived in many different areas.

Eventually, I began my life as a live-in student of the founder of Aikido, Morihei Ueshiba, in the small town of Iwama, in Ibaragi prefecture. I lived at the Aiki shrine with the founder, his wife, and their maid.

Previously, Mr. Ueshiba had visited my home town of Akita. My father, along with others, had studied Aikido under Mr. Ueshiba during these visits.

Although we had been poor, my father did give me a rich education. Along with my regular studies, I began practicing Judo in the second grade. In the fourth grade I began studying Kendo (the Way of the Sword). The fifth grade was when I began my practice of Aikido. That was the last year I lived at home.

The author, Gaku Homma, with his mother.

I have been living in Denver, Colorado, since 1977. Times have changed for the better. My family's situation has changed as well; they are now living in comfort. My only regret about the present is that I no longer receive packages from my mother.

During the last years of my mother's good health I received her packages regularly. When I would return to Japan, sometimes managing to have only two or three hours to spend at home, my mother would prepare a feast covering the table with food and stand outside waiting for me. She would tell me: "Gaku, when you were young, life was so hard I couldn't do this for you. Now the table is full." My mother's spirit was full of kindness and grace.

As chief instructor of Aikido Nippon Kan, I thank my mother and the elders I met while serving as curator of a folk art museum in northern Japan for the background knowledge I bring to my teaching. It is they who taught me about local folklore, traditional ways of preserving foods, customs, and the meaning attached to all aspects of these arts. It is because of them I can offer a unique experience to the students of Nippon Kan and now, through this book, to more people than can fit into my *dojo*.

During the first few years of living in the United States, I didn't share the foods from my mother's package. I considered them just simple, poor country foods, so I couldn't share them with my American students. Some of these foods smelled pretty strong to delicate noses and it was difficult to try to explain what they were, as some had no American counterpart. So I enjoyed my mother's packages behind closed doors.

One day a student of mine took me to a health food store. I checked out the Japanese section. *Hijiki, wakame, nori, miso,* and *soba* were all lined up on the shelf. To my surprise, I noted that although bearing expensive price tags, all of the products were of third-rate quality. "Americans won't eat this stuff. It is too low quality," I thought to myself and returned to Nippon Kan.

When I returned, I looked through my mother's package and decided to try cooking for my students. To my surprise and delight, they not only ate everything I gave them, but were very knowledgeable about most of the dishes and ingredients.

After that I opened my mother's packages with pride.

Thank You, Again I Am Able to Eat Today

Torii — shrine gate decorated with shimenawa.

R eal health, I think, is the health of the mind and the health of the body in coordination with one another. Without food, obviously, you cannot have either: it is a vital component for total health.

Food is a natural link between us and the earth that provides for us and keeps us alive. This very simple idea should not be forgotten. Food guarantees our health: the kind of food you eat is more important than you think.

This book does not deal with foods you may have seen in American Japanese restaurants or foods which were developed and eaten by the Samurai classes of Kyoto and Edo (Tokyo). In this book, I wish to portray the development of the food and culture of the country people of northern Japan.

Let's start with my diet. I am not a vegetarian. I eat pizza once in a while, hamburgers, fried chicken — I can enjoy any food that is edible. I do however maintain one very important policy: when you eat, enjoy what you are eating and say thank you. Thank you, again I am able to eat today.

I believe this approach should be tempered with moderation, obviously. In this chapter I wish to share some personal experiences in order that you may understand on what foundation I have based some of my views and opinions about foods and eating habits.

I wonder how many people reading this book are worried about where their next meal will come from. It completely changes one's perspective when sitting down to eat if you are aware how lucky you are there is food in front of you. It is easier to give thanks with feeling if you have experienced having had no food, having had to search for it, rediscovering basic instincts for survival.

If one has had this experience, it puts complaints about diet and nutritional fads into perspective. When these complaints disappear, you can begin to understand the true, natural value of simply eating.

When I came to the United States 12 years ago, I could not eat white bread. It gave me heartburn and hives. If I took a trip away from home I always carried rice balls along with me.

I couldn't eat tomato-based sauces and soups. Spaghetti was a challenge. My life in Japan had been fairly traditional and my experience with Western foods was very limited. I thought at the time that I couldn't control these reactions to certain foods, but now I realize I simply wasn't trying hard enough to meet the challenge of a new diet.

There are many instances when we as human beings react to something negatively when the cause of this reaction may be very far removed from the actual situation at hand.

Kids, for example, may resist when told to eat their carrots. They may not be reacting to the carrots so much as toward a strict parent. Someone who doesn't eat meat because he doesn't like the thought of killing has based his tastes on a moral conviction. There is nothing wrong with convictions, but I think it is interesting for all of us to stop and look at why we like or dislike certain foods and realize the powerful effect our attitudes have on our eating habits.

When I first came to the United States everything did not go as planned. My *dojo* (*dojo* means school, in this case the martial art of Aikido) was struggling to get on its feet. Dealing with this, culture shock, and strained relationships was a heavy weight on my mind. One way I unconsciously dealt with all of these new stresses was to hold on to my original Japanese diet. It was like a lifeline home, something familiar that held me together in a new world.

I was very stubborn. "I am Japanese. I won't eat bread or spaghetti" — like a kid who hates his lima beans. Everything else in my life was changing, had to change, so as a part of my need for my own sense of identity, I refused to change my diet. My struggle was with outside pressures; it had nothing to do with the foods themselves.

Today I can eat anything and that started with a realization. When I first opened the *dojo* my

Reaching people by sharing meals together. Student portrait of Gaku Homma holding chopsticks.

English was almost non-existent. Communication with my students was the major challenge. Aikido is a physical art, so teaching with body language worked fairly well. My task was to build a strong group out of my new students. The task seemed formidable, as human communications and entertainment were my weak points.

During those first years money was tight. Because all of my resources had gone into building the school, my students sometimes brought me food. It struck me that one way for us to communicate was to share our meals together. I felt this might not only bridge the communication gap, but would also be a chance to demonstrate to them another part of who I was.

After class I would bring my students home for dinner and drink. Usually there were more than 10 people crowded around the table. I would stay in the kitchen and cook the foods they brought me. Staying busy in the kitchen gave me a reason not to have to try my meager English. I was hoping that through cooking I could express my feelings toward them.

After everyone was full and had said their goodbyes, I would wearily, hungrily, check the refrigerator for something I could eat. Staring back at me would be one lonely light bulb. I would say to myself: "American refrigerators are for keeping light bulbs cold," give up, and go to bed.

Every night I fed my students. Their class fees went for groceries instead of rent. I don't know how we survived, but we did. You might be asking yourself why was he doing this? After you finish this book I hope you may understand.

Those first students became a very important foundation of Nippon Kan, and they are still with me as friends and advisors. They are here now because of a bond that began during those early days.

Often in the beginning I found myself relying on techniques I learned from my mother and from the elders who taught me when I worked at the folk art museum. I collected grasses from the river banks to eat. Mixing them with ingredients from my mother's package, I came up with some ingenious recipes.

One day while picking grasses I came to a great realization. I realized how lucky I was. I looked around me with true appreciation. I thought about the foods my students had brought me. Until now, I had just put the foods in the closet and cooked them for my students. If I could look at river grass with appreciation, there was no reason I couldn't eat the beautiful foods my students had given to me.

With this new mind I began to try the new foods. Once I resigned myself to an attitude of appreciation, my self as a whole moved forward. Not only did I have new-found respect for these foods, but a dawning respect for my mother's teachings about the "make-do" attitudes toward food and life that are the root of Japanese culture.

What is a Good Life Diet?

Kami Dana — folk art Shinto altar.

As you can tell by the last chapter, my introduction to American lifestyle and eating habits was unusual to say the least. I wanted you to understand what kind of experiences I have had so you can more easily understand my points of view.

When I opened my restaurant, Domo, in Denver, I never advertised it as a health food restaurant. It seemed simple enough to me: who would serve unhealthy food in a restaurant? I never thought of Japanese food as being special health food, so I never advertised it as such. It was my customers themselves that created the image of Domo as a health food restaurant.

After a few months, I noticed that an interesting clientele had begun to frequent the restaurant. They all seemed very health-conscious. Everyone had beautiful manners. Some even stacked their own plates and carried them to the dishwasher themselves. I wondered if these customers understood the crucial point that the most important thing to be thankful for was that their freedom to choose what they were eating was guaranteed.

I served many, many customers at Domo. Occasionally, there would be the customers with questions such as, "This is a health food restaurant. Why do you serve meat?" "Do you use organic vegetables only?" "What kind of oil is that?" "What kind of *miso* or *shoyu* do you use?" "Why do you serve the fruit with the meal? You're supposed to serve them at different times." "Tomato, eggplant, and green pepper seeds are bad for you."

I listened and thought to myself of all the people in the world who could not choose what they ate, of all the people who have nothing and die of starvation. We are lucky to have lives in which we can choose what we want to eat at any time.

As I listened to customers that were very worried about their diets, I worried that they would become seriously ill. Not from what they eat, but from worrying so much! Of course, I am also concerned about chemicals used in pesticides and preservatives. I agree we need to think seriously about the consequences of using chemicals, not only for what they may do to us, but to future generations as well.

But, let's not forget that one of the reasons we now have to worry about chemicals is because we as a society created the demand for products that contain them. If we hadn't, they wouldn't exist.

As consumers, we have demanded fresh fruits and vegetables year-round — in season or not. We have demanded meats that we can buy any time we wish, and foods that we can prepare in a few minutes or less. These demands resulted in the technological developments made in preserving and altering foods. In older times, foods that were caught or harvested and couldn't be eaten that day were preserved naturally to save for tomorrow.

Domo attracts a lot of attention.

Everything has escalated in our world. When our demands cannot be met by nature, science has rushed in to fill the need. This is simple economics. Instead of pointing our fingers at the mega-producers or at governments alone, we can start to change these trends by realizing that we are part of this cycle as well.

Supermarkets today supply us with every fruit and vegetable imaginable, all year round. It would seem strange to us if they didn't. It seems we are losing touch with the concept of seasons and what is naturally produced at what time. We have created the market for artificially produced products.

How do we solve this problem? If you don't like chemicals, don't eat! Of course, this is not a reasonable solution. So, what do we do? We rush here looking for "health food restaurants" and we rush there in panic looking for new vitamin supplements, succeeding only in worrying ourselves more and more. This cycle never ends.

Let's calm down and start over. During my Aikido training I had a great deal of experience with fasting. After a long fast, the most delicious thing in the world is half a glass of warm water. Understanding and appreciating a glass of water puts life in perspective. Worrying about this or that kind of new diet system is a luxury. Keeping our minds and our priorities in balance is part of our health as well.

Before you think about what you are going to eat, remember that we are products of the media. Companies launch large-scale advertising campaigns promoting new dietary programs every day. Foreign foods are exotic and can be used to arouse Americans' interest. Some Japanese foods have been built up to be super foods that they are not. The power of the media to control is frightening. Recently, oats were in the news as being the best thing for you. Now they seem to be on their way "out" and rice is on the way "in."

About 18 years ago, the Japanese government launched a wheat flour campaign. Suddenly everybody had to eat bread. Rice piled up in warehouses for three or four years. Japanese farmers, whose livelihoods depend directly on rice, had to be subsidized by the government. The entire economy began to rock. The next campaign? Eat more rice along with bread.

These campaigns are usually motivated by economics. They ignore the ability of the earth's natural seasons to produce sufficient foods, basing their projections on nutritional studies whose results keep changing. It is hard to know what we should believe in, yet we still believe.

Right now, *sushi* is popular. Heralded as the new low-fat, low-cholesterol health food, at $2 a bite, *sushi* has become a status symbol for yuppies. If it were true that *sushi* is the answer to all of our dietary problems, all Japanese people should be completely healthy. *Sushi* may be low in cholesterol and fat, but dip it in soy sauce and watch the sodium count go up. The important point to realize is that *sushi* is just another dining trend and should be recognized as such, not just followed blindly. Then we can enjoy *sushi* as *sushi*.

Before we sit down to give thanks for what we eat, we need to think about what food is. What a *meal* is. Most importantly, we need to think about what health is. Whenever we extend beyond the cycles of what the earth can naturally give us we break the natural circle. To find a really satisfying eating style we need to rid ourselves of the excesses that throw us off this natural track. If we are looking for watermelons in the winter, we haven't discovered a true appreciation for the balance of nature of which we are a part.

Many people believe Japanese "health foods" are today's alternative. In the next chapter I will discuss the roots of many Japanese foods.

Food: A Basic Means for Survival

Oshirasama — folk art religious altar.

The traditional Japanese diet is built on very simple foundations. As anywhere, foods are gathered from the mountains, harvested from the field, or taken from the seas. The core of the Japanese diet is in how these foods are preserved for storage and transport. The ways in which foods are dried, smoked, and pickled are the essence of both taste and nutritional content.

Because I am not a nutritionist, I cannot give you a complete technical breakdown on which vitamins and minerals are retained and which are lost through these preservation processes. What we can explore is the role these foods have had in the lives of Japanese country people. I doubt the mountain hunter and country farmers worried as much about mineral content as they did about putting something in their stomachs.

As recently as 15 years ago, the foods that are just now showing up in American health food stores were considered simple country foods in Japan. I can remember media campaigns in the newspapers and magazines of Japan that presented a completely opposite point of view than the one currently held here in the United States by many people. "If you eat only dried or pickled fish and vegetables, you will die of starvation. EAT MEAT! You need eggs and milk!" they claimed.

I was born in northeastern Japan where in the winter all of the villages became completely snowbound. Houses all had doors on the second floor as well as the first. When the snow piled up past the door on the first floor we just used the door up on the second floor! I think you can get an idea of just how much snow there was.

It was common for the Japanese army to parachute in relief supplies during those cold, quiet months. Nowadays with advanced snow removal technology the highways are kept clear. This gives the northern regions accessibility to fresh produce all year round.

Can you imagine what life must have been like 200 to 300 years ago? In these areas, it was not a question of how one spent the winter, it was a question of how one *survived* the winter. After completing the autumn harvest, a greater task was at hand. The villagers needed to pre-

Survival foods for winter. All vegetables were hung to dry under the eaves of the house.

serve the foods that would sustain them through the long winter months.

Vegetables and other edible roots were buried in holes lined with straw. Some vegetables were buried with salt or *miso* (soybean paste) and stored as pickles; many other vegetables and mushrooms were dried. Meat was dried like a "jerky" or packed in salt. Soybeans were also made into *miso* and *shoyu* (soy sauce). An ingenious variety of preservation techniques was created out of one necessity. Survival.

While reading through these processes, you may have noticed that almost all involve large quantities of salt. This accounts in part for the high percentage of the population that suffered from high blood pressure, stomach cancer, and strokes.

Clear, white skin is considered a symbol of beauty among Japanese women. Women from the northeastern region of Japan were famous for having skin of this translucent white quality. They also had round faces and swollen legs and ankles.

The women of northeastern Japan were envied for their beauty, but these traits were actually produced by vitamin deficiencies and an excessive salt intake. According to studies performed in my home town, common symptoms during these times were bluish-white faces, dark or red circles around the eyes, and dry skin. Various degrees of malnutrition have been documented for generations. Reports of sunken chests and distended bellies were common, as well as a marked lack of elasticity in the skin and muscles.

There were psychological imbalances as well. Stubbornness and short tempers were attributed to dietary deficiencies. I can remember as a child the on-going efforts of the local governments to try to improve the diet of the villages. For previous generations, the situation must have been perilously worse.

As the founder of a Japanese cultural center here in the United States, I have seen many people who are interested in Japan attracted to Nippon Kan's activities. I was surprised to find people in this country with bodily symptoms similar those of someone from the northeastern Japan of many years ago. Upon first meeting I could tell these people were strict vegetarians. I would sometimes ask if they were vegetarians, which would surprise them and make them wonder how I knew.

The Japanese "health foods" of today began as a means of survival against the harsh elements of nature. But early in Japan's history, the country farmers had to struggle not only with the elements, but with the political power structure of the times.

From the beginning of the Kamakura period (1192 A.D.) through the Edo period (1603 A.D.), Japan was organized politically under the feudal system. The country was divided and ruled by many different *hanshu* or lords of the clans. The *hanshu* in turn were subordinate to the *shogun* or leader of the central government. As with any political system, taxes played a dominant role.

The *hanshu* extracted taxes from their citizens not in the form of money but in bulk goods. Rice especially was used as legal tender. The *samurai* of the times were even paid in rice. This rice came, of course, from the poor farmers.

The *shogun* sometimes sent out spies to collect information about the harvests of the underlords. In this manner he was able to assess how many taxes he could demand. In this way he could also control those who were accumulating too much wealth and power by increasing their taxes.

The burden fell on the farmer. Not only rice, but vegetables, farm animals, and even crafts were confiscated for taxes. Tax collector humor compared farmers to beans. "You can always squeeze farmers and beans. There will always be one more drop if you just squeeze a little harder."

A poor harvest due to weather or war was no excuse for not paying the taxes that were demanded. When yield was low, tax collectors often took the farmers' very means for existence. Consequently, the farmers created methods for hiding their food that eventually became intrinsic to the foods themselves.

Secret storage caves were constructed deep in the mountains. Because the foods had to be easy to move quickly in the event of danger, the farmers began processing them for easy transport. *Miso* was dried and hung in balls. Different vegetables were dried, mixed with straw, and woven into baskets. Dried vegetables were mixed with adobe and sometimes built into the walls of the house! The vegetables would act to reinforce the adobe until such time they were needed as food.

The days of the *samurai* eventually passed, but the oppression for the farmer continued through many different styles of government and did not end until after World War II. What lies at the heart of the Japanese country peoples' ability to survive is a strong tenacity coupled with ingenuity. These skills were developed over centuries of oppression.

This history of Japan still lives in the country foods available today as Japanese "health foods." It is important today to learn from the long history of the Japanese farmer and bring the lessons to today's world. If we just eat these basic food components by themselves we might lose weight, but it is not a healthy diet. Much more important is to keep a balance in your diet.

The *hozonshoku* (preserved foods) created during these times may also not be the best tasting. The creativity involved in combining these simple ingredients to make a variety of subtle and delicious tastes becomes very important.

Part of the true essence of Japanese country cooking was carried in the hearts of the people who first created the foods. By experiencing their creativity in arranging these ingredients, we can truly enjoy the richness of these foods, emotionally as well as physically.

In the next chapter (in surprising contrast to this discussion) I will talk about the modern Japanese diet.

Chasing the American Dream

Konseisama — folk art religious altar.

In the section "What Is a Good Life Diet?" I expressed my thoughts on some of the attitudes I have encountered during my life in the United States. Now let us take a look at the Japan of today.

Anyone who has visited Japan recently can confirm what you see in Japanese magazines available here in the United States. The American and European styles and fashions are what is "in" in Japan. The beautiful, smiling models for the clothes and accessories are mostly European or American. The standard for feminine beauty these days is a thin body, long legs, large chests, white skin, high noses, and sharp minds. (Japanese girls with Mongolian ancestry have a tough role model to follow, as they are genetically characterized by long waists, short legs, small chests, and flat noses.)

American and European changes in fashion have instigated changes in the Japanese lifestyle as well. Traditionally, all Japanese people sat in *seiza* (kneeling position). Today chairs and couches are a popular means to show off legs. Twenty-year-old Japanese girls that visit Nippon Kan can't sit in *seiza* for even five minutes.

Following the lead of American and European movie stars, the campaign to adopt the ways of the West has been monumental. Twenty years ago, the popular image for Japanese men was to have a pot belly. A healthy-sized belly symbolized success, indicating that you were probably eating a lot of good food, especially a lot of meat, which was expensive.

When I was in elementary school, Japan was going through post-war rehabilitation. The country was getting back on its feet, but there remained a wide socio-economic gap between the families who were recovering and the ones that were still struggling. The government began a school lunch program as a way to ensure that children were getting something to eat and to try to close the gap between those who had a nice lunch to bring and those who did not.

Prior to this program, we all brought our lunches from home. My mother was older than the other kids' mothers and she filled my lunch box with tiny, traditional porcelain dishes and cups. The other kids had modern lunch boxes with jelly sandwiches and wieners cut to look like bunnies. I used to go home and complain about not having jelly sandwiches and wieners like the other kids. I think my mother was relieved when the school lunch program began.

Our government-issue school lunch consisted of one small cup of skim milk, *koppepan* (a submarine sandwich-sized loaf of bread), a pat of butter, and a bowl of soup. The students helped in the kitchen and as servers, rotating duty on a weekly basis.

Each student brought a large cloth napkin from home which he or she spread out on the table for the dishes to be served on. The other kids had napkins stitched on new sewing machines with fancy tulip or butterfly designs.

My mother gave me a hand-stitched napkin made from old clothes. I complained about this, too. Now as a grown man I finally appreciate all the work that went into painstakingly hand-stitching those napkins she made for me, and how beautiful they really were.

A lot of the kids had problems stomaching the new lunch, it being so drastically different from their usual diet. Some of the teachers also had trouble forcing it down, but they had to force smiles for the children.

Contests were created. A big ribbon went to the boy or girl who finished the most of their lunches. A big tally board was set up on a wall in the classroom. Some kids resorted to holding their noses and swallowing the food like medicine — sometimes without success.

As for me, I was a healthy, hungry boy who ate everything. I helped out a lot of my friends by cleaning their plates for them.

Before this program started, I remember the wintertime best for lunch times. All the students would bring their lunch boxes to the classroom and set them around the wood-burning stove to keep warm. I remember the aromas from all those different dishes mixing and filling the room before lunch....

During my elementary school years, American movies were very popular in Japan. And the Americans were so big! They were big because they ate meat. In the movies they all ate steaks. Through television, pro wrestling was introduced to Japan. Every house could not afford its own television so groups of televisions would be set up in high circles in the local parks. Thousands would come to watch. Interestingly, the Japanese wrestlers always won out over the American wrestlers. (The Japanese of post-war Japan were, in my opinion, suffering from a big man/little man complex.)

The Japanese wrestlers won because they ate meat every day. Between matches they would appear in meat and sausage commercials. The meat of those days was whale meat, the sausage was made of fish. Chicken or beef were far too expensive for the normal consumer.

There was a strong fascination with American foods. I remember my father buying a single bottle of Coca Cola and bringing it home to share with the whole family. After dinner we all sat and divided the drink into five tiny glasses. Nobody liked it — "tastes like medicine" was the general consensus. It wasn't until much later that we became aware of the problem with *chikuro* (cyclamates).

During my childhood years, the ambition of the nation as a whole was to be like America. It was the number one catalyst for economic growth in Japan.

Today that goal has almost been reached. Access to all facets of American culture has reached phenomenal levels. American foods, for example, from gourmet to fast food are found in abundance all over the country.

With the adoption of American culture and foods in Japan, the nation's afflictions and diseases have changed along with the lifestyle. Where it had previously been virtually unheard-of, heart disease is now a killer in Japan. Modern Japanese have had to join the search for a healthier balance in their lives. Executives no longer display pot bellies, but work out during lunch hour.

As pointed out in the section, "Thank You, Again I Am Able to Eat Today," the Japanese have also lost touch with their original diets because of the persuasive power of mass media. Globally we need to be aware of how easily influenced we all can be, and try to extract ourselves from the cycle of unnecessary consumption.

To balance mind and body, we need to refocus and appreciate the season-to-season gifts we receive from nature. If we eat what is given to us naturally, we can find truer nutritional fulfillment, as well as a truer understanding.

I am not going to tell you that Japan's *hozon-shoku* (preserved foods) will give you super power for a healthy life. I don't want you to believe that because these foods have been preserved with methods developed centuries ago that using these foods is the only diet to follow. If you were born in the United States, drink American water, eat natural American foods. These are your roots. Our challenge here is how to blend Japanese foods and cooking methods with American produce and lifestyle. Please do not forget the ground on which you stand.

Having lived in both Japan and the United States, I have the unique opportunity and responsibility to offer my honest opinions. I am not here as a salesman for "A Beautiful Japan." My opinions are just those of one man who was born and grew up in a small town in the Japanese countryside.

Chapter

2

THE
BACKGROUND OF
COUNTRY COOKING
– FOLK ART & CUSTOM –

The Foods of the Noble, Samurai, and Merchant Classes

Butsudan — Buddhist altar.

J apanese lifestyles are changing very rapidly. It has become difficult to trace the past through live artifacts.

I have been lucky, in that by working for the Lake Ogawara Folk Art Museum I have had access to living artifacts well over 100 years old. In the area where I was raised, there are still standing (protected by government-backed historical preservation programs) 300- to 500-year-old farm houses. The experiences I am about to

Zen priests making soba.

relate come directly from my time as a museum curator.

Earlier I explained that the focus of this book is on the country foods and country people of Japan. As a comparison, though, I wish at this time to give a brief background of the foods customarily enjoyed by the high-ranking elite of Edo (Tokyo) and Kyoto. We have access to records dating back to 650 A.D. that describe in detail the lifestyle and eating habits of the noble classes. Keep in mind that the lifestyle of the nobles was built on the backs of the farmers, fishermen, and mountain people forced to support them.

Historically, Japanese society has freely adopted traits it deemed valuable from other cultures. Early in Japanese history, Japan had close relations with China. Japan yearned to assimilate the Chinese culture, as it was older and more developed at that time.

During the Meiji period the source was Europe. After WWII the role model was the United States.

In 650 A.D. the eating habits of the Chinese imperial court were adopted by the nobles of Japan. The high-ranking drank milk, ate cheese and butter, and used a lot of oil for deep-frying foods. Their main staple was brown rice.

The common people on the other hand survived on a dish called *zakkoku,* which consisted of the husks and hulls left over after processing the brown rice, mixed with deccengrass, foxtail, vegetables, corn, and beans.

With the coming of Buddhism, new religious philosophies began to penetrate the minds of the Japanese people. For a thousand years from the coming of Buddhism, red meat was discouraged for religious reasons. After the religious prohibition waned and until the Meiji period began in 1868, apprehension about consuming animal flesh still prevailed.

The first official mandate making it a crime to eat most meats (675 A.D.) declared the flesh of horses, cows, dogs, monkeys, and birds off limits. It is interesting to note that an exception was made to this rule for the consumption of deer and mountain pigs (wild boar). During this time it was common to see deer and boar semi-domesticated, living in the farmyards like the chickens of today. Shrines that serve as a sanctuary for deer have their roots in this period. In 721 A.D. another mandate was passed that banished the consumption of deer and boar as well.

Under the new Buddhist laws, milk, cheese, and other dairy products were still allowed for consumption.

The people of the imperial court and associated nobles needed to find a replacement for the meat and chicken they were no longer allowed to eat. Because of their status, they still had access to expensive foods. Consequently, *so* and *daigo* were developed, made from what we would call today butter or cheese.

Over the course of history, families in power fell and the society of the *samurai* emerged. Although the parties in power changed, the diet of the rich did not.

The year 1192 A.D. marked the beginning of the Kamakura period. Zen Buddhism had gained immense popularity with the *samurai* society. Because Zen Buddhism forbade the consumption of any warm-blooded animal, the diet of the

Zen priests eating.

times was heavily affected. The typical diet consisted of *kezurimono* (shaved dried bonito), *awabi* (abalone), and other fish and shellfish, *umezu* (juice from pickling plums), *namasu* (thin sticks of Japanese white radish), and *kanbutsu* (lightly salted, dried fish) flavored with a mixture of soy sauce and *miso* called *hishio.*

The roots of today's Tokyo-style *sushi* can be traced to this period. Raw fish was pressed together with cooked rice and allowed to stay in a press for a few days. The natural fermentation process created a slightly sour taste. Today vinegar is added to the rice to reproduce the original flavor.

These foods were very simple in accordance with the religious mandates of Zen Buddhism. The basic ingredients of these foods are still used in the modern Japanese diet.

For example, before 1338 A.D., which marked the beginning of the Muromachi period, rice was similar to the rice you would find today in a Chinese restaurant, and it was cooked by steaming. That rice was called *kowai* or *kowameshi*. We still use this method of steaming to make special festival rice cakes called *mochi*.

Although the rice has changed, I can remember my mother calling these special rice cakes *okowa* after the original *kowameshi* of ancient times. After 1338 A.D. most foods began to change into forms that are more recognizable today. *Himei*, the rice that was introduced at that time, is the same as the rice used for cooking today.

Under the continuing influence of Zen Buddhism the Japanese diet consisted mainly of cooked vegetables, rice, and an early form of *miso* (soybean paste) called *name miso* or *lick miso*.

During the 14th century *miso* soup, made from soybean paste, was introduced. Other new varieties of tastes were also developing. The Japanese began using *shoyu* (soy sauce) and *wasabi* (green Japanese horseradish) to flavor their foods. *Karashi* (hot yellow mustard) and *kosho* (pepper) were imported from China with expensive price tags.

Tofu (soybean cake — also called at the time *shira kabe* or white adobe) was introduced by Zen Buddhist priests. Today nearby most temples are small stands offering tofu hand-made by the priests.

In 1603, during the Edo period, major changes were taking place due to the emergence of the merchant classes. Money had completely replaced rice as legal tender. Rice from the farmers was sold to merchants who in turn sold it plain or as polished white rice to the people of the cities and towns. The trend of processing brown rice into polished white rice gained pop-

ularity because it was more profitable. It digests more readily and has to be eaten more often every day.

This system of commerce has developed into the rice economy of modern Japan. Today the government buys the rice from the farmers and distributes it. The scale is different, but the same basic economic system has been in place for centuries.

This has been a brief historical overview of the foods of the Japanese imperial court, *samurai* classes, and later the wealthy merchant classes. Historically Japanese foods have come from many parts of the world. Depending on the trade agreements of the time you can trace some Japanese foods to China, Holland, Portugal, and other countries.

With this brief overview to provide context, let's turn to the main focus of this book: the traditional farmer, his life, and foods.

The Traditional Japanese Farmer and His Way of Living

Irori — Sunken fireplace.

The lifestyle I will be discussing in this chapter no longer exists in rural Japan, but the tastes and methods of the past are still present as part of modern daily life.

When I was a curator of the Lake Ogawara folk art museum, I was fortunate to be able to talk personally with elders who still lived a very traditional country lifestyle.

In 1964, around the time the Olympics were held in Tokyo, the government began a campaign encouraging farming families to improve their lives and join the 20th century. The farmers who could afford to made plans to demolish dwellings that had been lived in for hundreds of years. This most did without regret, thinking of the future rather than the past.

When we heard about a planned demolition at the museum, we would move in as quickly as possible and try to have the house moved instead of destroyed. It would take us up to a month to disassemble the house, move it, and rebuild it. During these projects we found many artifacts including folk art crafts, utensils, tools, and valuable old wood beams and posts.

The house of a traditional farmer, fisherman, or mountain person is called a *jomin minka* by professional folklorists. The architectural styles varied by geographic location and economic position. We used these architectural clues to draw conclusions about the region from which the original householder may have originated. We could trace the movement and integration of different villages by tracking and dating the blending of certain architectural styles. If a house of a certain type was in one location and another type was in a second location, and yet another house in between had a style that mixed the two, this told us a great deal about the history of the area.

The area I grew up in, Tohoku and other parts of northeastern Japan, is an area that endures harsh winters. I want to recreate for you a traditional northern farmhouse, focusing on how the structure of the house related to the families who lived inside, and their relationship to each other and the world around them.

Although I say farmhouse, remember that traditional farmers also went to the mountains for

Jomin minka.

lumber, hunted and fished, and took care of farm animals, as well as tending their fields. The duties of the farming families were not restricted to just farming.

The farmers' houses, or *jomin minka,* were built to support a large family system. It was not uncommon for one *minka* to accommodate up to three families spanning generations. The inside structure of the traditional *minka* was organized by generations. The oldest couple living in the house had their living quarters behind the *butsuma* (Buddhist shrine room). This was the place in the house reserved with great respect for the elders.

Financial control of the household was the responsibility of the eldest son. He and his fam-

ily lived in a room next to the kitchen. The upstairs was inhabited by younger sons and their families. If the household was very large, a third floor served to accommodate the younger families. If there was a change in the family structure, if for example the oldest members of the family died, everybody changed rooms, and the roles that went with them.

As you step into a *jomin minka,* you find yourself in a dirt-floored entry area called the *doma.* Especially in the areas enduring hard winters an *umaya* (horse stall area) was located adjacent to the *doma.*

On the other side of the *doma* was the *nagashi* (kitchen). Some of the houses were very small and did not have a *nagashi* inside the house; a nearby creek would provide water to wash and prepare foods. Next to the *nagashi* was the *kamado* (kitchen adobe fireplace). The *kamado* was used to make hot water to boil vegetables and to cook rice. In rural areas the

Nagashi — kitchen.

kamado remains a status symbol. When an aging couple retires and the new householders (the oldest son and his wife) take over the position, it is called *kamado o yuzuru* ("I give my *kamado* to you"). The term *kamado mochi* or *kamado ga ookii* (a lot of *kamados* or a big *kamado*) means that you are rich. The control of the *nagashi* and *kamado* was the symbol of leadership. That is why the oldest son and his family slept next to the kitchen.

If you step up from the *doma* you enter the area called the *joi* which serves as both a living room and dining room for the families. In the center of the *joi* is the *irori* (square sunken fireplace), which serves not only as a place for cooking and eating but as the hub for family communication.

The first image that may come to your mind when you think about Japan is one of rooms covered with *tatami* mats. In the country farmer's house, *tatami* had no place in the *joi*. Around the *irori* was a *mushiro* (rice-straw mat) to sit on. Everyone else sat on the wood floor.

The fire in the *irori* was never put out. At night the embers were covered with ash and earth and saved for morning. Most of the family cooking took place over the *irori*. In this small space one could bake, steam, smoke, and broil different foods. Hanging from the ceiling over the center of the *irori* was the *jizaikagi* (retractable kettle and pot hanger). At right angles with the *jizaikagi* near the ceiling was a number of bamboo or wood poles fastened in a grid pattern with rope and called the *hidana*.

Hanging from the *hidana* were tubular woven-bamboo baskets about two feet in length called *venkei*. The *venkei* were stuffed tightly with rice straw and used like pin cushions to store skewered meat or fish that had either been

Above: Irori area in a jomin minka.

Above and right: Irori area in Nippon Kan's Japanese rooms.

cooked and needed to keep warm or was there to be smoked.

The daily harvest of fresh vegetables, fish, and fowl would be cooked in the large cast-iron kettle hanging from the *jizaikagi*. If there was an overabundance of meat or fish on a particular day, it was skewered on bamboo and stuck in the *irori* pit near the fire. In this fashion, the meats' excess fat and juice would run down the bamboo stick and dissipate.

Sometimes fish or fowl were marinated with salt and *miso* or *tamari* (juice from making *miso*), flash-seared on both sides to seal in juices and flavor, and stuck into the *venkei* to be smoked. The foods that were stuck in the pit could be used for that evening's dinner while the food, usually meats, left stuck in the *venkei* would keep a couple of extra days. This is the origin of *teriyaki*.

Potatoes and other edible roots were placed directly in the ash to bake or wrapped in leaves first. Examples of similar fireplace cooking can be found in cultures and civilizations around the world, throughout the ages.

For the traditional Japanese farmer every part of the kitchen, every realm of life for that matter, was inhabited by gods, or living spirits. The *kamado, irori,* and *nagashi* had religious as well as physical functions.

Every part of the farmer's life was ruled by the gods. Everything in life was inhabited by what is called in Japanese folk religion *ke,* which could be translated to mean "living spirit." Every object, animate or inanimate, every force of nature, all possessed *ke*. All objects and forces possessed both bad (negative) *ke* and good (positive) *ke.*

Just to misuse a tool would cause the bad *ke* spirit to be released. Obviously then, to take the life not only of animals but of plants was taken very seriously. Any butchering was done by spe-cial, professional butchers. On a specific day, at a specific time, facing a specific direction, all of which had been selected according to the religious calendars, these butchers would come for the slaughter. The bad *ke* spirits were not angry with these professionals because they had been selected to devote their lives to this task and worked very closely with the priests.

When meat, fish, or vegetables were cut, both the good *ke* and the bad *ke* would be released. The word for *nagashi* (sink) is derived from the word *nagasu,* which means to wash away.

Meats or vegetables were always cut near the sink because it was important to keep the good *ke* with the cut foods and wash away the bad *ke*. This washing away was a cleansing process not only for the meats and vegetables but for the farmers themselves. It helped them deal with the guilt they might have been feeling for taking the life of the food for that day's meal.

This subject in itself could fill volumes; therefore it is better left for the professional folklorists. Instead, I have another interesting story about life around the *irori*.

To say goodbye, we say *sayonara*. If you directly translate the word *sayonara* it means "the person on the left says it is so." This is a strange way to say goodbye but the roots of the expression came from *irori* life.

After a long day of working at various tasks, the farmers and their families would return home and gather around the *irori* for a meal. This was when all of the sons reported the day's events to the eldest in charge: "the rice will be ready to harvest on the east side soon" or "the mountain mushrooms have begun to come up" or "the deer have come down from the hills." In this way the head of the family could use the information to give guidance for the next day's work.

The *irori* is the center. Where you sit in relation to the *irori* is also very important. If you look from the entrance of the house, the person you see facing you squarely is the oldest male member of the household. The position occupied by this person is called *yokoza*. On his right side sits the female householder. Her position is called *kakaza*. On his left sits his oldest son or any special guest invited for the meal. Then in succession on his left sit the other sons. The wife of the oldest son cooks and serves the meal.

The other wives and children eat together near the *nagashi*. This area, called the *kijiri*, was also where the firewood was kept. It was an important job for the children to carry a steady supply to the *irori*. After dinner everyone turns to evening chores.

Sayonara — "the person on the left says it is so" — means that, at the end of the meal the oldest son (the person on the left side) agrees that the day's business has been discussed, and everyone understands and is in agreement with the directives given for tomorrow. It also means good night, thank you for this meal, and we will retire to our evening chores.

So, in Japan the word for goodbye is a starting agreement for tomorrow. The words "good bye" in English have a completely different meaning.

The meaning of the word *konnichiwa* (hello) also has a wide variety of meanings different from English. One translation is "what is today's." Generally reconstructed, when small tenant farmers gathered in the yard of the landowner's house in the early morning they would say *konnichiwa*, which implied "What is today's work?"

The *irori* was the symbol of the Japanese family system. All family life revolved around this central point. The *irori* gave witness to the happiness and tragedies of these country farmers' histories. The *jomin minka* described here was one for a large extended family. These farmhouses usually had separate *doma*, *nagashi*, *irori*, and family living space. There were also many smaller farmhouses for single families, where the *kamado*, *irori*, and living area were all in the same small room. An elder told me that during the winter when it was very cold, whole families huddled together around the *irori*, covering themselves with a patchwork blanket called a *donjya*.

During my time as a curator I collected stories and personal histories as well as artifacts.

The lives of these villages were directly dependent on nature. When nature did not smile on them, if the weather was bad or the crops failed, there were direct and sometimes cruel repercussions.

I once had the opportunity to speak with a 96-year-old *samba* (midwife). She told me stories of a long famine she had survived. During this famine, the food reserves had been exhausted and even the salt was gone. The place where the wife sits to cook at the *irori* is called *kakaza no goza*. This spot is covered by a *mushiro* (small rice-straw mat). Sometimes food was spilled onto this mat while serving. The famine mentioned by the *samba* was so severe that these mats were chopped and eaten. The rice straw inside the hanging *venkei* were also eaten for the juices they had collected.

The saddest and harshest reality of famine was most evident at birth. With the fear of starvation looming, the thought of another mouth to feed sometimes became overwhelming. In these times of desperation, a baby girl had more value than a baby boy: if given absolutely no other choice, a girl could be sold to become a house maid. During birth, after determining the sex of the infant, the midwife would ask the mother if she wanted to deliver the baby. Infanticide, of course, was illegal if the baby was completely separated from the mother. During the worst of times, some did not survive delivery. In small village cemeteries you can find tiny rock statues with red aprons marking the graves of miscarriages. Of course, in modern Japan this no longer occurs, but these stories are acknowledged by elders of the villages.

As I have said, entire family histories have unfolded around the *irori.* Throughout Japanese history the *irori,* if not as a physical reality, has remained part of the Japanese makeup as a symbol for gathering, communication, and sharing. Today it is considered normal routine for Japanese businessmen to gather after work to eat and drink and discuss the business and frustrations of the day. If you watch a circle of businessmen in Tokyo, even the positions in which they sit based on their relationships to one another is reminiscent of the *irori.*

When I was a child we did not live in a farmhouse, but we did have an *irori.* During the Edo period (1603-1867), the area in which I lived was part of the castle grounds of the ruling monarch. The house where I was born had been the quarters for the castle supervisor during those times. This whole area has since been turned into a park.

Compared to a farmer's house, our *irori* was small and shallow. Charcoal was used for fuel to warm the room, make hot water for tea, or for tea ceremony.

As a kid I used to collect *ginnan* (ginko nuts) and *kuri* (chestnuts), and bury them in the ashes to bake. You had to make a small cut in the chestnuts and hit the chestnuts with a hammer before burying them. I found out the hard way, of course, that if you don't do this, they explode and leave tiny burn marks all over the *tatami* mats. I can still see my father's angry face when he heard that story from my mother.

The *jizaikagi* from the *irori* of my home is now hanging over Nippon Kan's *irori* in Denver.

In the next chapter we will discuss cooking utensils and tools and the customs surrounding their origins and uses.

Utensils and Customs for Their Use

Hidana and Venkei and Jizaikagi.

Farmers

You can see by examining the lifestyle of the traditional farmer that simplicity was a key factor. Few utensils were used for traditional Japanese cooking. Every member of the family worked from dawn to dusk, so complicated, time-consuming recipes were simply not feasible on a daily basis.

The religious calendar of the farmer included special holidays. These special days were called *hare no hi* and were spent cooking and enjoying more elaborate dishes. For the farmer, the regular daily meals consisted of *zakkoku,* rice husks and corn mixed with foxtail, decengrass, and beans. This was the staple food of the Japanese farmers. It is very different from the white rice served today in Japanese restaurants.

A large *tetsu nabe* (cast-iron pot) was hung over the farmer's fire. Potatoes and fresh vegeta-bles were boiled — and maybe a few dried vegetables and mushrooms — then mixed with *zakkoku* and seasoned to make a porridge. Fish or fowl were not eaten every day. Pickles might be served as a side dish.

Few utensils were needed to prepare this simple meal. A cast-iron pot, a big wooden ladle, a cooking knife, small wooden plates, and serving bowls were all that were necessary. For more elaborate preparations only a few other utensils were needed. A *suribachi* (earthenware mortar with wood pestle), *seiro* (steaming basket), *oroshi* (grater), and a *zaru* (bamboo basket for holding and washing vegetables) were common. *Irori* cooking was easy, you just threw ingredients into the pot! The side dishes as well did not involve complicated processes.

One important accessory was the wooden covers for the *tetsu nabe.* According to religious teachings, once the vegetables were cut, the bad *ke* had to be washed away. If you didn't cover the pot while cooking, the bad *ke* would return and enter the vegetables again. The wooden covers prevented the good *ke* from escaping and the bad *ke* from getting back in.

Just before the vegetables and meats reached a boil, a brown film appeared on the surface of the water. This film, called *aku,* was skimmed and thrown away; it was said to be the remnants of bad *ke.*

Where once religious explanations were given as reasons for covering vegetables and removing impurities, we now cover vegetables to ensure proper cooking and remove *aku* because it tastes bad and makes a dish look dirty. Chicken or beef that has been raised on foods treated with chemicals release much more *aku* than organically raised produce. So it is also for health reasons that we follow these steps.

For the traditional farmers it was probably easier to accept the religious explanations. This was merely a way to teach the people what they should and should not do. In this manner, folk tales and customs were born.

The skillful way in which the traditional farmer prepared foods brought out their natural flavors. Meats, fish, and vegetables were not overly prepared, but were kept in pretty much their natural states; therefore few utensils were required. Wet seasonings were added at the last minute to maintain the natural taste of the foods.

Tetsu nabe — cast-iron pot.

Above: Traditional Japanese dishes.

Left: Seiro — steamer.

Below: Suribachi and surikogi — mortar and pestle.

From left: shuki (sake pot), tetsu bin (kettle), kashiki (food container).

Left: Oroshi — grater.

Umakazari. For good luck through the year, images of horses decorate the house.

Even foods that have been pickled or preserved with salt possess much of their original flavor when well washed and cooked. Fish or fowl skewered and roasted near the fire keep the juices, nutrients, and flavors while excess fats run down the sticks.

The most popular dish at Domo restaurant was teriyaki chicken. For this dish I borrowed the traditional farmer's method of *irori*-style cooking. I marinated the chicken overnight and then hung it over the grill *venkei* style for four or five hours (still a short time; eight hours is more traditional). My customers used to exclaim over the nice brown color of the skin and the tender, juicy meat inside.

Let's go back to the traditional farmer's lifestyle so you can more easily understand why eight hours was usually needed to cook the chicken. Without refrigeration, an important consideration when hunting deer or pheasants was how to keep the meat fresh. When hunting, the men tried to trap the animals alive (live ani-mals keep better). After butchering, the farmers either had to consume all of the meat or figure out ways to preserve it. In winter, of course, the problem had an obvious solution. The rest of the year ....

At dinner the first evening the meats would be seared. Some would be eaten, and some were put in the *venkei*. After dinner the fire would die down but would not go out completely. While the farmers slept, the chicken slowly cooked. The next morning they had chicken like I served at Domo.

If there was still more meat than could be eaten at these two meals, the rest was marinated in *miso* and *tamari*. The marinade would keep the meat from spoiling during the night. The next morning the meats were rinsed lightly, seared, and put in the *venkei* for the duration of the working day. When the family returned from their chores the meat was ready to eat.

With all the work to be done, no member of the family had a lot of time to spend cooking. Methods were created and timed to coincide with their busy workday schedules.

Fishermen

Fishermen, like farmers, had vegetable gardens, but their livelihood of catching and killing fish set them apart from other members of society. Their lives were restricted by numerous folk religious taboos, rules, and ceremonies.

Remember that during this time there were no extended weather forecasts or radar. The fishermens' boats were small and allowed for fishing close to shore only. The advice of elders and the experience of the captain was all they had to guide them. Many boats were lost at sea.

The fishermen left each morning before sunrise carrying white rice balls seared in the fire or wrapped in leaves or bamboo bark to keep the inside from drying. Mixing the rice first with *umezu* (pickled plum juice) also kept it from spoiling.

Two hundred and fifty years ago *kuromai* (brown rice) was a coveted food of the wealthy. The farmers ate the *kuromai* of the lowest quality, that rejected after sorting. White rice at that time was reserved for special Shinto ceremonies. Why then were the fishermen eating white rice? The people believed that the bad *ke* released when the fish were killed placed the fishermen in grave danger. Eating this special white rice while they were in the boats was supposed to protect them. This was one of the religious reasons. A more worldly reason was that fishermen leaving for work never knew if they would return. The fishermen's wives would give them the luxury of white rice in case it might be their last meal. The white rice also metabolized quickly, providing them with the energy they needed.

I think you can appreciate the ingenuity of these simple people. A good way to protect themselves from the tax collector was to explain that they needed white rice for spiritual reasons. Even the tax collector couldn't deny people the right to follow their religious beliefs.

Farmers and fishermen still eat *zakkoku* as a main staple. (The fishermen only ate white rice while they were fishing.)

We have been talking about white riceballs but haven't yet discussed the utensils used by the fishermen. It is important to understand what they ate and why before we talk about the utensils. Earlier I mentioned the 96-year-old midwife I met when I was a curator. She told me another interesting story about white rice.

After the birth of a baby the mother was given a fresh bowl of white rice to ward off any sickness or bad *ke*. The white rice was also considered a bonus for the mother, a gift for a courageous delivery. Today there remains a ceremony in which raw white rice is put in a bamboo tube and shaken over a mother about to deliver. The ties between Japanese religion and white rice are many and strong.

I mentioned the fishermen mixing *umezu* with their rice. *Umezu* is the juice from pickling plums, and for a long time it was said to keep foods from spoiling. *Umeboshi* (dried pickled plums) are still an integral part of the Japanese diet. The fishermen of course ate fresh fish with their *umezu* rice balls. The fishermen would split the fish in half from the inside out. They didn't use knives. They would dip the fish in *tamari* or *miso*. Sometimes *tamari* was mixed with *wasabi* (Japanese green horseradish) and used as a dip. *Wasabi* is still used as a sterilizing agent. This might remind you of the *sashimi* and *sushi* found in restaurants today.

Ten hours by boat south of Tokyo is Hachijo Island. Another four hours south of that is a smaller island on which I lived for three months studying the customs and collecting artifacts from the people there. At that time, about 50 native people were living on that tiny island. For three months I ate what could be called the original *sashimi* lunch, and it wasn't exactly by choice. A boat came from Hachijo Island about every four days. There was no port, so during bad weather the boat didn't try to come at all. The local people would take freshly caught fish, split them open with their fingers, pull out the bones, and wash the fish in fresh seawater. They would then dip these foot-long fish in a sauce and eat them raw.

Accompanied by the local *sake*, this meal tasted pretty good, but after eating it day after day, just looking at fish made my stomach ache!

Mountain vegetables, boiled and served with a sauce, completed the meal. This very traditional meal required no knives or plates. Large, empty shells were used to serve the sauce and fish and were discarded afterward.

We have already discussed the concept of *ke* and *nagashi,* i.e., washing away the evil in a farmer's life. This case involves *ke* as well. Bad *ke* was released when you killed a fish. If you used a knife, the bad *ke* would transfer to the knife, so it was better to use your fingers. After the meal, everyone again washed their hands in the ocean to be rid of the bad *ke.*

At first I had trouble understanding why these people wanted to live on this small island. It began to make more sense when I learned that political prisoners had been sent into exile on this island during the Edo period. These people were the descendants of those originally forced to live here against their will. I think that even though the island was uncomfortable, these people would not be happy returning to the mainland their ancestors were forced to leave so long ago.

One day a fisherman from another island paddled up in his boat only to be stopped by an old man who wouldn't let him land. The old man yelled, "You can't come here, this is my island!"

His son had to jump in to avoid a fist fight. Territorial rights were heartfelt.

The daily menu for these island people obviously included fish and shellfish. They didn't catch them for commercial use and there was always a fresh supply, so there was no need to develop preservation methods. Their diet was supplemented with mountain vegetables, potatoes, and other edible roots.

Larger fish had to be sectioned and cleaned with a knife. This was done in one single designated area of the house. The knife, baskets, and cooking bowl used to prepare the fish were kept separate from other utensils. In Akita, my home town, the utensils used for preparing fish and other meats were also kept separately. This custom still exists.

I think that although now the island people may have caught up with modern ways, like mainland Japan their daily menu and preparations have roots steeped in folk religion.

A dish that was found on both this island and in my home town was called *kayaki* or *kai yaki.* *Kayaki* means shell bake. A large scallop shell is placed over the fire and filled with fish, *tofu,* and seasoned vegetables. *Miso,* soy sauce, or *shottsuru* (juice from pickling fish) are added for taste. During the wintertime the people from my home town eat *kayaki* and wash it down with locally brewed sake. Only someone who has visited northern Japan during wintertime knows how delicious this is.

Mountain People

The relationship between the Japanese people, wood products, and the forests that produce them goes back to the Stone Ages. The mountain people of Japan spent most of their time harvesting timber for use all over the country.

In this section we will discuss the foods the mountain people lived on and how they were preserved for storage and transport. Their markets were the wild forests and rivers themselves, which provided fresh vegetables, fish, and meats.

In the northeast section of Japan the Pacific Ocean and the Japan Sea are divided by a mountain range named the Owu range. In that range, especially near Akita prefecture, the people whose livelihood depends primarily on hunting are called the *Matagi*. (Depending on location, other peoples were called the *Yamadachi* or the *Kobiki*.) These people also farmed, but they were takers of life. So their lives, like the fishermen, were restricted and controlled by religious customs.

What kind of utensils were used by these mountain people? How did they cook their meals? The owner of the Lake Ogawara folk art museum asked us to go to the mountains and research these and other questions.

At this time in the early 1970s, knowledge about these subjects was disappearing. Someone would be pointed out to me: "That person over there is the last traditional *Matagi*, acknowledged as capable of passing down the true traditions of the past." Or I was told in my inquiries: "The last *takasho* (traditional falconer) just died." Like a candle, the knowledge of these peoples' customs and habits was flickering low and dying.

We went deep into the mountains to meet the *Matagi* and to chronicle their customs and lifestyle. We collected many hunting tools which are still on display at the Lake Ogawara folk art museum.

Every part of the *Matagi's* life was controlled by the mandates of folk religion. The religious calendars chose which days it was safe to go to which places, or what day was a good day to set out on a long trip. Hunting equipment was selected by the season according to what prey was available.

The *Matagi* have been using flintlock rifles for only the last 100 to 150 years. It is the only fir-

ing weapon they used, if they used one at all. During earlier times, only the *samurai* were allowed to carry weapons. Still, as of 15 years ago it was a matter of pride for the *Matagi* not to use rifles. The *Matagi* carried many different kinds of traps and used their environment to capture prey. If they did use a weapon, it was a spear or a bow and arrow. It was part of *Matagi* honor to want an even match with the animals they sought. To use traps or falcons one needs to be acutely aware of animal behavior. Then it becomes a true a match of wits between the *Matagi* and their prey.

In late autumn the animals were fat in preparation for winter. With the leaves fallen from the

Nokogiri — saws (above).

Yaseuma — frame pack (above); *Shoiko* — shoulder bag (right).

Waraji — rice straw shoes.

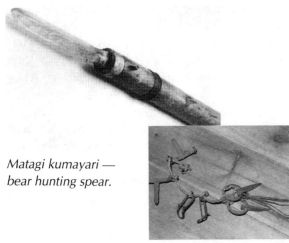

Matagi kumayari — bear hunting spear.

Kana kanjiki — snow shoes.

Right: Candle stand and draw knife.

Left: Kanjiki — snow shoes.

trees, this was the best time for hunting. During the winter, dogs were used to hunt bears. The dogs would find the bears' hibernation cave, arouse the sleeping bear, and signal the *Matagi.* The *Matagi* would simply spear the sleepy animal as it emerged from the cave. If the bear was not so sleepy, the dogs were sent in to agitate him and make him stand up. When the bear stood up the hunters would stab him in the chest, causing the bear to fall over and impale himself on the long spears.

I have in my collection *Matagi* spearheads that weigh almost nine pounds and are up to two feet long. The shafts that were attached to these blades were about 10 feet in length. When the *Matagi* would go on their hunting trips deep into the mountains, they would carry only the spearheads with them, fashioning the shafts from wood they found upon their arrival.

The dogs used by the *Matagi* were of the Akita breed. In the United States today there is a very large Akita dog organization. I raised many Akita puppies as a child. Akitas are known for their curled tails, beautiful round faces, and their calm, loyal nature. Although Akitas come in many shades of black and brown, I have heard that in the United States only white Akitas are

prized. Akitas with mixed colors were used to hunt in autumn; white Akitas were used in winter.

To withstand long hunting trips, the *Matagi* needed food, especially in autumn and winter when there were not a lot of fresh foods to be found. The only flavoring they carried was a dried ball made of soybean paste called *miso dama.* On the hunting trips all the *Matagi* had to do was add hot water to make miso again.

The main food the hunters carried included what is called *hoshi meshi,* which was a cooked and dried mixture of decengrass, foxtail, corn, and rice. Stone-ground decengrass or foxtail flour mixed with water and steamed, called *dango,* might also have been included.

The *Matagi,* like the fishermen, were allowed to eat white rice to counterbalance the effects of the bad *ke* that was released when an animal was killed.

My home town is still famous for a dish called *kiritampo. Kiritampo* is white rice that has been cooked and wrapped around a wooden handle about 16 inches long. The handle is secured in the *irori* next to the fire to sear the outer layer of the rice. Then the handle is removed.

The *Matagi* packed this same *kiritampo* for their long hunting expeditions. Originally the *Matagi* added mushrooms they found under the autumn leaves to complete the dish. Today we add *tofu* and other ingredients to make a dish that can be found in the finest traditional restaurants.

The *Matagi* had a lot of equipment to carry on their hunting trips, and they had to think about hauling out their kills. To reduce weight, utensils were kept to a minimum. For digging holes in the snow, a *suki* (spade); to plow, a *kua* (hoe). Depending on the season, a *manno* (rake) might be carried. All of these tools could be used for cooking as well, the point being to conserve space, time, and energy. Meats were dried or smoked, so the only utensil needed was a knife. *Sansyo yogu* is the Japanese word for the few tools of the mountain people.

The image that comes to mind when thinking about Japanese foods is usually one of *sushi*, *tempura*, and *sukiyaki*. The name *sukiyaki* comes partially from the mountain people. *Suki* means a spade, *yaki* means barbecue.

The *sukiyaki* we see today was first made after the Meiji period. At that time beef as a rule was not being eaten. The word *sukimono* refers to a person who delights in collecting or enjoying unusual, interesting things. After the Meiji period the trend from America and Europe was to eat beef. The people who joined this new trend ate beef out of large, flat, cast-iron pans. There was no name for this new dish. It was named *sukiyaki* for the spade the *Matagi* used for cooking and the trend setters who enjoyed it.

The *Matagi* and other mountain peoples' lives were controlled by their gods. Like the fishermen they were "takers of life" and lived by strict religious codes designated by the folk religion of the times.

The mountain communities were isolated during their time not only by the remoteness of their location. Although respected, the *Matagi* were isolated because they killed in order to survive. This discrimination has as far as I know disappeared with the religious taboos that were the source of the initial segregation.

One important conclusion to be drawn from this chapter is the inseparable relationship between folk religion and lifestyle of the traditional farmers, fishermen, and mountain peoples of Japan's not-so-distant past.

In the next section we will explore religious events still celebrated in Japan today and the foods that are enjoyed with them.

Traditional Events and Foods

Nagashi — kitchen.

*T*he Role of Traditional Events in Today's Modern Society

There are many traditional events and celebrations that retain important roles in the lives of modern Japanese people. There is also a great deal of tradition that has been lost. To understand the life of the Japanese of today, we need to understand what has occurred to cause the disappearance of so many of Japan's historical traditions.

The substantial growth of the Japanese economy has drastically changed the Japanese lifestyle. This economic growth has had its effects on the family as a traditional unit of society.

Traditionally, entire families — grandparents, their children, and their children's children — all lived and worked together. Every member of the family had his or her duties, and every working hour was spent doing the chores necessary to maintain the family household. The grandpar-

ents especially maintained vital roles in the working family unit. The elders took care of the children, prepared meals, tended the family gardens, and mended tools. At sunset when outside work was no longer possible, the younger adults returned home for dinner. After dinner the family engaged in *yonabe* (night work).

The men used rice straw to make *nawa* (rope), *waraji* (shoes), and *kago* (baskets). These and other crafts were also made of bamboo, the under-layers of tree bark, and vines. The women spun thread, wove cloth out of jute, cotton, and silk, and sewed.

As a curator I disassembled and reconstructed many traditional farm houses. One interesting point that affected the lives of these people was that they had no glass for windows. The windows were either covered with a solid wood shutter that was pushed up and held in position with a stick, or they were covered with tanned or waxed paper held on frames that slid back and forth. Try to imagine what life was like in the evenings with no light except for the moon and the glow of the fire.

Although these farmers had *andon* (paper-covered lamp stands), the oil used for these lamps was made from pine tree sap and was very expensive. (This reminds me of a park in the center of my home town that had many pine trees that were hundreds of years old. All of these trees show massive scars from when, during oil shortages in WWII, all pine trees were tapped to make fuel for fighter planes.) Candles were used for important religious ceremonies and were not for everyday use. In the shadows, therefore, the entire family gathered together and worked on their crafts until late into the evening.

At sunrise everyone rose to start their daily chores around the house, in the gardens, and in the fields. I can remember eating an early breakfast before sunrise and watching the farmers leaving for the fields.

Today, with the Japanese GNP one of the highest in the world, the effects on the farmers' lives have been tremendous. The farmer's newfound prosperity has led to advanced mechanization of their daily routines. Their work is done by state-of-the-art equipment, cutting their work time substantially. Modern farmers usually pursue side businesses since the demands upon their time have been lessened. Mealtimes that used to coincide with the rising and setting of the sun are now dictated by other work schedules. The family doesn't need to spend its evenings doing nightly chores. Today they watch TV. It is not uncommon for some farmers to buy their rice and vegetables at the supermarket.

Once the farmers had a self-sufficient lifestyle, trading or selling foods to buy only simple necessities. There is a vast difference between this and the typical lifestyle of the Japanese families of today.

The 18th Olympic games held in Tokyo in 1964 was a turning point in recent Japanese history. The games brought a flood of international exchange and exposure.

For the people of the cities, Japanese lifestyles before 1964 resembled America in the 1950s in many respects. When a woman married she stayed at home. (Even today among established, traditional families a high percentage of the women choose home-making over a professional career.) Every afternoon, a pretty apron covering her dress, a shopping basket in one hand and a child in the other, the wife would go to the market for her daily shopping. By 6 p.m. the evening meal was prepared and she waited for her husband to return. This paints a typical portrait of life at that time.

After the Tokyo Olympics, the Japanese standard of living began to escalate. Japan became a country inspired by consumerism. In "modern families" both the husband and the wife began to hold jobs outside the home. At 6 p.m. now both are getting off work. The wife stops by the market on the way home and buys pre-cooked packaged dinners while the husband spends an hour or so socializing with his business associates. The wife rushes home and throws the packaged dinners in the microwave (which is being paid off in installments). The rice cooker, preset to cook at 5:45, blinks on. Just as the husband walks through the door the wife tears open a pouch of instant *misoshiru* and adds hot water — looks so real and tastes so good.

Children have also been affected by the new, faster-paced lifestyles of modern Japan. After attending regular daily school, a kid goes to *juku,* a private school. Children study constantly to prepare for entrance exams to schools with higher curricula.

About 10 p.m. the kid returns home and heads directly to the tiny kitchen crowded with the latest in modern appliances. From the large refrigerator the kid pulls out a TV dinner and pops it in the microwave. Then he sits down to eat alone, as his parents have already gone to bed.

In this household there is no lack of convenience with all of the new appliances and services, but at what price? With all family members working so hard to keep up with the payments and making ends meet, very important family communication has been lost. What is sacrificed is the important time that families spend preparing and eating meals together.

Behind the tremendous growth of the Japanese economy lies this tremendous sacrifice. What is even more frightening is the fact that this escalating game of "chase your tail" is considered normal behavior. This example is not from the lives of the wealthy. Families that are financially independent are not in the majority in Japan. In most middle-class families both husbands and wives are working.

In the days of the traditional farmer every evening was spent sitting around the *irori* discussing the events of the day and planning for tomorrow. We have traded this tradition for economic growth. We have replaced happy families with the problems that arise from lack of daily communication. The problems that plague a modern world — juvenile delinquency, divorce, marital problems, abandonment, suicide, etc. — all stem from basic lack of communication. Whether around a table or around a fireplace, eating together, sharing together, talking together is an important part of a healthy family life.

While working from dawn to late in the evenings, the busy farmers found time to eat with and spend time with families and friends. Under the auspices of folk religion there were many scheduled events where people gathered together and celebrated with food. Many of these celebrations have survived.

It is hard to say whether we celebrate an event so we can eat or eat to celebrate the event! Weddings, funerals, memorial days are all good reasons to gather. The Japanese also celebrate flower- and moon-watching in special ceremonies. Each event for whatever reason was and is always accompanied by special foods and drink.

The presence and importance of foods at these festivities stem from folk religious ideology. The special foods prepared for a certain event were first offered to the gods. Remember these are country traditions; these offerings were not necessarily made in elaborate temples only — under someone's favorite tree, or in the family house in a special place was acceptable.

After the gods had "eaten a little bit," the people removed the offering and shared the special foods among themselves. The feeling that they were "sharing a meal with the gods" brought them closer together.

These events, especially for the children, became interesting and mysterious. When sharing the delicacies, stories and religious guidance were naturally passed down from one generation to another.

Similarly, in the United States the spirit of Thanksgiving is shared over turkey and pumpkin pie. These events did not necessarily all take place in the house. Moon-watching celebrations may take place in the garden, cherry blossom celebrations outside under the trees. Any place can be appropriate for celebration.

I recently read in an article that in about 1280 A.D. Marco Polo was made aware of Japan while in China. The books he read stated that the Japanese gathered around coffins and ate the flesh of the dead. During that period in Japan it was true that after the interment of the dead the villagers gathered at the covered grave and ate and drank. This custom must have been distorted in translation until finally reported as eating the flesh of the dead.

Seasonal Events and Celebrations

A most popular event still held in Japan occurs on March 3rd. This is the girls' festival *hina matsuri*. In every traditional house today, there is a beautiful doll of a Japanese girl. Traditionally these beautiful dolls were no more than stick figures made of paper and rice straw. According to custom, the young girls would rub the dolls over their bodies to draw out any uncleanliness and then throw the dolls into the river. This was another form of *nagasu* (washing away evil or bad *ke*). I collected these dolls as a curator.

To celebrate *hina matsuri, yomogi* (mugwort) is mixed with rice to make special rice cakes called *yomogi mochi. Yomogi mochi* was used to get rid of worms, and to help with female disorders. *Yomogi* was the herb used to cleanse the body during the festival. As a kid during school track and field contests, we used to rub *yomogi* on our legs for good luck in hopes that we would run faster.

The theme of each festival and its accompanying foods naturally fit together. The foods for this festival are sweet. Steamed sticky rice is mixed with *mirin* or cooking *sake* and ground until soft, and then fermented. This produces a special *hina matsuri* drink called *shirozake.*

On this day, the cleansing dolls and cleansing foods are offered to the gods by placing them in front of shrines all over the village. It was customary for the children later to form groups and scour the neighborhoods collecting the food and dolls. In this manner it looked as if the gods had taken away the offerings that had cleansed the girls. This custom is called *hina-arashi* and was quite a treat for the children.

May 5th is the day for *sekku,* or boys' festival. On this day large kites shaped like carp are flown in hopes for good health and luck for the boys while they are growing up. White rice flattened into balls stuffed with *anko* (cooked sweet red beans) are wrapped in *kashiwa* (oak leaves). These special rice cakes are called *chimaki* or *kashiwa mochi.*

Steamed, sticky rice is mashed, rolled into balls, and wrapped in *sasa* (bamboo leaves).

This is called *sasamaki.* The *sasamaki* is dipped in sweet *kinako* soybean powder and eaten.

Kashiwa and *sasa* are used to keep the foods sterile and provide models for the boys. In the autumn, the *kashiwa* leaves do not fall off the trees, even after they die. The bamboo leaf always stays green. These leaves then not only keep the foods clean but also represent everlasting good luck for the boys when they become householders, and hopes for a strong, tough spirit.

During the earlier days there was only vague knowledge of the medical causes of disease, so religious explanations were given instead. The religious leaders of the community were also the persons responsible for prescribing herbs to aid the ill. Summer brought on a lot of illnesses due to the increasing heat and humidity. The cause of illnesses at that time was not linked to germs, but to evil spirits. When a certain illness broke out, a certain evil spirit would be accused and festivals would be held to drive off the unwanted spirit. For this reason, summertime is filled with festivals.

Many delicacies from the ocean are eaten during these summer festivals, such as *hamo* (sea eel) and *tako* (octopus). In my home town

Yaki mochi. Grilling mochi.

Shimenawa. For the New Year, the house is decorated with paper images of all the household items and farming tools.

we ate a lot of *kasube* (a variety of dried fish cooked with sweets until soft). *Koi* (carp) is also cooked in this fashion.

There are books that date back to the middle of the Edo period in 1750 A.D. that served as a kind of "Farmers Almanac" for the common people. According to these sources (although there was not much oil in the diet to begin with) one should not partake of any oily foods. During the summer months they reportedly blamed oils for diarrhea, therefore there were many taboos and rules applied to particular oily foods. In actuality, the hot summer months weakened the people's stamina, and the temperature and humidity caused food to spoil more rapidly. Insects were also a large contributing factor for disease.

The foods of the summer festivals were not nutritionally or medically oriented. The events were specifically held to ward off the bad *ke*. The foods were chosen because they were reportedly the favorite foods of the "good gods" who had the power to rid the land of the bad *ke*.

Autumn, according to the lunar calendar, falls in July, August, and September. In Japan, August 15th is the day of *chu shu no meigetsu* or the moon-watching festival. A more general term for this festival is *otsukimi. Tsuki mi dango* (rice cakes filled with sweet red beans) is a popular dish at this festival. These rice cakes are not made of sticky rice as usual, but of regular white rice ground to a powder. Sometimes *tsuki mi dango* are made into balls, sometimes they are flattened. A thumb print is pressed into the center to resemble a navel. This is called *heso mochi. The heso mochi,* along with apples, Japanese pears, grapes, sweet potatoes, and boiled chestnuts, are arranged on trays and given as offerings to the moon. This is just one of the many harvest festivals.

In my home town area, August 15th was too early for harvesting the fruits so we celebrated what is called *mame meigetsu* on September 15th. The principal food offered for this festival was *eda mame* (green soybeans) along with boiled chestnuts, other fruits, and sweet potatoes. The festival's name is derived from the word *mame* (bean). In another area, the festival may be named *kuri meigetsu, kuri* meaning chestnut, or *imo meigetsu, imo* meaning sweet potato, depending on the major crop produced. All of the different harvests were offered to the moon.

For *mame meigetsu,* wild flowers are gathered from the mountains to make decorations. *Susuki* (eulalia), *kikyo* (Chinese bell flower), and *kiku* (chrysanthemum) are most commonly used. Moon-watching festival decorations especially must incorporate these important flowers. When I was a child an old woman peddler would carry these flowers down from the mountains and sell them around the town.

Because the house where I was born was in an ancient castle area, I could easily find these flowers close by. I remember that this season was not only colored by wild flowers, but insects as well. Dragonflies — bright red dragonflies — would cover the power lines until they were completely red as far as you could see. The dragonflies would land on my hat by the handful. They were everywhere. I remember the beauty of an autumn sunset, the bright red dragonflies against the fire-red background of the setting sun. It unsettles me now that the dragonflies are gone.

The sliding doors of the veranda were opened. We would set out the offerings of special food, light a candle, and watch the moon. For me as a child, the moon took a very long time to cross the sky and set. I waited impatiently for the moon to set, for then we could eat. The usual routine for kids is to go to school, play, eat dinner, and go to sleep. On this special day, I was allowed to stay up very late waiting. I tried to stare down the moon, to make it set faster so we could eat the festival treats.

"Can you see the rabbit making mochi *in the moon?"* — *my mother's voice* …. Now I am 40, and when the full moon rises over the Rocky Mountains, I reminisce about my childhood in Japan. I don't see the rabbit making *mochi* when I look at the moon, I see my parents' smiling faces.

Acknowledging the New Year

The Japanese celebrate the New Year from January 1st to January 3rd. Although these are the main days of the celebration, preparation starts many days before. As early as December 12th the New Year's activities begin with *susuharai.* During *susuharai,* everyone pitches in to clean up the shrines, temples, offices, streets, parks, etc. After December 20th, families make *mochi* to use in the offerings given on January 1.

Kadomatsu decorations made of bamboo and/or pine boughs are set in front of the houses. In Aomori prefecture on December 25th or 26th, the head of the household would go to the mountains and cut down a pine tree. This tradition is called *matsu mukae.*

Depending on the sign on which the New Year would fall, each new year also had a direction associated with it. The direction of the New Year would dictate the direction in which the head of the household would set off to find his tree. He chose a tree that was not bearing pine cones and whose branches grew in tiers numbering 3, 5, or 7 only. After praying before the tree, he would bring it home and set it outside for one night. The next day the tree was brought into the house and decorated.

Over the tops of the house entrances, *shime-nawa* (Shinto paper) and rice rope decorations are strung to ward off or absorb bad *ke.* These *shimenawa* are made in the shape of all the farming family's tools, including the barn!

Kagami biraki marks the end of the New Year's celebration on January 20th (or January 25th, depending on the locality). For *kagami biraki,* the *mochi* left as offerings at the beginning of the festivities are broken and eaten.

Why is the Japanese New Year's festival so long? During the Meiji period (1868-1912) the government ordered the change from the lunar to the solar calendar. The change had inherent problems, considering that 1000 years of scheduled events would no longer match the seasons. Customary harvest festivals would no longer correspond to the time when the fields were ready to harvest or the flowers ready to bloom.

Everyone obeyed the government's orders and began celebrating New Year's on January 1 by the solar calendar. It was a quick change. New Year's day by the lunar calendar falls about one month after the January 1st of the solar calendar. Would it not seem strange if the American government decided to change daylight savings time from one to three hours? Changing from the lunar to the solar calendar had this effect multiplied many times over.

The celebration of the New Year has deep meaning which has not changed for centuries. In

Shimenawa, mizuki ofuda. New Year's decoration.

rural areas even now, the lunar calendar is more valuable and important than the solar calendar; therefore in the country, traditional New Year's celebrations start in February.

There is one side benefit from having two New Year's celebrations. Many young people leave the country and go to work in the larger towns and cities. During the New Year's festivities in January, most government and business offices close down. Like Christmas time in the United States, the shops and restaurants are filled with people enjoying the holiday. These businesses are manned by the young people from the country. In February when everything has calmed down, the rural young people return home to celebrate. So, unlike the United States where it is hard to find gas or an open grocery store on Christmas day, Japan has a natural solution to this problem.

On December 15, the Japanese begin cooking the traditional foods for the New Year's celebrations. These are called *osechi. Daikon* (Japanese white radish) and carrots are cut into long thin strips and soaked in salt and vinegar to make light vinegar pickles called *namasu.* Black beans are cooked and sweetened to make *kuromame. Kazunoko* (herring fish eggs) are seasoned lightly with soy sauce. Herring wrapped in *kombu* (kelp) is cooked and sweetened to make *kombumaki.* Small anchovies flavored with soy sauce and sweetened makes *tazukuri.* Sweet potatoes are mashed to make *kinton.* These are the traditional *osechi* foods. They are not chosen for their nutritional benefits, they are meant for good luck.

The main dish for New Year's is *nabemono* (one-pot cooking). It is also part of the tradition to eat *soba* (buckwheat noodles) and *udon* (wheat noodles). The New Year's soba is called *toshi koshi soba* (literally *connecting the years soba).* This *udon* is called *tsunagi udon* (or *tie*), *udon* meant to symbolize tying or linking the old and new years. I will explain *soba* and *udon* in more detail in a later chapter.

On the Shinto altar, two large round flattened *mochi* are placed one on top of the other. Gifts from the mountains and the sea — kelp, dried fish, oranges, and spring lobster — are placed on the shrine's altar and decorated with pine tree branches and bamboo.

At midnight on December 31 most people go to the neighborhood Shinto shrines to pray. There is always a crowd, and if I am in Japan, I have to go. (At Nippon Kan in Denver, we hold a ceremony as well.) People continue to visit the Shinto shrines for the next three days. At the front of the shrine is a donation box into which everyone donates the *yen* equivalent of a dollar or two. Pulling a rope that rings a bell, they clap their hands together twice and make a wish for the new year. Some have joked that Shinto priests have a good business. In only three days they can make enough money to survive for an entire year!

Baked *mochi* in a light soy sauce-flavored soup is traditionally eaten on January 1st. To eat these rice cakes is called *zoni*.

On the first day of the New Year, the children receive *otoshi dama,* which is a small envelope of celebration money. The adults spend the day visiting family and friends, or entertaining guests. Together, they eat the *osechi* and drink to

Kine and usu.

celebrate the New Year. With so many people visiting each home, other main dishes are prepared and shared as well. The meaning associated with *osechi* is to share together in these foods of good luck. The sharing is most important, and guests are encouraged to partake in their host's hospitality.

These descriptions typify the relationship between Japanese celebrations and their foods. In the northeastern part of Japan alone there are more than 100 scheduled events, so it would be difficult to describe them all. Most Japanese traditional foods are religiously related to particular festivals and events.

All celebration foods were offered first on the Shinto altar, then removed and eaten. This did not mean that the people were asking the gods to eat first, followed by the villagers. The feeling surrounding this custom was that the foods retrieved from the altar were foods given by the gods, that the gods were sharing these foods with the people.

Foods and events are still tied together in modern Japan. For example, if there is to be a baseball tournament *katsudon* (deep-fried pork cutlet on a bowl of rice) is eaten. The word *katsu* means to win or "today is a good luck day so we must eat meat." For birthdays and starting a new semester at school, *sekihan* (steamed sticky rice with red beans) is eaten. Usually around the dinner table family members discuss the happenings of the day and the plans for tomorrow. Naturally, when someone says "tomorrow I have a special event," one of the parents prepares for them the appropriate food for good luck. In this way special events, daily events, and foods remain tied to one another.

In the next section we will talk about how to enjoy eating Japanese foods.

How to Enjoy Eating Japanese Food

Jomin minka.

Generally, there are no set rules for enjoying Japanese foods. It depends on where you are, and who you are with. Manners are practiced so that everyone enjoys the meal. Manners provide a framework where all can be comfortable relating to and dining with one another. This is one of the basic concepts behind the manners we practice. Making each other comfortable is an important part of the meal's enjoyment.

Where it gets interesting, from an international perspective, is when certain manners that people practice in one part of the world may make someone else from another part of the world feel very uncomfortable.

I have lived and worked in Laos and Cambodia. In this part of the world, it is expected that guests burp loudly to show their appreciation to their hosts for a fine meal.

In Singapore, in mid-level restaurants, chicken and fish bones are spit onto the floor. After the customers have left, the waiters hose down the floors with water. In parts of China to leave a messy table means the meal was delicious.

In Japan, noodles and soups are eaten noisily, with loud slurping sounds. I have witnessed in the United States what is completely taboo in Japan: blowing your nose at the dinner table.

I think it might prove to be an interesting discussion if people from each of these countries gathered together to talk about manners.

I purposely picked out these "bad habits" from each country to prove a point. At their place of origin, there is absolutely nothing wrong with these habits — in fact they are expected. Instead of becoming disgusted with the manners of another country, a more positive approach may be to try to understand someone else's point of view.

What scares me the most in this age of unlimited international exchange is that some of the bad examples are being accepted as common behavior, especially when made by professional chefs. In Japan the chef holds a very high position. It concerns me that in the United States I have seen chefs that were unqualified in both technical skill and manners.

In the United States, in certain Japanese restaurants, the chefs put on an entertaining show in front of their customers. I am sure many Americans believe that this is how food is served in Japan. For example, *hibachi* grill chefs in the United States cook rhythmically and very fast. In Japan, the *hibachi* grill is completely different; most Japanese people have never seen this style of cooking. This is American-style Japanese food. Flipping food onto customers' plates or juggling knives in the air cannot be found anywhere in Japan.

This is the United States, and this is fine for entertainment, but a seriously trained chef from Japan would consider this performance alarming.

I have seen *sushi* chefs in the United States making *sushi,* stopping to throw the pads of rice behind their backs, catching them again and striking dramatic poses. I don't think that something as important as the food that is going into a customer's mouth should be played with. A real *sushi* chef would be surprised.

Sushi chefs that clown around to entertain their customers are a favorite with many people, but they were probably not trained in Japan. I am not trying to be overly harsh, but I am very concerned about anyone handling raw fish without the proper training and licensing.

In Japan, to graduate as a *sushi* chef takes about three years of study. After this training and passing a government examination, one still needs the recommendation of an established *sushi* restaurant owner to open his own establishment.

Watching a truly professional chef may not be as entertaining, but food preparation is a serious business. It is better for him to concentrate on his job. A true chef may have the time to laugh or smile with a customer while taking an order but usually not for long, then it's back to work. Look at the actions of a real chef. The attention and skill he gives to his work is his gift to you.

I would not want you to imitate any bad manners you might have learned in front of other Japanese people. It would reflect badly on you. This is why I have wanted to make this point.

In Japan, there are many manners associated with eating. The first item we need to deal with are chopsticks. You cannot separate Japanese cuisine from the use of *hashi* or chopsticks.

Oriental foods are served with chopsticks. Japanese chopsticks are round or square and pointed at one end. Chinese chopsticks are longer and are not pointed.

In Japan, men's, women's, and children's chopsticks are different in length and decoration. Rice bowls are also different sizes. The chopsticks served in restaurants are made of wood or bamboo. The wooden chopsticks you have to pull apart at one end are called *waribashi*. *Waribashi* are hygienic because once they have been pulled apart they can't be used again.

In a restaurant, you can tell if bamboo chopsticks have been used many times by dark stains from soy sauce visible at the tips. This may surprise you, but the mistake made most often is with *waribashi* chopsticks.

When I was running my restaurant I used to watch everyone — men, women, and children — pull their chopsticks apart and rub them vigorously together like a chef sharpening a knife. "You have to do this first" I heard people being coached by their friends.

This is a big mistake! When I have gently asked my customers why they are doing this, they either shrug or tell me it is to remove splinters. I am not sure that rubbing chopsticks together would remove splinters. If I asked them why, they would tell me that the splinters poked their mouths. Such a scary answer! While working on this manuscript, I happened to see on a television morning news show a story about a major Japanese company switching from wood to plastic chopsticks for environmental reasons. This is a good idea. What surprised me was to then listen to the commentator explain on national news how one must rub wooden chopsticks together to remove splinters!

Chopsticks are meant for picking up foods and carrying them near your mouth. It is considered bad manners to touch your mouth to the chopsticks. Think about the knife and fork, the same holds true for using them.

Where then did this bad habit come from? If you rub chopsticks together the splinters stand out more. If you are using lacquered chopsticks or other chopsticks with a smooth finish, it is difficult to eat slippery foods. It is easier to use the wood ones with splinters to help hold, for example, noodles.

People stop at noodle stands all over Japan to quickly eat a bowl. Because they are usually in a hurry, even though it is bad manners, they rub their chopsticks together to make the splinters stand out more. This way they can eat their noodles even faster. This, then, is where "chopstick rubbing" originated.

It is not considered bad manners in Japan to make slurping noises while eating noodles, especially in noodle stands where there are not usually even any chairs (you just stand up and eat). Who cares about the noise?

In regular Japanese restaurants, however, it is considered bad manners to rub your chopsticks together. When I was a child, we used to pretend our chopsticks were knives and forks and try to cut something "knife-and-fork style." My mother soon told us to stop because by copying this action, the chopsticks rubbed together and this was bad manners.

Somehow this noodle-stand tradition has found its way all over America. Maybe this custom was spread by *hibachi* grill chefs jokingly pretending to sharpen their chopsticks like knives, pretending like I did as a child.

The next time you go to rub your chopsticks together, look closely to see what the rubbing accomplishes. Whatever you want to do is fine.

Once we have separated the chopsticks, there are a lot of taboos such as: *Name bashi* — licking food off the ends of the chopsticks; *mayoi bashi* — not being able to decide and moving from dish to dish picking at the foods in them; *sashi bashi* — stabbing foods with your chopsticks; *utsuri bashi* — putting a bite of a side dish in your mouth and then another bite of a different side dish without eating a bite of rice in between; *komi bashi* — using chopsticks to stuff your mouth with food; and *seseri bashi* — picking your teeth with your chopsticks.

These are the most common taboos associated with using chopsticks.

Even more offensive than these is to pick up a bowl while you have chopsticks in the same hand, or to hold chopsticks and talk with your hands, waving the chopsticks around in the air or pointing with them.

When I was growing up, we all received very strict training in manners. If I did something that was bad manners my mother or my older brother would slap my chopstick hand.

When you are being served a meal, your chopsticks should lay horizontally in front of you at the close edge of the table, pointed ends pointing to the left. Your rice bowl is on your left side and your *miso* soup is on the right side. In American Japanese restaurants, when serving dinner they usually serve a salad and then a *misoshiru* or *osumashi* (clear soup) before the meal. In Japan, unless you order it specially you will not receive a salad with dressing. The Japanese enjoy mixing the tastes of the soup with the side dishes so the soup is served with the meal.

Sometimes you might notice to your dismay that the soup bowl cover won't come off. This is caused by a vacuum created as the soup cools. The way to get the cover off is to release the vacuum by squeezing the sides of the bowl between your thumb and first two fingers, allowing air to enter. Then just lift off the lid.

If you are served *sashimi* (sliced, bite-size pieces of raw fish), it is important to follow these steps. *Sashimi* is accompanied by a small plate called a *nozoki*.

Use your chopsticks to mix about 1/2 teaspoon of *shoyu* (soy sauce) and a small amount of *wasabi* (Be careful, this *wasabi* can be hot, and a little goes a long way).

Pick up and hold the *nozoki* in your left hand and your chopsticks in your right hand. (If you are left-handed and find it too uncomfortable to use your right hand, use your left!) Pick up a piece of *sashimi* with your chopsticks and lift both the small dish and the *sashimi* to your mouth. This is not considered bad manners in Japan and is good "dribble protection" in case you drip or lose the piece of *sashimi*! A helpful reminder is, do not fill the *nozoki* to the brim with soy sauce, as you are asking for trouble!

When you are eating *sushi*, do not add *wasabi* to your small dish of soy sauce. The reason you sit at a *sushi* bar in front of the *sushi* chef is to explain to him how much *wasabi* to put on your *sushi* for you. If he puts too much or too little on, just ask him politely to adjust the amount. He should be agreeable to this.

When eating rice hold your rice bowl in your left hand, your thumb supporting the side and four fingers underneath; do not hold the other side of the bowl with these four fingers. Allow the bowl to rest on these fingers, your hand palm up. Raise the rice bowl to the center of your chest, not under your chin, and take a bite of rice with your chopsticks.

Leaving your rice bowl on the table (or worse, putting soy sauce on your rice) and eating out of the bowl is considered extremely bad manners. The bowls are not well balanced, and they will tip over if you try to eat out of them without picking them up.

When you are ready to drink your soup, put down your rice bowl, pick up the soup bowl with your left hand, and raise it to your mouth to drink. It is not considered bad manners to drink from the bowl. You can pick out the soup's delicacies with your chopsticks while holding the bowl at about chest level.

A spoon is used with a few Japanese dishes, but soup bowls are not the right shape for spooning. Be careful not to use a spoon with soup or try to put a spoon in your soup bowl while it is sitting on the table — it will tip over.

In Chinese restaurants the food is served on plates, and it is awkward to use chopsticks. When I go to a Chinese restaurant I use a fork, as it is more comfortable.

Chopsticks are most useful when you are holding a bowl of rice in your left hand. Then chopsticks can be used to select a bite of a side dish, carry it to the rice bowl and then to your mouth, or to place it on a small dish. From a flat plate sitting on the table it is a long way to your mouth — using chopsticks is difficult. Notice that in Chinese restaurants everyone sits in a hunched-over position trying to get their mouths closer to the plate!

Traditionally in Japan the use of the utensils and the shape of them naturally match. When customs are mixed, sometimes the utensils don't work well with one another.

When you are a guest in a Japanese home, it is acceptable to ask for more rice and soup if you wish. You may ask for more rice, or leave one bite of rice uneaten and place the bowl on the tray your hostess is holding. This signifies that you are finished. Be careful not to grip the bowl with your thumb inside. You can only ask for *misoshiru* a second time. This is very formal; if it is a casual situation the rules are not as strict, yet manners are important in all situations.

If you have asked for more rice (asking for seconds is called *okawari*), place your chopsticks again horizontally in front of you pointing to the left and wait. When you receive your second helping, take the bowl with both hands and place it on your tray or the table in front of you. Then you can pick it up to eat.

All Japanese dishes were meant to be eaten together with a bite of rice, not individually. The foods are flavored with this in mind.

When you pick up a bite of a side dish, put it in the rice bowl held in your left hand, then pick up the bite of the side dish with a bite of rice and eat them together.

Many times I have seen people eating side dishes alone, or putting soy sauce directly onto their bowl of rice. This is extremely bad manners and is hard for Japanese to understand.

The majority of Americans have experienced Japanese foods in restaurants rather than in people's homes. When you go to a Japanese restaurant, you can order what you want and if you don't like it, just leave it on your plate. When you visit a Japanese family, the menu has already been set and sometimes there may be something you can't eat.

The best approach is to be honest with your host by asking for a small plate. Turn your chop-

sticks so that you use the other ends. This is a show of respect and cleanliness. Use your chopsticks to remove the food you can't eat and place it on the small plate. This is a sign of respect.

If you don't know what something is, politely ask your host; it may be an interesting topic of conversation. Ask again for a small plate, turn your chopsticks around, and use the other ends to take a small piece and place it on your small plate. Then turn your chopsticks around again, pick up a bite, and try it.

Cooking methods and ingredients vary depending on what part of the world you happen to be in. If a Japanese family invites you to dinner you can probably expect to eat Japanese foods. It is up to you to be a polite guest and not wrinkle your nose at a new dish.

I have invited many people to dine with me at Nippon Kan. The successful executives I have invited usually are interested in the meal and try to challenge everything on their plate. It is this kind of attitude I think that made them successful.

When a Japanese family invites you to their home, the table may be set with your main dish placed in front of you, accompanied by a few empty side dishes. In the center of the table large plates filled with different side dishes will be placed. If there are chopsticks in these dishes, use those. If there are not, turn your chopsticks around and use them to serve your own plates. This is the most polite approach. If your host tells you you don't need to turn your chopsticks around, it is like telling you you are family, which is a gracious gift for a host to impart to a guest.

After the meal there is one more thing to remember. This is in regard to *tsumayoji,* or the toothpick. When you have finished eating, putting a toothpick in your mouth to chew on while you are talking is considered very bad manners. If you need to use a toothpick, hold your left hand over your mouth as a shield and use your toothpick quickly. Do not leave a restaurant with a toothpick in your mouth. This is not only bad manners, it is dangerous!

Manners are different, depending on the formality of the situation, who you are dining with, and where the meal is being eaten. Even here in the United States, manners vary from one coast to the other.

In Japan classes are offered to high school students on how to eat Western foods properly. Your knife is in your right hand, your fork is in your left. After cutting a bite of food you push it onto the back of your fork.

No, that is European; if I do that in the United States I attract attention. "Don't cut your food with your fork," they said in high school. But everyone does it in America!

As these examples show, it is difficult to know what the right thing to do is. It might be easier to learn if people from different countries ate together, made mistakes, and learned from each other about the manners from their homelands.

Chapter

3

THE BACKGROUND OF JAPANESE STAPLE FOODS

Basic Wet Seasonings

Abura shibori — oil press.

Today in Tokyo you can find foods from all over the world. Bookstores stock publications on cooking from all parts of the globe. Weekly magazines include international gourmet sections, and television broadcasts include world gourmet reports. Japan has reached a state of *hoshoku no jidai* or gluttonous saturation.

This book is not about the new International gourmet cuisine of modern, urban Japan. This book focuses on the roots of traditional Japanese foods and cooking methods.

Someone visiting Tokyo today might think that there are no such traditional foods. Japanese families who invite Americans into their homes for extended visits do so because they are interested in American culture. It makes sense then that the lifestyle of these families is usually Westernized. Homestay families in consideration of their guests serve Japanese foods that Americans might be familiar with, like *tempura* or *sukiyaki*.

The adventurous traveler that gets off the beaten track knows, however, that there is a whole other culinary world outside of mainstream Japanese restaurant cuisine.

I have entertained guests at Nippon Kan who have experienced the backroads of Japan, and they have been delightfully surprised to find what they now consider real Japanese food, right in the middle of the United States.

The foods available in Japan have changed drastically over the last few years. I have been living in the United States for 12 years, and each time I return to Japan there is an obvious change in the Japanese diet. Many of the young Japanese people do not know the original shape of the fish they buy. Everything is presliced and prepackaged, so they do not have a chance to learn. Even many of their mothers' generation are unaware of the old traditional recipes.

This section focuses on traditional Japanese seasonings. A major foundation for all the flavors in Japanese cooking is the *dashijiru* or soup stock. What makes *Kokyu Ryotei* or *Kokyu Kappo* (top-level traditional Japanese restaurants) exceptional is the way in which they prepare their *dashijiru*. Top restaurants use traditional methods only.

American Oriental markets reserve large sections for *dashi* or instant soup stocks and flavorings. While the packaging might have cute designs and a catchy Japanese name, they can't disguise the fact that their flavor comes mostly from MSG (monosodium glutimate).

MSG has found its way into most Japanese staple ingredients; it is hard to avoid on either side of the Pacific. Some Japanese and Chinese restaurants advertise that they do not use MSG, but if you know the taste, you can quickly tell whether an instant *dashi* has been used, even what brand. MSG is difficult to avoid in restaurants, too.

Making *dashijiru* from original natural ingredients takes more time than opening a package, but the flavor is much better and the spirit involved in spending the time, planning ahead, and taking care adds to the *dashijiru's* richness.

Creating a meal start to finish, going through each step and completing them successfully, is a testament to the ingenuity of mankind. Just pouring a package of powder into a pan and adding water has no story. Taking shortcuts saves time, but we lose the experiences that make us rich within. We also miss appreciating the efforts of the chef, or miss sharing tips and secrets about recipes handed down from generation to generation.

In the next section, I will go into *dashijiru* or soup stock in more detail. But first, I want to explain where Japanese flavors and seasonings originated and how they developed into the flavorings that are popular today.

Traditional Japanese flavorings can be divided into two general categories:
1) Seasonings derived from salting during storage.
2) Seasonings created as by-products of the process of preserving or fermenting foods.

Umezu — Pickled Plum Juice

The phrase used when checking the flavor of a dish in progress is *anbai o miru*. (*An* is a word for salt, *bai* is the word for plum, *miru* is to look or see.) Flavors derived from the pickled plum are ubiquitous in Japanese cooking.

If you are at all familiar with Japanese food you can easily recognize a form of the pickled plum called *umeboshi:* this pickled plum is dried before serving. *Umezuke* are plums that have been pickled but are served in their juice. You dry *umezuke* to get *umeboshi. Umezu* (the pickled plum's juice) is widely used for flavoring. The phrase *"anbai o miru"* implies, "Is there enough *umezu?"*

Kame — pickling jar.

Currently, brewing rice vinegar is replacing *umezu* as a means to create sour tastes. But *umezu* and *umezuke* still have many uses.

Plums are usually pickled with *shiso* (perilla). *Shiso* aids digestion and is said to prevent hardening of the arteries. It is a popular herb for protecting against certain poisons from fish. You will now understand why *shiso* is served abundantly in sushi restaurants.

Sanmi — Vinegar

The pickled plum is naturally sour. In this section, I will discuss how foods that are not sour in their natural state develop a sour or sweet-sour flavor during the processes used to preserve them. These products, when taken from different stages of the preserving process, are then used as a flavoring to produce a sour or vinegar taste.

Preserving the vegetables of autumn harvest is a very important task in rural Japan. As previously mentioned, some vegetables are dried or buried in holes lined with rice straw, but mostly the vegetables are pickled.

In autumn during October and November, about the time the persimmons turn red and ripe, the work in the rice fields is almost completed. The task of preserving the vegetables begins. If you took a walk through the countryside at this time of year, you could see the farming women down at the creekside, each with hundreds of *daikon* (Japanese white radishes) piled by their sides. (Even that creek is hard to find in the over-developed Japan of today.) These women, armed only with a brush made of rice straw, wash each *daikon* in the icy waters of the creek.

The *daikon* were usually dried before pickling. The radishes were tied into groups with rice-straw rope called *nawa* and dried on large scaffolds. Up to 200 *daikon* could be seen on these scaffolds, which stood on the north side of the house where the winds were strongest. After the *daikon* had dried, they were ready to make into *tsukemono* (pickles).

Because the autumn leaves had already fallen, the countryside was painted with only the colors of the red persimmons and the walls of hanging white *daikon*. This image heralded the coming of winter.

Above: Daikon and persimmons hung to dry.

Left: Tsukedaru — pickling tub.

The cold north winds took about a month to dry the *daikon*. Occasional frosts also helped with the drying process. Once the *daikon* were dry, they were taken down and packed with salt and *nuka*. *Nuka* are the husks and remnants left over after making white rice, containing important oils and proteins for the pickling process.

Of course, some of the *daikon* were pickled directly before drying; the method used depended on the intended duration of storage.

After taking down the *daikon, susuki* (eulalia) grass was fastened together with thin ropes to make large mats. These mats were hung on the "drying fences" to act as protection from the cold north wind and snows of winter.

Vegetables used for pickling include *daikon, hakusai* (Chinese cabbage), *nasu* (eggplant), *kyuri* (cucumber), and *ninjin* (carrots), to name a few. The preserved vegetables supplied the villagers for the entire winter. Some of the pickles were "short term" and some were "long term". The pickles meant for long-term storage were dried first before pickling. Fresh vegetables that have been pickled eventually release their water, thus ruining their flavor.

After being stored for two to three months "long-term pickles" develop a light sour taste. Pickled *daikon* or cabbage can then be used to make dishes with a lightly sour flavor. Vegetables pickled for long-term storage, however, have to be washed carefully before being used for cooking.

For example, lightly sour Chinese cabbage mixed with *tofu* and chopped *negi* (Japanese onion), simmered with water, *miso,* and *sakekasu* (rice wine lees), makes a delightfully sour dish. (I think it's delightful. I suppose it depends on your tastes.)

The *tsukemono* we have been discussing date back centuries. In the old Imperial courts, *tsukemono* were called *gako*. In the area around my home town, the local colloquialism for *tsukemono* is still *gakko*. Both the name and the pickles have survived centuries to be served daily on the modern family table.

The traditional Japanese farmer ate many things provided by nature. *Sansai* (wild herbs and vegetables) and varieties of mountain mushrooms were also pickled for the winter.

In the autumn, more than twenty varieties of mushrooms are gathered, dried, and pickled with salt.

When it is time to use the mushrooms for cooking they are soaked in water to remove most of the salt. A trace of saltiness blends with the natural flavor of the mushroom, making a delicious flavor on its own. No other seasonings are required.

Kinoko (mushrooms) and salt make an exceptionally nice *dashijiru. Tsukejiru* (juice from the pickled mushrooms) is also used as a seasoning.

When I was a child, I would go mushroom hunting with my father and brother. My mother, a very traditional woman, declined to go on these outings because this was customarily men's work.

Each grove of trees was the home for different kinds of mushrooms. If you were not familiar with the mushroom seasons, or when and where each variety grew, it was difficult to find them. The farmers and mountain gatherers always knew where the mushrooms were but kept this a guarded secret. After overhearing a neighbor talk about where he had found mushrooms, we would try the same place. We rarely found many mushrooms, but while searching we found mountain *yamabudo* (mountain grapes), *kuko* (Chinese matrimony vines), *matatabi* (silver vine), *kuwa* (mulberry), and *kuri* (chestnuts) — all of which we had uses for.

As a child, it was just as much fun to find these treasures as it was to find mushrooms. *Kuko* and *matatabi* are useful for making herb medicines. My neighbors would buy them from me to make their own remedies.

In the early spring when the trees began to bud, entire families would go to the mountains to gather *warabi* (bracken), *zenmai* (osmond), *taranome* (Japanese angelica tree buds), and *takenoko* (bamboo shoots).

The first bulbs to break the surface after the winter snows melted belonged to the *fuki* (butterbur) plant. These bulbs were seasoned with *miso* and roasted, or made into *sunomono* (any vegetable, fish, meat, or shellfish seasoned with sweet vinegar is called *sunomono*). This way, we could enjoy literally the first tastes of spring.

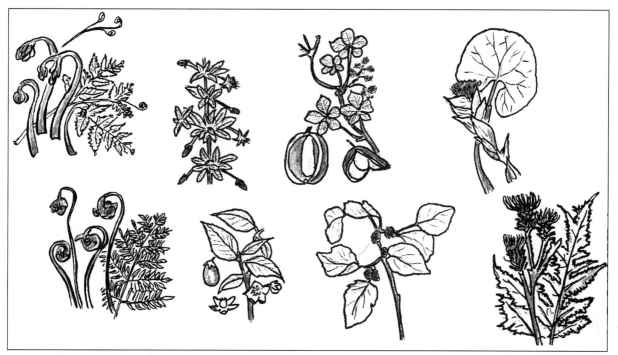

Top row left to right: warabi, kuko, akebi, fuki. Bottom row left to right: zenmai, matatabi, kuwa, azami.

Spring got to everybody in Northern Japan. I remember my mother, a very traditional woman, would greet me at the door when I came home from school. One day she did not greet me. I finally found her out on a long slope by our house wearing peasant trousers and collecting a special variety of thistle used in *miso* soup. Although a traditional woman who would not hunt mushrooms, she too enjoyed the first gathering of spring.

Another person who enjoyed the gathering of spring was a friend of mine named Mr. Maeda. Although he was 75 years old when I met him, I still had trouble keeping up with him on our forages into the forest. Decades of experience had made his eyes sharp — from twenty feet away he could discern a desired herb, vegetable, or mushroom from the surrounding vegetation.

Miso and Tamari — Soybean By-products

Making *miso* was traditionally a community effort that began May 21st or 22nd (*haru higan* or the spring equinox).

Soybeans were soaked overnight, boiled, drained, and poured into a large tub. Men wearing rice-straw shoes to protect their feet crushed the beans. The women then shaped the crushed beans while they were still warm into pyramids, squares, or balls, depending on the locality. After the shapes cooled they were tied with rice-straw rope and hung under the eaves of the house. When the naturally occurring fungus began to grow on the *miso,* it was said that "the flower had opened." After this occurred, the *miso* was transfered to the *misodaru* or *miso* tub. Salt was added and the tub was covered.

This original method is simpler than the method used to produce *miso* sold commercially today. It also has a saltier taste.

Japanese Country Cooking   67

To make modern commercial *miso, koji* is added as a catalyst to start the fermentation process. *Koji* is malted rice or sometimes barley, although rice *koji* is the most popular. *Shiro miso* or white miso has a high percentage of *koji. Aka miso* (red miso) has a lower percentage. (I will explain more about *koji* later in this chapter.)

It was my job as a child to crush the boiled beans used to make *miso.* The crushed beans were then poured into a wooden tub, mixed with *koji,* covered, and left to ferment for an average of six months to a year. The traditional farmer still keeps a storage shed for the tubs of *miso* and other pickles near his house. Not too near his house! The most obvious reason for storing *miso* away from the family home was the pungent odor created during the fermentation process. City people sometimes use the phrase "you smell like *miso*" to mean you come from the country.

Sometimes on larger farms, *miso* was stored for up to eight years. To have old *miso* in your house meant that you had a large, prosperous family.

The farmers used a large cedar tub to make *miso.* Just before it was time to make the *miso,* the tub was carried outside to sit in the rain, or sometimes it was weighted with rocks and soaked in the river to swell the wood tight. The tub was then laid on a large platter to catch leaks and covered with a wooden lid. From time to time, the cover was removed and the *miso* stirred. When the *miso* was uncovered, the layer of mold that had formed on the top was stirred in, enhancing the fermentation process.

In American Japanese markets there are many varieties of *miso* available. The difference between them depends on where they were made, what kind of *daizu* (soybeans) and *koji* were used, the amounts of *koji* and salt, and even the weather at the time. Of course, I believe the most delicious *miso* is the long-fermented variety that comes from traditional homes.

Misodama at Nippon Kan.

Misodama hanging under the eaves.

Preservatives are added to today's packaged *miso* to keep it fresh while being shipped, stored, and redistributed. Because *miso* is a product of fermentation, fermentation will continue if it is exposed to air. I have seen month-old packages of *miso* in organic health food stores that were not vacuum-sealed that had no mold on the top. I have trouble believing this *miso* was a totally organic product.

While the *miso* is fermenting in the tub, juices leak from the bottom and are collected underneath. This juice is called *tamari* or *taremiso* — used to make soy sauce. In the United States, there is a product named *"tamari."* This is completely different from the original *tamari* collected from the fermenting *miso.* If you have experienced Japan, you know that American *tamari* and Japanese *tamari* are like American *futons* compared to Japanese *futons:* the names are the same, but the two are fundamentally different.

Shoyu (soy sauce) was traditionally produced as a cash crop to be sold in the cities. The mountain people and country farmers couldn't afford *shoyu,* and used *tamari* or *taremiso* as a flavoring instead.

Because real *tamari* is very difficult to find in the United States, the recipes that originally used *tamari* in this book will call for *miso* or *shoyu,* or a mixture of the two.

Shottsuru — Salted, Pickled Fish Juice

If directly translated, *shottsuru* means "salty juice" and can be applicable to the juices derived from pickling wild vegetables, ocean products, or even mushrooms. Here, however, *shottsuru* applies to pickled fish juice.

The end of November and December in my home town of Akita was the season for *hata hata* or sand fish. Thousands and thousands were caught at sea or were washed up on shore in what looked like an invasion.

The Japanese written character for *hata hata* depicts a lightning fish. During the season of the *hata hata,* the northeastern region of Japan is frequented by lightning storms. When the lightning storms began, my mother would say, "Tomorrow *hata hata* will be cheap."

She was right. Early the next morning the peddlers came pulling carts or riding three-wheeled motorbikes pulling carts full of large wooden boxes overflowing with slippery *hata hata.* The *hata hata* have no scales, so the small fish slid everywhere. The fish were extremely inexpensive. An entire box might cost only the equivalent of 20 cents or so.

During the spawning season, a female *hata hata* could carry a *burikko* (egg sack) the size of a man's fist. After a storm, the seas washed these egg sacks onto the beach. My brother and I would ride our bicycles down to see miles and miles of beaches covered with the egg sacks. There would be so many you could not see the sand where the waves were breaking.

Today the ocean currents have changed and the *hata hata* do not come to Akita like they used to. Now they are imported from Korea. One single native *hata hata* now is about 300 *yen* or $2.

For many years *hata hata* was the source of winter protein in Akita and the surrounding areas. Most families bought abundant supplies and pickled them with salt, or with salt and *nuka* (rice bran). A favored delicacy was *sushizuke,* which was *hata hata* mixed with *koji* and white rice in large quantities (sometimes 60 gallons). The mixture was left in a large press to pickle. As the *koji* and white rice fermented, the vinegar produced preserved the fish. The press kept poisons from forming by limiting the access to oxygen.

To avoid the tedium of eating the same fish each day, villagers prepared the *hata hata* in a variety of ways. The fish was enjoyed fresh by lightly salting and broiling. It was also marinated with *miso* or *tamari* overnight and broiled, or flavored with *shoyu* or *sakekasu* (rice wine lees) and poached in a pot. Today Akita is famous for a local dish named *shottsuru nabe.* The primary flavoring for this dish, cooked in *nabe* fashion (using one pot), is from the *hata hata* and its pickling juices.

In Oriental markets here in the United States, *shottsuru* (pickled fish juices) are called fish sauce. Usually these sauces are made from the juices from pickling sardines and anchovies. This fish sauce can be used to make delicious soup stock or noodle dishes.

Sardine or anchovy fish sauce is an important flavoring and nutrient all over Southeast Asia. Traditionally, many kinds of fish were pickled and the juices used as *shottsuru* for cooking. Today in Japan *shottsuru* is made from *hata hata* or *ami* (mysid opposum shrimps). *Ami* has been part of the Japanese diet for centuries, and it is interesting to watch it gaining popularity in the United States.

Kanmi — Sweets

Traditionally, sweets have not played a major role in the Japanese diet. The only sweets found in earlier times were naturally sweetened foods such as sugar cane or sugar beets.

Three hundred years ago, crystal sugar candy was imported from Holland and Portugal. These novel candies were enjoyed by the *samurai* and the wealthy but were not for the mouths of the common people. The sweets of the farmers came naturally or were processed with very simple techniques. There were no candy factories. Today tooth decay is on the rise among the young people of Japan, a problem that did not occur until recent times.

Traditionally, sugar was not consumed directly. The country people found their sweets in dried vegetables and fruits. For example, after the harvest in late October and November, the branches of the persimmon tree are heavy with red, ripened fruit. Entire families used to gather the fruits, peel, and dry them outside in the cold autumn air. These dried persimmons are called *hoshigaki.* These fruits never completely dried but stayed soft and chewy on the inside. After hanging for a time the persimmons would develop a white powdery covering that indicated they were ready to eat.

There are two varieties of persimmons: one kind is always sweet, and the other is bitter until dried. Persimmons were a very important source

Homemade sake pot.

Sake and sakazuki next to the irori.

for sweet flavors for the traditional country people, especially during the long winter.

One day, an old man standing at a heavily laden persimmon tree said to me, "No matter how starved we have ever been for something sweet, we have always left the last few fruits, the ones highest up in the tree, as gifts for the crows." The crows were once believed to be messengers for the mountain gods. "See how today all these ripe persimmons remain on the tree. Japan must be doing very well these days to let them fall to waste. I am not sure if this is good or bad," he said with a solemn look.

If you buy fresh persimmons and they taste bitter, put them in a plastic bag whole with whole apples and store them in the refrigerator for one or two days. The bitterness disappears. This helpful hint comes from the elders of rural Japan — they don't know why it works, either.

The sweeteners used the most were maple syrup and honey. During my time as a curator my territory included Lake Towada national park in northern Honshu. This was a beautiful area in which to enjoy the four seasons. In the fall the maple trees are in full glory. In the old days, said my friend Mr. Maeda, he had been able to extract syrup from any tree in sight. Today, environmental concerns prohibit this, and most syrup must come from the market.

Traditionally, and still when I was a curator, maple syrup was extracted to sell as a cash crop or to be used for barter. In this area field farming is difficult due to the rugged mountain terrain. People from this area survived on what the mountains could provide. *Hachimitsu* or wild honey was a very important cash crop, and commanded a high price.

After being granted permission by the local environmental control office, Mr. Maeda and myself went hunting for wild honey while researching traditional honey-gathering techniques. Deep into the mountains we traveled. After finding a hive we approached it carefully. I was completely covered with protective netting. My old friend, with no protective clothing at all, marched up to the hive, carefully pulled out a bee larva, and popped it into his mouth. "I just added two years onto my life," he exclaimed. We ate one or two, but left the rest for the hive.

This area was also home to a poisonous variety of pit viper called *mamushi*. They were highly sought after and used to make *sake*. You've heard of the worm in the bottom of the bottle. The viper's unborn young are highly prized for their nourishment and powers to increase male sexual prowess.

Another interesting sweet is called *saruzake* (monkey *sake*). (Don't worry; they don't put the whole monkey in a bottle.) You may have seen wildlife specials on television featuring the monkeys of northern Japan famous for enjoying bathing in hot springs. These monkeys' natural habitat is near my home town in Akita.

The monkeys gather fruits and nuts before winter and store them up high in holes in the trees. The fruits and nuts are chewed to a pulp by the monkeys before they are stored. The moisture from the living tree and the cold temperatures outside provide ideal conditions for the fruit to ferment.

Saruzake is very sweet with a nice color and viscous consistency. It is also very high in alcohol content. The monkeys stirred the liqueurs with sticks, only poking in a finger to taste — that was enough.

When the snows were deep, we could wear snowshoes and hunt for monkey *sake*. Having found one of their caches, we gave the monkeys food in exchange for what we took, and left more than a third of the liqueur in each tree for them.

At that time, the price of monkey liqueur was about $45 for a shot-sized glass. Brokers who sold these various fruit and other herb liqueurs made quite a handsome profit.

Since we have been talking about *sake,* another story comes to mind.

Rice or barley (rice being the more popular of the two) is steamed and mixed with *kojikabi* (a mold that changes starches to dextrose) to make *koji. Koji* you remember is used as a catalyst to make *miso* and *shoyu.*

Because of the high starch content in rice, if this *koji* is brewed and distilled, it becomes quite sweet. This unique sweet taste from fermenting *koji* is the basis for making *sake* (drinking rice wine) and *mirin* (cooking rice wine).

Today *sake* is drunk all over the world. In the old days, *sake* was too expensive for the farmers and common people. The farmers drank *nigorizake,* which was homemade *sake.* This *nigorizake* did not go through the final filtering-separation process, so it was not clear like the *sake* we see today.

About 60 or 70 years ago, a new government liquor law was instigated to control the production of homemade *sake.* It became illegal to brew *sake.* Of course, unlawful brewing continued. In my home town area, the local word for *nigorizake* is *doburoku* or *ohho.* This *doburoku,* brewed in secret under penalty of law, was most delicious. Today it is no longer illegal to produce *nigorizake* to be sold in liquor stores as long as the producers pay an alcohol tax.

About 15 years ago when I was a curator, we visited many old traditional farmers' homes. Many times on these visits *doburoku* was offered, accepted, and enjoyed.

One cold day, a farmer gave me a large bottle of *doburoku* for a gift. After leaving his home, I returned to the train station to wait for the train.

It being so cold, I entered the station to join the others gathered around the coal stove to keep warm. I forgot that I would be quickly warming the *doburoku,* too.

"Boom!" The cork to the *doburoku* bottle shot out, the aroma filling the tiny waiting area. Everyone looked at me with questioning eyes. "Do you have what we think you have?" There was only one thing I could do. I walked over to the stationmaster, borrowed a *chawan* (tea cup), and shared with everyone. Because the stationmaster was also a farmer, the rules in this country area were flexible enough for the occasion to be a happy one.

From an old farmer I heard an amusing story. One day a jeep pulled into his small farming village. From the jeep stepped a man obviously from the city wearing a suit. The old farmer instantly assumed that this was a government agent looking for home-brewed *sake.* He ran to the back of his home warning all the neighbors as he went. All the farmers at the same time poured their batches of *doburoku* into the creek, turning it white.

As it turned out, of course, the stranger was an interested buyer of *doburoku,* not a government agent.

Nigorizake has been made from *genmai* (brown rice) since the Edo period. The clear *sake* you see today does not have as much history behind it.

Sake also has a religious function. The *sake* used in shrines is called *omiki.* Today, clear *sake* is used in shrines and called *omiki,* but originally herb liqueurs were used for this purpose. The exorbitant price of these liqueurs caused the change to clear *sake.*

Farmers and mountain people made many different varieties of liqueurs by fermenting different herbs and fruits together to create many unusual tastes. The most widely used sweet ingredient produced by fermentation is *mirin*. To make *mirin, nigorizake* is filtered to separate the clear *sake* from the dregs or lees (the latter is called *sakekasu*). Distilling this *sakekasu* results in *shochu* (distilled spirits). *Mirin* is the result of fermenting and straining *shochu*, adding it to steamed sticky rice and *koji*, and fermenting the lot together. *Mirin* is the most popular sweetener used in Japanese cooking.

One day while visiting a liquor store in Denver, I was surprised and amused to find a row of *mirin* bottles lined up next to the *sake* and plum wine. I hope no one took this home to drink! *Mirin* belongs on the market shelf next to the soy sauce and sesame oil: it is for cooking, not drinking.

Abura shibori — oil press.

Abura — Oils

There is on display at the Lake Ogawara Folk Art Museum an antique wooden tool used for extracting oil. As shown in the illustration, the mechanics are simple. The food to be pressed was placed between two pieces of wood, and wedges were hammered into place with a big wooden mallet, driving the pieces together.

In the Lake Ogawara area, this method was used to make rapeseed oil, a popular cooking ingredient. It is obvious by examining this simple method of extraction that the oil was produced in small quantities. The traditional Japanese farmer was never able to produce enough oil for deep-frying foods.

You may be questioning why we are including oils in a section dealing with flavorings and seasonings. There are many sources for natural oils in Japan. From sesame seeds we obtain *goma abura*, from Japanese nutmeg we obtain *kaya abura*, from corn we obtain *kimi abura*, from peanuts we obtain *rakkasei abura*, and from soybeans we can make *daizu abura*.

Few oils are used in traditional country cooking. Oils were made to sell as a cash crop; they were too expensive to indulge in. When making country dishes, a little bit of oil might be used for sauteeing or a few drops mixed in to enhance the smell and taste. Therefore, traditionally these oils were treated as a flavoring more than as a method for cooking other foods. This definitely contrasts with Chinese cooking, which uses a lot of oil.

At my restaurant, 24 ounces of vegetable oil and 10 ounces of sesame oil would last for two weeks. The vegetable oil I used as an anti-rust agent, the sesame oil I used as a flavoring. If a Japanese country food restaurant used only this much oil, think how little was used in the households of rural Japan.

Our bodies need oils to remain healthy. How then did the traditional farmer get the oils he needed? The traditional farmer ate the foods that contained the oils in the first place. If you eat rapeseed flowers, corn, soybeans, and sesame seeds, your body will get the oils it needs.

Animal oils, although not eaten in abundance, added to the farmers' total oil intake. Late autumn was hunting season for birds and rabbits. Other four-legged animals were eaten only on special days. During hunting season, *to nabe* (rabbit stew) was popular. Oil rising to the top while the dish was cooking indicated that it would be tasty and nourishing. In late autumn, animals have much fat stored for winter. Humans as well, especially those whose lives are closely bound to nature and the seasons, want to pad themselves with extra fat for the winter for protection from the cold.

Hare no hi, or the special days designated for eating meat, did not all fall only in autumn in preparation for winter. Special days were also held in spring during rice-planting time or late summer during or after a harvest. Although these special days were religiously oriented, they also corresponded to times when the people were expending a great deal of energy. These holidays allowed them to eat the meats that gave them the energy they needed to perform the tasks at hand. The country farmers' diet followed the rhythms of both the seasons and the work load.

This concludes the section on basic Japanese seasonings. Of course, all seasonings and tastes vary slightly depending on location and lifestyle. The seasonings we buy in the markets today in the United States are individually mass-produced. Originally, however, these seasonings were by-products of food preservation processes. The byproducts of these processes were gifts to be ingeniously utilized by the country people of Japan. Interesting flavorings such as soy sauce or *mirin* were discovered as the foods were pickled, fermented, or salted. These by-products have since found a honored place in the Japanese diet.

Interestingly, these seasonings are still undergoing change to suit current tastes: witness "lite" soy sauce and reduced-salt *miso*!

Basic Soup Stock Ingredients

Kamado — kitchen hearth.

Soup base or soup stock is called *dashijiru*. The word *dashi* directly translated means to "take out." In other words, from good ingredients, one can extract good tastes.

The quality of the *dashijiru* determines the quality of a finished dish. However, you can create delicious soups using the juices from preserved foods (as explained in the previous section) or even vegetables and meats alone. Especially in *nabe* cooking (cooking with one pot), cooking all the ingredients together makes for a delicious taste, even if *dashijiru* is not used.

Of course, just throwing anything into the pot won't necessarily create a pleasant taste. The ingredients need to have an affinity for one another. For example, pork and *gobo* (burdock), and chicken and *shoga* (ginger) blend together nicely.

It is difficult to set a lot of rules for making *dashijiru*. If you asked an old farmer for such rules he would be surprised: he put *dashijiru* together without thinking.

For anyone who is trying this for the first time,

following a cookbook with "The ABCs of How to Make *Dashijiru*" will tend to narrow your range of possible tastes and experience.

If you go to the market you can buy any number of pre-made mixes called *dashi*. A person familiar only with instant *dashi* would not recognize the taste of traditionally prepared *dashijiru*. A true *dashijiru* reflects the tastes of the chef. *Dashijiru* varies from house to house: everybody has a different idea of how to make it. If everyone had exactly the same tastes, we would not be making full use of our creative senses.

In the recipes in this book, the amounts listed for the ingredients are standard guidelines. This is especially true for those amounts given for water, seasonings, and *dashijiru*. These, as well as the cooking time, should be adjusted to suit your personal tastes. Part of the enjoyment of cooking is the learning process itself. If you prepare a soup and it tastes too bland or weak, or if the ingredients are overcooked or undercooked, make adjustments the next time.

As a child I remember the peddlers hawking their wares from house to house in our town.

Most of the *dashijiru* for any particular area was composed of local ingredients. The recipes in this book are basically from the northeastern part of Japan, so they seldom include, for example, *katsuo* (bonito) — a fish indigenous to the southern islands of Kyushu and Shikoku. Since this fish had to be imported from the south, it was expensive and so not used as widely as ingredients readily available locally. I am sure recipes from Kyushu include *katsuo* as a main ingredient.

Interestingly, all the ingredients used to make *dashijiru* are preserved. If you try to make *dashijiru* with the same fresh ingredients, it simply doesn't taste right.

Early farmers discovered that foods preserved for the winter made a good-tasting soup stock when cooked again in water. After that they continued to preserve their foods, but now they saved some to make *dashijiru* for soups and other dishes.

Niboshi, Yakiboshi, Ebi, and Katsuo Dashijiru — Dried Sardines, Grilled and Dried Sardines, Shrimp, and Bonito

Today, most fish *dashijiru* is made from anchovies and sardines. In the past, char or horse mackerel were also used. The *niboshi* (small sardines, anchovies, mackerel, or char) were boiled on the beach and laid out in the sun to dry. Broiled and dried fish is called *yakiboshi*.

These fish range in size from a half inch to four inches. The Japanese name for a fish changes depending on the size. The size we used for making *dashijiru* was about two inches. Each size has a cooking method best suited to bring out the most delicious taste. Each household has its own tradition concerning what size is best, so naturally, *dashijiru* varies from house to house.

Misawa City is located in northern Honshu. This is the home of the Lake Ogawara Folk Art museum, of which I was a curator. The city is surrounded by water: the Pacific Ocean on one side, Lake Ogawara on the other, and Mutsu Bay to the south. The Hakkoda range of mountains

Dashi ingredients:
1) Kezuri bushi
2) Yakiboshi
3) Kombu
4) Daizu
5) Shiitake
6) Kampyo
7) Niboshi
8) Hoshi ebi

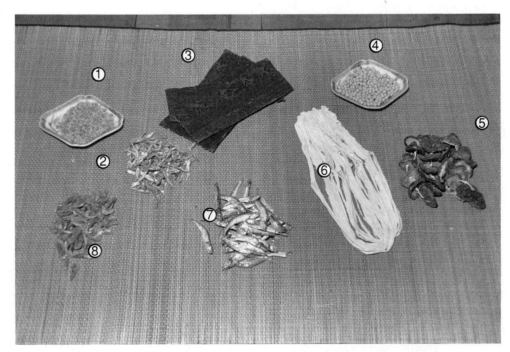

to the north completes the framing of the city. I was lucky during my time as curator to be living in such a beautiful area. I got to know the local fishermen well while doing my research there.

One day, I arose with the fishermen and headed for the beach. The nets were cast and the fishermen and their neighbors began hauling them in. Waiting on the beach was a cast-iron pot big enough for four people to use as a hot tub. A bonfire was built under the pot. After the nets had been hauled in, the horse mackerel and sardines were separated by size and the smallest ones put in large baskets, which were lowered into the pot. After they were cooked, the fish were spread on mats to dry. These smaller fish became *niboshi.* The larger fish were divided equally among the fishermen and neighbors who had helped pull in the catch for that day's meal.

Today, these larger fish are cooked commercially by the hundreds. Traditionally, however, these fishermen took the day's catch home and cooked them individually. The ones not eaten that day were dried: when it was time to cook them later they were first soaked in water. After soaking the fish, the fishermen accidentally discovered that this water made a nice soup base.

When using *niboshi* and *yakiboshi* to make *dashijiru,* either gut the fish and leave the fish in the soup, or use the fish whole and remove it after the *dashijiru* is made. Japanese cookbooks today suggest using the whole fish then removing them. When I was growing up, it was commonly held that eating the whole fish made your bones strong. We always kept the fish in our *miso* soup made from *niboshi* or *yakiboshi.* My mother even purposely put extra fish in my soup.

If you did remove the fish, they were collected for a few days (a lot of *miso* soup was eaten, so a lot of fish could be collected), cooked with soy sauce, *mirin,* and *sake* to make *tsukudani* (a popular side dish).

Many different kinds of fish could be caught from Lake Ogawara. These fish were preserved by boiling, broiling, drying, and pickling. Many shrimp were also caught. These were used to make *dashijiru,* too.

In Japan, another fish popularly used to make *dashijiru* is *katsuo* (bonito). Bonito was not readily available in my home town because the waters were too cold. Long ago *katsuo* was graded by location, each area producing a fish with a different taste.

Today, deep-sea fishing expeditions go far out into the ocean, track, catch, and freeze the fish before returning to Japan. There is no longer a specific character associated with the fish based on where it was caught.

We usually see bonito in the United States Oriental markets in the shaved form. But because bonito is getting rarer and more expensive, shaved tuna is becoming a common substitute.

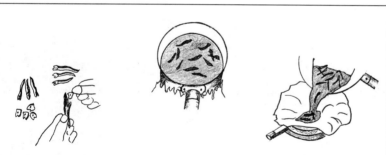

HOW TO MAKE NIBOSHI DASHIJIRU (MAKES 4 CUPS.)
4 1/2 cups water, 2 lbs. sake, and 20–25 1-inch niboshi or yaki-boshi.
  A. Remove heads; pinch out stomach area.
  B. Soak fish in sake and water for 7 to 8 hours. Over high heat bring almost to a boil and turn off flame.
  C. Strain through cloth or fine-mesh strainer.

Dried products increase two to five times in size when soaked in water.

Shiitake Dashijiru — Black Forest Mushroom Soup Stock

In the United States you can buy fresh *shiitake* (black forest mushrooms) year-round. Fresh mushrooms are not used to make *dashijiru*, however. Dried *shiitake* mushrooms called *hoshi shiitake* make a far better soup base. *Shiitake* mushrooms are graded according to where they were pro-duced, size, shape, etc. The best quality *shiitake* are called *donko* and are small, firm, and circular.

Today in Japan these *donko* are imported from Korea. They are less expensive, which has forced many domestic *shiitake* farmers out of business. This in turn has caused a decreased supply of Japanese *shiitake* mushrooms, which has in turn caused an increase in demand for more imported *shiitake* from Korea. Some *donko* are still produced in Japan, but they are quite expensive.

Today, behind the family house somewhere in the corner of the back yard, stands a *hodagi.* The *hodagi* is made of oak, cut into about four-foot-long beams leaned against and secured to a top central post to form a triangular framework. The *hodagi* is placed in a damp, shaded spot.

Small plugs with tips laden with *shiitake* fungus are hammered into the undersides of the beams. Using this method, a family can raise enough *shiitake* mushrooms to eat fresh or to dry.

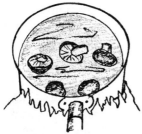

HOW TO MAKE SHIITAKE DASHIJIRU (MAKES 3 CUPS)
4 cups water, 5–7 medium shiitake mushrooms.
A. Soak mushrooms in 4 cups water for 7 to 8 hours.
B. Bring almost to a boil, turn off heat. Remove mushrooms.

HOW TO MAKE KOMBU DASHIJIRU (MAKES 3 CUPS)
4 cups water, 1 oz. kombu.
A. Soak kombu 7 to 8 hours in water.
B. Bring all ingredients to a boil over high heat and continue to boil 5 to 6 minutes over low heat. Turn off heat. Remove kombu.

My home too had a *hodagi*. This *hodagi* attracted slugs and snails so it was my job, not my sister's, to collect the *shiitake*. She was afraid of slugs.

Wild *shiitake* can be found growing on chingua pine, oak, or chestnut trees in both spring and autumn. Fresh, wild *shiitake* lightly salted and barbecued is most delicious.

The *shiitake* has gained attention in this country recently through reported medical findings indicating that the *shiitake* helps to prevent certain cancers and reduce cholesterol levels.

Traditionally, *shiitake* was a popular present to be given on New Year's and *Bon* (August Buddhist festival). Any house was happy to receive such a gift.

Kombu Dashijiru — Kelp Soup Stock

Dashikombu (a variety of kelp) is the sea vegetable used to make *kombu dashijiru*. There are different grades of *dashikombu*, the best to be found in the waters off the island of Hokkaido, Japan's northernmost island. Here the long, cold winters provide the right environment to produce quality sea vegetables.

Consistent with the theme of farmer survival, this *dashikombu* was first dried to use at a later date. After making *dashijiru* we used *dashikombu* in other dishes. *Kombu* can grow up to 24 to 26 feet in length and about two feet wide. This variety is too large for eating.

The best *kombu* for eating is about four inches wide and less than eight feet long, with a deep black color. Sometimes a white powder forms on the surface of packaged *kombu.* Don't worry, just wipe it off with a wet paper towel: it consists of evaporated minerals from the *kombu.*

The Japanese eat many sea vegetables. These vegetables are collectively called *kaiso.* One major use of sea vegetables is in the making of gelatin by-products, including *tokoroten* (gelid-

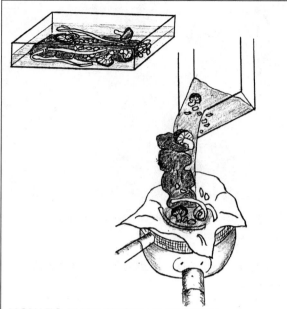

HOW TO MAKE SHOJIN DASHIJIRU (MAKES 4 CUPS)
5 cups water, 3 Tbsp. soybeans, 1/2 oz. kanpyo, 4-5 medium shiitake mushrooms.
A. Combine ingredients and soak for 7 to 10 hours.
B. Cook over medium heat, but do not boil.
C. Strain through a cloth or fine-mesh strainer.

ium jelly), *kanten* (Japanese isinglass), and *ego* (agar products).

Shojin Dashijiru — Vegetarian Soup Stock

Shiitake mushrooms and sea vegetables are used for *shojin dashijiru.* This *dashijiru* relates back to early Zen Buddhism. Today we could call it a completely vegetarian *dashijiru.*

A good *shojin dashijiru* includes *kanpyo* (dried gourd shavings) and *daizu* (soybeans). Large *kanpyo* can measure 2 to 3 feet in diameter. These gourds are peeled and dried.

I have a friend who farms *kanpyo* in Tochigi prefecture, an area famous for *kanpyo.* He still uses a foot-powered machine to peel the gourds and hangs the *kanpyo* in his yard in long rows to dry. This area is also famous for thick bamboo plants. It is a beautiful sight to see the wind sway the green bamboo in time with the fluttering of the drying, white *kanpyo* strips.

In the United States, the available packaged *kanpyo* is very white. This *kanpyo* has usually been bleach-dried with chemicals. *Kanpyo* that has been dried naturally has a creamy color, smells nice, and is uniform in size.

Gara Dashijiru — Fowl and Meat Bone Soup Stock

After you have stripped the flesh from a chicken, what remains is called *gara*. For pork it is called *ton kotsu*, and for beef, the remaining bones are called *gyu kotsu*.

In recent times in Japan, the word for chicken is *tori*. Originally, any bird, pheasant, turtle

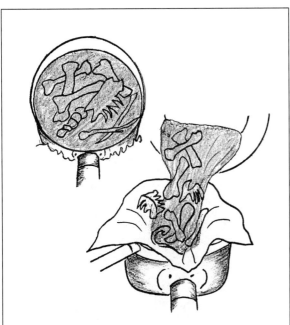

HOW TO MAKE GARA DASHIJIRU (MAKES 5 CUPS)
8 cups water, 1 lb. chicken bones and sinew, 1/2 oz. ginger.
A. Combine all ingredients and simmer over low heat for 2 to 3 hours. Remove aku.
B. Strain through cloth or fine-mesh strainer.

dove, or such was called *tori*.

There are two types of *gara dashijiru*. 1) The *gara* is removed after the *dashijiru* is made, leaving the "broth" only, and 2) pieces of meat with the bones are left in the stock.

We will discuss this further in a later chapter under *naberyori* and *nabemono* (one-pot cooking), but these dishes usually include chopped meat with the bones inside. Noodle dishes are prepared with the clear *gara dashijiru*.

Conclusion

This section has offered an explanation of the various different types of *dashijiru*. The most important point to understand is that the ingredients used to make *dashijiru* were not originally processed with this intention. The primary objective was to preserve the foods themselves.

Earlier in the book we talked about basic seasonings. When preserving certain foods, a unique taste is created that can be used for flavoring without using *dashijiru*. The line between which foods should be used directly and which foods would be better combined with *dashijiru*, is a difficult point to distinguish in country cooking.

My favorite *dashijiru* is *kombu* and *shiitake*. I use it every day. I make it by soaking the *kombu* and *shiitake* for 5 to 6 hours. You don't necessarily need to follow the step-by-step process shown in the charts. If I use some of the *dashijiru* for making soup, I just refill the jar with a little more water so I have a fresh supply every day.

After the vegetables have been used to make *dashijiru*, they can be chopped and used in other cooking recipes.

Another favorite *dashijiru* of mine is made by placing *niboshi*, *yakiboshi*, *kombu*, and *shiitake* in a gauze bag and lightly crushing the ingredients. This bag can then be cooked in water. This is fast, easy, and most economical. You can achieve a variety of tastes by adjusting the mixture of the ingredients.

This *dashijiru* is the most popular of all Domo products. After using these "*dashijiru* bags," the leftover *dashijiru* can be removed and used to fertilize your houseplants.

It is important to think about how the taste of the *dashijiru* will balance with the other ingredients in the soup. Sometimes the soup will taste better without any *dashijiru* at all. A good example is *hakusai* (Chinese cabbage). When boiled it makes a nice broth by itself.

Traditional Foods Preserved Naturally

Miso Dama, Konnyaku Dama

This chapter focuses on major food groups that are preserved via drying, salting, or pickling. Foods that are pre-prepared and then refrigerated will be discussed in a later chapter (under country meals).

Jikasakumotsu — Garden Vegetables

Garden vegetables are grown around most family homes. Prior to about 1900, the varieties of vegetables grown were limited. Depending on location, *daikon* (Japanese white radish), *negi* (Japanese onion), *konsai rui* (edible roots), *nappa rui* (greens), *kabocha* (pumpkin), and *uri rui* (gourds) were the main vegetables grown in Japan.

When I was a child, lettuce and celery were not available. These vegetables are called *yoyasai* (Western vegetables). Traditional Japanese vegetables are called *wayasai*. Of course, more *wayasai* was grown than could be consumed, so the rest were harvested for preserving.

Many different methods were used. Vegetables were pickled in salt, dried, boiled and dried, or buried in straw-lined holes in the ground.

Traditionally, the dried leaves of the *daikon* plant, *hoshina,* were popular fare. Today, because of the abundance of food in Japan, *hoshina* is rarely eaten. In earlier times, like when I was a child, *hoshina* could be found hanging from the eaves of most houses.

The area around Misawa City used to be very poor because rice could not be grown due to the lack of a fresh water supply. An irrigation system was installed by a man named Inazo Nitobe (1862–1933), whom martial artists know as the author of *Bushido.*

Before this irrigation system was developed, *hoshina* was eaten frequently. *Hoshina* mixed into *miso* soup gives the illusion of fullness. When I was a curator, I discovered a folk song called *Hoshina Jiru* that told about troubled times and of having to eat *hoshina.*

The stem of the *daikon* radish was also eaten. When tied and hung, the stems would dry until they looked like sponges: only the fibrous skeleton would remain. This is called *shimidaikon* and can be ready for use after soaking again in water. This drying method was and is an important way to save foods.

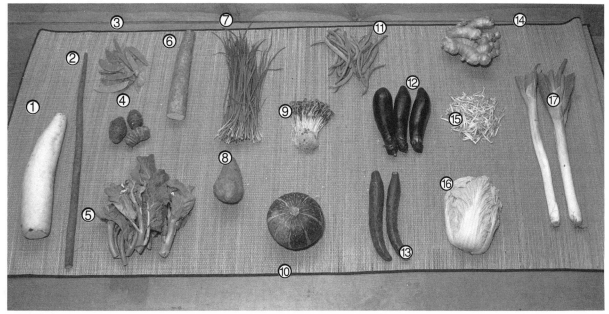

Wayasai available in the United States. 1) Daikon, 2) Gobo, 3) Kinusaya, 4) Satoimo, 5) Nanohana, 6) Nagaimo, 7) Nira, 8) Satsumaimo, 9) Kaiware, 10) Kabocha, 11) Saya Ingen, 12) Nasu, 13) Kyuri, 14) Shoga, 15) Moyashi, 16) Hakusai, 17) Negi.

If you think about what you have read here, you realize there must have been a lot of products hanging from the eaves of the traditional farmer's house. You are correct. In addition to the dried vegetables we have been discussing, farmers also hung dried fruits, fish, meats, *shimitofu* (freeze-dried tofu), *misodama* (dried balls of miso), and *konnyakuimo* (Devil's tongue potato).

When I worked at the Lake Ogawara Folk Art Museum, we saw many traditional houses that still had their dried produce stored under the eaves. I feel lucky to have witnessed this, since this kind of tradition is so rapidly disappearing.

Sansai to Kinoko — Wild Herbs, Vegetables, and Mushrooms

Not nearly as abundant as garden vegetables, wild produce could be found in the mountains or even bordering the nearby fields. Common people who did not want to worry about taking care of a garden or didn't want to show taxable property could supplement their diets with these wild vegetables. All you had to know was how

to find them. These wild herbs, vegetables, and mushrooms also had their own methods for preservation.

After the long winters of northeastern Japan, the villagers would head to the mountains carrying baskets to collect the first buds of spring. The purpose of these outings was to gather, but more importantly, everyone was delighted to get outside and enjoy the first days of spring.

In the area where I grew up, the bamboo is about an inch in diameter and 8 to 10 feet tall. A sea of bamboo covers the surrounding hills. During the winter the snows are heavy and the winds fierce. Avalanches are not uncommon. The bamboo growing on the hillsides contorts to conform to the sliding and drifting snows. This means that the bamboo usually grows along the ground downhill for a foot or two before it finally turns upward toward the sun.

When the snow melts, it is time for gathering *takenoko* (bamboo shoots). During spring, bamboo grows at the rate of about one foot per day.

This spring harvest is still important to today's country people. *Takenoko* are highly regarded and constitute an important cash crop.

As I have explained, the bamboo conformed its shape to the drifting snow. Therefore, when walking downhill one walks with the curve and it is easy to move through the forest. When you try to return, however, the bamboo is curved toward you, making it difficult to penetrate. It takes about three times the amount of time to get out of the forest as it did to get in. One needs to plan for this time element. The people who regularly gather mountain vegetables, mushrooms, and bamboo shoots are usually secretive about the whereabouts of their gathering, so if an accident does occasionally occur, it is not discovered for quite some time.

One of the most prized and expensive mushrooms in Japan grows in the Rockies in relative abundance. The Japanese Americans that live in this area are serious about the hunt for the *matsutake* mushroom.

A few years ago I was assisting and coordinating a story being done by a major Japanese newspaper on the *matsutake* of Colorado. We interviewed many Japanese Americans, but not one person would tell us where the mushrooms could be found! If someone had given directions, I think they would have been questionable anyway, given the secrecy of mushroom hunters. In Japan a *matsutake* mushroom the size of a child's fist can fetch 20 to 30 American dollars, the best ones even commanding a price of 100 dollars each. In Japan the professional mushroom gatherers pick only mushrooms of the right

Hoshina and other sansai examples. 1) Mizuna, 2) Hoshigiku, 3) Takana, 4) Imozuru, 5) Yuri, 6) Renkon, 7) Kiriboshi Daikon, 8) Sengiri Daikon, 9) Nasu, 10) Daikon no ha

Making dried kinoko at Nippon Kan. 1) Shiitake, 2) Kikurage, 3) Hokitake.

size, leaving the ones too small and the ones too big for another day.

In the spring in Japan there are many kinds of wild herbs and vegetables to be found. Gathered and used fresh they make wonderful side dishes, or they can also be pickled with salt, boiled and dried, or just dried. For example, *zenmai* (osmond) is mixed with water and ash, boiled, rinsed, and dried. When dried it shrinks to one-third its original size.

Warabi (fernbrake) and *fuki* (butterbur) are mixed with ash and water, boiled, and left under cold running water for 2 or 3 days. There being no running water indoors, the vegetables were traditionally lowered into a nearby creek. After this they are salted or pickled. When it is time to use them you need only to soak them in water to remove the salt. Interestingly, if you add salt to water, the salt is leeched from the plants much faster. We call this *yobi shio* (calling out the salt). The ash works like baking soda to soften the vegetables.

Warabi, fuki, and *zenmai* are now sometimes processed with chemicals and enhanced with food color. (The plants have original-looking coloring added back in.) I am not sure why they try to make them green again, but they look unnatural to me. Usually *hozonshoku* (preserved foods) lose their original color and turn brown like summer grass.

Fuki thrive in moist areas. The plants usually grow up to two feet high with leaves resembling small umbrellas as large as one foot in diameter. The flower comes up from the ground before the leaves; the leaves actually emerge in a different spot. These leaves we call *fukinoto.* Akita *fuki* is famous in Japan. The plants grow several feet tall, and the leaves do grow as big as umbrellas. There is an old folk song that says, "In case of rain we don't need umbrellas in Akita." *Fuki* is boiled and often added to *miso* soup or used in other dishes.

In Japan on January 15 (some areas January 7) *haru no nanakusa* (the seven grasses of spring) are traditionally gathered from around the yards, chopped, and mixed with *okayu* (see breakfast recipe section). The dates of January 7 or 15 are for the areas of Japan with warm climates. In my area the grasses don't come up until late April or early May. The grasses do not all come up at the same time. Only one or a mixture of a few can be used to season *okayu. Seri* is especially popular.

These wild grasses include: *seri* (Japanese parsley), *nazuna* (mother's heart), *ogyo* (cotton weed), *hakobera* (chickweed), *hotokenoza* (henbit), *suzuna* (turnip grass), and *suzushiro* (wild radish). These grasses grow as weeds. The grasses are dried and used to make herb tea. The flowers are picked off flowering adult plants and eaten. The most delicious ones I have found in Denver are *hakobera* and *hotokenoza*.

Traditionally these grasses were mixed with *genmai* (brown rice) or *zakkoku* (farmer's porridge). Today, white rice mixed with water to create an oatmeal-like consistency is combined with these grasses and lightly salted to make a special *okayu.*

These special celebration dishes are explained in more detail under Traditional Celebrations in Chapter 2.

Late summer is the season of the mushroom. The Japanese mountain forests are cool, and the high humidity provides a good environment for more than 40 varieties. Unfortunately, only a few of these wild mushrooms can be found in the United States.

These wild mushrooms can be cooked and eaten fresh but are usually dried or pickled with salt. Dried *shiitake* mushrooms, oyster mushrooms, and black mushrooms are fairly available in the United States. I have also seen portabello, cremiri, tree oyster mushrooms, and morels in gourmet stores.

In the United States, it is difficult to find mushrooms that have been pickled in salt. If you do manage to find some, soak them to remove the salt before cooking. I think you'll find they make for a novel taste.

Kaiso — Sea Vegetables

My home town of Akita boasts one of the largest markets in Japan. Fresh produce is brought in daily from the mountains, fields, and oceans. The market covers three square blocks, and is divided into sections for fresh fish and shellfish, fresh vegetables, dried mushrooms, dried vegetables, *kanbutsu* (dried fish), and *nerimono* (ground fish cake products).

Sea vegetables have their own section. You can imagine how many varieties there must be to fill an entire section. More than ten stores are required to hold them all.

As soon as you step into the sea vegetable section you are surrounded by smells of the beach and ocean. In addition to the vegetables themselves, there is a myriad of products made from sea vegetables like *tororo, oboro,* and *sukikombu.* What I have found available in the United States Japanese markets is *arame* (an edible seaweed variety), *nori* (laver), *hijiki* (a variety of brown algae), and *mekabu* (a kelp shoot).

When testing the quality of sea vegetables, check the color and the smell. Interestingly, Japanese markets in Japan place the fresh sea vegetables in the fresh fish section. In the sea vegetable section the products are all dried, pickled, or cooked. The sea vegetables we distribute out of Denver my sister buys from this market and ships to us by air. When we open the packages the smells from the beaches of Japan permeate the room. It always makes me homesick for the sea. Colorado has no ocean....

Harvesting and gathering *nori, hijiki,* and *arame* from the oceans and the beaches is tradi-

tionally women's work. This is extremely hard work, especially when it is cold.

Wearing rice-straw sandles tied tightly to their feet, the women carry baskets and wait on the beach watching the tide go out. As the waters recede down the pebble beaches the women run down and quickly search among the gravel for *isonori.* As the waves come in they run back up to higher ground, only to run back again with the next receding wave.

Kaiso. 1) Kanten, 2) Itowakame, 3) Nori,
4) Itokombu, 5) Funori, 6) Mekabu, 7) Mekabu
after soaking, 8) Itawakame, 9) Itawakame
after soaking, 10) Hijiki,
11) Hijiki after soaking.

When we see *nori* it most resembles a sheet of carbon paper. Women toss the *isonori* on screens and spread it uniformly to dry. When it has dried it is peeled off.

Handmade *isonori* of this good quality is very difficult to find in the United States. Even in Japan most of the *nori* is produced in Korea and imported.

If you look carefully at a sheet of *nori* you can see there is a front and a back side; the screens leave tiny impressions on the backside; the front side is shiny. When you are making *sushi* or rice balls, put the shiny side on the outside. Good quality *nori* has a nice smell and is almost black with hints of purple. If the color is completely black or completely purple or moss green, either food coloring has been added or it has been mixed with another sea vegetable.

Nori is susceptible to humidity. Once you have opened a package of *nori,* wrap it tightly and store it in the refrigerator.

Kelp, unlike *isonori,* is harvested in the ocean instead of on the beaches. Traditionally, a fisherman went out to sea in a small one-man craft. In his left hand the fisherman held a glass-bottom box with which he could see under the water to locate the kelp beds. In his right hand he held a scythe with a long handle. While maneuvering the boat with one foot on the rudder, the fisherman would reach over the side and cut the kelp loose.

As a child I remember the peddlers from Hokkaido. They sold the kelp called *kombu.* *Kombu* was sold both in large pieces and in smaller shavings. Very fine, thin shavings are called *tororo* and wide shavings (like wood shavings) are called *oboro.* When added to *misoshiru* they melt, turn a little sticky, and taste very good.

Tororo and *oborokombu* have for centuries been credited with cleansing the digestive system. Because they are low in calories and fat and are very filling, they are popular with today's youth as a diet food. Freshness is very important. If they are not fresh they won't melt or taste very good.

There are other kinds of seaweed that become sticky when heated. Two examples are *mekabu* and *gibasa.* To prepare them, place in boiling water until they soften, rough chop, and add soy sauce and vinegar.

Today the *kombu* peddler is gone. In earlier times the peddler played a vital role in the development of Japanese culture and social development. The peddlers traveled from the sea to the mountains, promoting communication between villages and encouraging exchange of ideas and customs. The peddlers' paths widened to become roads, inns were built to house travelers, villages grew and changed. The exchange of food lies at the base of this cultural development.

When I was a curator, one of the important assignments given to me was to trace the origin of road networks in a given area. Before there were real roads or highways, how did the people travel from one place to another? Where were the trails?

One clue we used were ancient, hand-carved utensils kept at some of the larger traditional farms. These sets were hand-carved out of wood by professional carvers called *kijishi.* For our research we documented the characteristics of the collection of utensils specific to each area. Somewhere on the box's cover would be the name of the *kijishi* and the date the item was made.

By piecing together this preliminary information we could begin to track the lives of the *kijishi.* We could tell where one stayed, how long he stayed, what year he stayed in a particular village, how many families he made utensils for, and which village he moved to next. By tracing the dates and mapping the villages, we could begin to map the routes connecting the villages at that time. By this method of research, it is also possible to trace the development and history of customs, foods, religion, and language.

When I was a child many different kinds of peddlers came to my home, sometimes only once a year. I remember the herb and medicine peddler best. She would bring a box to the house that had a small inventory of medicines individually packaged inside. When she returned the next year she would count what medicines had been used and mark a tally sheet on the side of the box. We were charged only for the medicines we had used. I remember the medicine peddler well because she gave all the kids paper balloons after making a sale. I still have that medicine box with me at Nippon Kan in Denver. Now it sits on my desk holding my stamps and seals.

My mother always gave peddlers tea and we listened to stories and information from other towns. These peddlers walked all over Japan. They knew a great deal of information about the towns along their routes. During the Edo period the *bakufu* (Japanese feudal lords) sometimes hired peddlers as spies.

Gyo Kai Rui — Fish and Shellfish

As I have previously explained, there are many ways to preserve fish. They can be soaked in salted water for a few days then left to dry or directly hung to dry, boiled and then dried, salted and dried, or even marinated with *miso* or *tamari* (to give the fish a subtle undertaste) and dried. These are called *himono*. Sometimes the fish are not completely dried but only half-dried then broiled and eaten. Fish that are half-dried are called *namaboshi* and have a large section reserved for them at the market.

The smell of half-dried fish being broiled is rather hard to handle even for Japanese people but the taste is delicious. On the other hand, fish that have been dried completely (*hoshizakana*)

have no smell. *Tara* (cod), *karei* (flat fish), *ika* (squid), and *fugu* (bufferfish) are examples of fish that are completely dried. Traditionally these fish were "freeze-dried" by the cold winds from the north. When dried, they are very hard and very light. They must be soaked in water before they can be eaten or cooked. When the fish almost regain their original shape and plumpness they are ready to be cooked.

Another way to enjoy these fish is to eat them dried, like a jerky. As students, when we gathered to drink *sake* we snacked on dried flat fish or cod. We would have to hit them with a hammer to soften the fish a little, though. The light, salty taste of dried fish complements *sake* nicely.

Originally, during the season when the fish were feeding near the shoreline, rough seas would sometimes wash them ashore. During winter it was too cold outside for these fish to spoil, and the strong salty winds helped to "freeze-dry" them. Fishermen just walked down the beaches and collected them in baskets. This does not happen much any more.

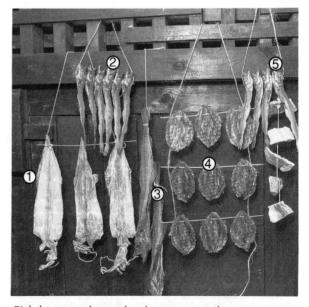

Fish hung to dry under the eaves. 1) Ika, 2) Hata hata, 3) Hokke, 4) Fugu, 5) Tara.

Kokumotsu Rui — Cereals and Grains

Historically, the traditional farmer's main staple food was the lowest quality *genmai* (brown rice) and *gokoku*. *Gokoku* is a general term that encompasses the following five major foods: *hie* (decengrass), *awa* (foxtail), *mugi* (barley), *kimi* (corn), and *mame* (beans). With this limited number of ingredients, a wide variety of finished products was produced.

One very popular product was and is *soba*. Buckwheat flour was mixed with water and Chinese yam, kneaded into a dough, rolled out, cut into thin noodle strips, and boiled. These noodles were then eaten with a *soba* broth or cut into strips and hung to dry.

Wheat flour mixed with water and a little salt, kneaded, rolled out, and cut into noodle strips is called *udon*. *Udon*, like *soba*, can be boiled and enjoyed in a broth or dried. Both are readily available in the United States markets.

The most delicious noodles are cooked immediately after the dough is made. In the Japanese countryside, the dough is prepared two or three hours before mealtime. The dough is rolled out with a three-foot-long rolling pin called a *nobebo*, precisely and rhythmically cut into strips, dusted with flour, and boiled.

1) Soba, 2) Somen, 3) Harusame.

Soba is rich in amino acids, strengthens veins and arteries, and prevents high blood pressure. In Japan, *soba* is eaten to counterbalance foods of high caloric content. If you are eating too many calories a day it is recommended to eat *soba* daily.

When *soba* is boiled, the minerals and amino acids are released into the water. This leftover water is called *sobayu*. If someone drinks this *sobayu* straight or mixed with soup broth, people might say, "Oh, he is a gourmet: he knows how to eat *soba*." Traditional *soba* restaurants serve *soba* with a small pot of *sobayu* on the side.

There are many traditions and customs associated with *soba*. *Toshikoshi soba* is traditionally eaten on New Year's eve. *Toshikoshi soba* directly translated means "from one year to another" *soba*. It represents a wish for long life. *Hikkoshi soba* or house-moving *soba* is given to all the new neighbors when you move into a new house.

The rolling pin my mother used when I was a child is still with me at Nippon Kan in Denver. The ends are worn from generations of hands. If rolling and chopping the dough into noodles sounds like too much trouble, just make dumplings by pulling off bite-size amounts and dropping them into boiling water.

Soba and *udon* are very popular with Japanese people. If you have been to Japan you know that noodle stands and restaurants can be found at almost every train station and all over any town. Traditionally, however, these noodles were eaten on *"hare no hi"* or special days only.

Hiyamugi and *somen* noodles are made from the same wheat flour. These are much thinner, so to keep them from breaking a little bit of oil is added before they are dried. These noodles have the best texture when after about one year the oil has dissipated. They can be kept for long periods and are convenient when moving or packaging for distribution.

Rice or sticky rice are ground into flour and made into *mochi* (pounded rice cakes) and other rice flour desserts. These too were traditionally eaten only on special days. Rice was not used on regular days; *hie* or *awa* were used instead.

In the Misawa City area, I discovered green soybeans or regular soybeans that were ground into a flour to make *mochi*. These rice cakes were flavored with sweet *miso* and broiled.

From *hie, hie mochi* is made. From *awa* comes *awa mochi*. Corn is made into *kimi mochi*. Originally all of these were made as offerings to the gods.

For journeys, these rice cakes were wrapped in bamboo leaves or oak leaves to keep them from drying out and to protect them and keep them from spoiling. Today, these kinds of wrapped cakes are sold as souvenirs at country resorts.

Mame Rui — Beans

The most popular product made from soybeans is *tofu,* and I will go into *tofu* in greater length in the section on products used daily. Here we shall explore how to save fresh *tofu* for future use.

A block of *tofu* can be cut into half-inch squares and freeze-dried to make *shimidofu*. Another common name is *koyadofu* — named after Zen monks who lived on Mt. Koya near Kyoto who first discovered this process.

We don't need to go back this far in history to find *shimidofu*. It was common practice for farmers to hang *tofu* under the eaves of the house to dry. Although *tofu* came from China, the making of *shimidofu* is Japanese.

The *shimidofu* available in the markets today is sometimes processed with ammonia. There is a three-month shelf life for *shimidofu*. If it is too old it won't soften again when soaked in water. Of course, it also doesn't taste very good.

If the temperature where you live drops below 32° Fahrenheit for consecutive periods you can make *shimidofu* yourself. You can't make it in the freezer. You need to set it out where strong cold winds blow. *Tofu* turns yellow when it is freeze-dried. Don't worry, this is natural.

Tofu was also preserved through pickling in salt. In Japan, *tofu* pickled in salt is no longer available. Salt pickling is still popular in China and other parts of Southeast Asia.

Yuba.

Very healthful but not as popular is a soybean product called *yuba* (dried soymilk film). *Tofu* is made by bringing soybean "milk" to a boil. As it boils, a thick film forms on the surface. This film is picked up on a cloth and laid out to dry. The resulting food is *yuba*.

I have served *yuba* to people visiting from Japan and had them ask me what it was. *Yuba* is popular in China and other parts of Southeast Asia and is eaten fresh or can be dried. *Yuba* is available in the Oriental markets in the United States, but chemicals have usually been added during production.

Speaking of chemicals, I can remember during the years I was in elementary school Japan was having a problem with cyclamates. At the time cyclamates (called *chicuro* in Japanese), a common sweetener, were found to be carcinogenic. The issue had already been raised in the United States, but the Japanese government had chosen to ignore it. Eventually, consumer organizations rallied and *chicuro* was replaced with sugar. At that time there were no laws against the use of cyclamates.

I have brought this up because now in Japan chemical preservatives are falling under closer and closer scrutiny. These efforts have been spearheaded by consumer groups. What does surprise me is the products that are making their way into the United States from Japan. Some of the products have labels written in Japanese with directions and ingredients only loosely translated into English. US government import control agents need to look more closely at labels that list only vague accounts of ingredients. Chemical preservatives that are no longer allowed in Japan are still being found in products exported to the United States. Please check the labels carefully for preservatives, and check the expiration dates before buying. There can be a fair amount of time between when products are shipped from Japan and when they end up on the shelf in the U.S. In one particularly bad case I saw products that were two years old.

Products Used Daily

Ishiusu — stone grinder.

T ofu — Soybean Curd

Americans frequently ask me what Japanese people eat on a daily basis. Sometime I get disappointed looks when I tell them. I think they expect me to describe some strange, exotic dishes never heard of here in the United States. In the larger cities and towns of Japan today, the younger generation's diet is not so different than here in the U.S. Milk, cheese, and ham are common sights in most young family homes.

Visiting a home in the country which continues to practice the old customs is a slightly different story. In these homes (almost stubbornly) mostly traditional foods are served. If there is a difference between the traditional households of the past and present, it is in the way the foods are procured, not the foods themselves. Instead of making most everything at home, the people of the countryside visit the grocery store. The flavors therefore are not quite as fresh and good as they used to be.

When I was a child, the *tofu* peddler came by early every morning blowing his horn and yelling, *"Tofu, tofu!"* in a loud voice. His bicycle was equipped with a metal washtub filled with fresh water and the *tofu* he had made himself that day. He also carried other products, like *age* (deep-fried soybean puff), *yakidofu* (broiled *tofu*), *atsu age* (deep-fried *tofu* cutlet), and *konnyaku* (devil's tongue yam cake).

The *tofu* peddlers made *tofu* in larger blocks than you buy in the United States. One block was called a *cho*. You could buy a half or quarter *cho* if you wished.

The *tofu* peddler was very familiar with our family and knew how much *tofu* or *age* we used daily. Knowing how much we needed, he filled the time with pleasantries and friendly conversation as he filled our bowl with the day's supply.

Traditionally, the old *tofu* makers used the mineral *nigari* (bittern), found naturally in fresh sea water, as a solidifier during processing. The *tofu* found in the supermarkets is made with man-made solidifiers. The nutritional value of mass-produced *tofu* is rather less than *tofu* made in the traditional fashion.

Tofu was brought to Japan by Japanese priests who went to China to study Buddhism. Today, for example, near the old temples of Kyoto there are *tofu* shops and restaurants that date back many, many generations.

From its introduction, *tofu* was eaten by the people of the imperial courts. It was not until the Edo period (1603-1867) that *tofu* became popular among all classes. Since those earlier times *tofu* has become a major part of the Japanese diet, one of its daily foods.

When I was a curator, I spent some time with an old man who made *tofu* for me in the style that was originally taught to him. I was surprised; his *tofu* was so hard you could tie blocks of it up with a rope and carry it. Naturally, the solidifier he used was *nigari* from fresh ocean water.

Proverbs regarding *tofu* have been told for generations: something impossible is said to be "like breaking your teeth eating *tofu*" or "like picking up *tofu* with a pair of tongs." A spoiled person "has his *tofu* peeled." Remarking that anyone can change: "even *tofu* gets tight if

cooked long enough." I heard these proverbs on more than one occasion from my parents!

The owner of one large *tofu* company in Denver told me about the first time he took a fresh *tofu* sample to one of the large local markets. The buyer took one bite and said, "This is not *tofu.*" The new *tofu* maker was surprised and returned home to make another batch, believing in the traditional techniques he knew well. Again the buyer took a bite and said, "This is not *tofu*, it is not sour. I have real *tofu* brought to me from California by truck. This *tofu* does not taste like the *tofu* I get from California." I started laughing before he finished the story. The *tofu* shipped from California had begun to spoil en route. The buyer, not having anything to compare it to, thought all *tofu* was supposed to taste sour!

Fresh *tofu* is a food high in nutritional value. However, because it has a high water content, it spoils easily. When you are buying *tofu*, I recommend you buy it at a store that has a good turnover rate, to make sure it is fresh. A bulging plastic cover indicates that gas is being released and the *tofu* is no longer fresh. After you have opened the package, submerge the *tofu* completely in fresh water. *Tofu* absorbs odors easily, so it needs to be covered. If refrigerated, *tofu* should last for three or four days.

While I was running my restaurant, young mothers sometimes asked me for raw *tofu* for their children, but I always boiled it first. Like a *sushi* chef serving raw fish, it was my responsibility not to serve anything that might have spoiled.

Tofu has been promoted here in the United States as a "new age" food that is very good for you. Please remember that *tofu* distributed on a large scale and produced with chemical solidifiers may not be quite the same as the traditional product you may have read about. I suggest you boil the *tofu* just a little bit before serving, especially to children.

Tofu products. 1) Yakidofu, 2) Ganmo, 3) Tofu, 4) Atsuage, 5) Koyadofu, 6) Age.

Okara — Soybean Mash

If you visit a *tofu* factory you will notice that the process results in two products. *Unohana* or *okara* is the soybean mash by-product. It used to be that the small *tofu* maker would give *okara* away. At large *tofu* factories today it is sold for animal fodder.

Although the nutritional value of *okara* is high, it has always had the image of a by-product and was not marketable. This has been a problem for *tofu* makers. With two products of similar nutritional value, one was in demand with his customers, and one he kept in the back room!

Today *okara* has become a popular diet food because it is filling, nutritious, and low-calorie. Larger Japanese markets in the U.S. now carry *okara.*

When I was a child, the *tofu* shop gave *okara* away, but to use in cooking you needed to add many other ingredients. Therefore people used to say that *okara* was free but expensive.

Natto — Fermented Soybeans

Natto is a very popular item on the Japanese breakfast table, but either you love it or you hate it; there is no middle ground. *Natto* is boiled soybeans that have been fermented by introducing the *natto* fungus. Open a package of *natto* and the first thing to hit you is a very strange aroma. If you stir it, it becomes sticky. Someone watching this might say "yech." The translator of this book, Emily, is one of these people. Although she has lived in Japan and traveled extensively in Southeast Asia, she says, "*Natto* is not for me."

Like the *tofu* peddler, the *natto* peddler came every morning. Now *natto* is available throughout Japan, but in the past, because of the growing conditions needed to produce it, many people had not eaten *natto* in southern Japan.

Some of the visitors I have had at Nippon Kan, especially the young visitors who lived south of Osaka, had never tasted *natto.*

The weather in northern Japan is favorable for the *natto* fungus. Traditionally, it was common for the farmers to make their own *natto* at home. I have tasted homemade *natto* from many different parts of Japan. Like most traditional foods, the taste and texture varies depending on the location and the family recipe.

The first *natto* was discovered, it is thought, when soybeans stored for safekeeping became contaminated with water and created the appropriate environment for the *natto* fungus. Historically, many Japanese foods were discovered accidentally, such as in the course of storing or preserving foods.

Since its initial discovery, the process has been isolated and developed into a controlled procedure.

To eat *natto,* pour it from its container into a bowl and stir vigorously with chopsticks until it turns sticky. Then add *miso* or *tamari* and *shoyu* or *umeboshi* (pickled plums) to suit your taste. Spoon it over rice and eat. Although some people may not agree, I find it tasty.

I met a very old woman in Denver who was a wonderful traditional Japanese cook. She knew all of the techniques for making homemade *sake, natto, tofu, umeboshi,* and *tsukemono* — everything in her kitchen was homemade. Sometimes this old woman would make *natto* and bring it to my home. It did not taste like the *natto* available in the grocery stores. She fermented the soybeans in a styrofoam cup using plastic bread wrappers for a cover. She then wrapped the cups in layers of crumpled newspaper as insulation to keep them warm. So you see, traditional Japanese methods can have a place in modern America.

Konnyaku — Yam Cake

I am not quite sure how to classify *konnyaku:* it is one of Japan's most unique foods. *Konnyaku* is made from *konnyaku imo* (devil's tongue potato). This potato is dried and powdered then boiled and mixed with ash water. After it has been mixed with the ash water it has the consistency of gelatin; if you accidentally drop it, it won't break but it cuts and chews easily.

There are two types of *konnyaku.* The first is poured into a rectangular mold and is called *itakonnyaku.* If you take this *itakonnyaku* and put it through a push-slicer you get the second kind of *konnyaku,* which is called *itokonnyaku,* or yam cake noodles.

Konnyaku has become a popular diet food in Japan because it has few calories, yet it is very filling. *Konnyaku* is also served in temples as part of a special diet known as *shojin ryori.*

The *itakonnyaku* that is available in the markets is either brown, speckled, or creamy white in color. If it is too white, the *itakonnyaku* has been bleached with chemicals. I prefer to use the brown *itakonnyaku* in my cooking. If you do buy bleached *konnyaku,* soak it overnight. I recommend boiling it briefly before use.

Konnyaku. 1) Itakonnyaku, country style, 2) Itakonnyaku, 3) Itokonnyaku, or shirataki.

Kaiso — Sea Vegetables

The Japanese harvest the seas for many products used daily. Foodstuffs taken from the seas are very seasonal, and are therefore associated with certain times of the year. *Agar agar, tengusa,* and *tokoroten,* for example, are made as summer foods when people's appetites are small. If sweetened, they can be enjoyed as desserts; if sprinkled with ground ginger, vinegar, and soy sauce, they can be used as another side dish.

In my home town area, the peddlers sold *tokoroten,* which is made from *tengusa,* a sea vegetable. Peddlers sold *tokoroten* in small blocks. Carefully, they would remove the blocks and put them in a push-slicer to make noodles. I remember when I was a kid, the peddler pushing a block of *tokoroten* through the slicer into my bowl.

Wayasai — Japanese Vegetables

This category of vegetables includes those originally found in Japan and those imported long ago from the Asian continent.

Today, many Oriental vegetables are available throughout the United States. The increase and variety of Oriental vegetables available can be attributed to the increase in Southeast Asian immigrants over the last several years.

When I shop for Oriental vegetables here in Denver, I visit the Chinese, Korean, and Indochinese markets. The variety is good, and the prices compared to the Japanese market are lower. The grocers usually have first-hand experience on how the vegetables are grown and give good advice on selecting and preparing them. This is different from a produce person in a grocery store, whose product knowledge may stop at the cardboard box it comes in.

The Asian markets in Denver have the atmosphere that reminds me of the neighborhood markets of my childhood. The shopkeepers greet you at the door, welcoming you inside with friendly manners. The owner carries her grandchild on her back while she bustles around the store.

Many Japanese vegetables are now being grown in the United States by those who brought the seeds from Japan. *Kabocha* (Japanese pumpkin), *daikon* (Japanese white radish), *imo rui* (potatoes), *nihonnegi* (Japanese onion), *kinusaya* (snow peas), *sayaingen* (green beans), *shiso* (beef steak leaves), *nihonkyuri* (Japanese cucumber), *nihonnasu* (Japanese eggplant), *aburana* (rape seed plant), *nira* (Japanese scallion), and *gobo* (burdock) are *wayasai* that are easily found in the Denver area, for example.

For the recipes included in this book, it is not necessary to always use Japanese vegetables. With a little ingenuity, other vegetables can be mixed with Japanese flavorings and methods of preparation to create delicious dishes. Using vegetables other than Japanese varieties creates dishes that are more familiar to the American palate. Anyway, the Japanese vegetables called for may not be available in your area.

Today in Japan, especially in the cities, people go to the market to buy their vegetables. When I was a kid, the farming women came by each house pulling carts or carrying packs loaded with that season's fresh produce and flowers. I believe these farmers still visit my family home.

I remember my mother would invite one farmer's wife onto the porch for tea and a visit. While they chatted, my mother would order the *daikon* she needed for pickling this coming winter, and also ask about having *susuki* mats (the mats used as wind and snow barriers) delivered later that fall. It was a warm, relaxed conversation between my mother, who had grown up in the city, and this hard-working woman from the farm. Today, our lives benefit from many modern conveniences, but relationships like this one have been lost.

These visits reinforced our connection with the rhythm of the seasons. Now that watermelon

Gaku Homma headed for the fields at Iwama, Aiki shrine (1967).

Aikido founder Morehei Ueshiba's wife, Hatsu, resting in the garden (1967).

and strawberries are available in the winter, we have lost this connection with the changing seasons. We miss enjoying the first new fruits and vegetables to come in each season.

Personally, my first experience with gardening was while living at the Aiki shrine with the founder of Aikido, Morihei Ueshiba, and his wife.

In the early morning, the founder would walk through the gardens looking over the growing vegetables, selecting a few ripe ones here and there for an assistant to pick for morning breakfast.

The first new vegetables of the season had to be saved and offered at the Aiki shrine ceremony held every month. When there was an abundance, we carried the extra vegetables to the Tokyo Aikido school headquarters. Heavily laden with a large cloth sack on my back and the founder's favorite brown leather bag, a souvenir from his first trip to Hawaii, we would set off for the city. I was in high school at the time and found this all rather embarrassing.

One major point about vegetables in Japan is that traditionally they were never eaten raw. If not boiled, they were at least dipped in boiling water or rubbed with salt and then boiled to protect against parasites. Vegetables were boiled quickly and the *aku* (the brown or grayish residue that results from boiling meats and vegetables) was removed to enhance their appearance.

Vegetables began to be eaten raw in Japan after Western foods became popular. When I was a kid, the only raw vegetable we ever ate was sliced cabbage. The closest we came to having salads were *ohitashi,* which are vegetables boiled very quickly and flavored with soy sauce and other condiments.

I will go into more detail about *ohitashi* under breakfast recipes in Chapter 5.

Chapter

4

THE
BACKGROUND OF
COUNTRY COOKING
– BASIC PREPARATION –

Basic Preparation

Cooking at the irori.

Holding one bottle of *sake*
I sat down upon a garden rock.
In my sake cup
The moon's reflection I can see.
Beside me sits my shadow, as my friend.
I do not sit alone, for we are three.
Unknown Chinese poet

I have always been impressed at the depth of emotion and humanity of this ancient poet, as he sat reflecting over a cup of *sake.*

You have probably had the experience in which the same meal tastes different depending on different circumstances. A hamburger consumed alone in a tiny apartment will not taste the same as hamburgers enjoyed with friends in a beautiful national park. The atmosphere and mood surrounding a meal can change the taste of the foods being eaten. For example, simple foods can be a feast when shared by a family that is happy together. The most elaborate meal cannot be enjoyed if it is served at a table where parents argue with one another.

Your emotional state and your communication with those you share your meals with are just as important as the food you eat. The home environment has a great effect on all of us, especially on the development of children.

Nippon Kan holds aikido classes in Vail, a ski resort town west of Denver. Sometimes when we go to visit, we stay at the local instructor's home, usually bunking on the living room floor. Early in the morning, trying hard not to wake us, the instructor's two teenage daughters sneak into the kitchen. As I lay dozing in the living room I can follow their actions by the sounds I hear. There, the refrigerator door is opening and closing, yes, the sound of cupboard doors snapping open and shut. That's the rattle of plates and cups. The sound of cereal being poured into a bowl, followed by the gurgle of pouring milk and the crunch of adolescent chewing. I have visited families all over the United States, and I think these are pretty common "kids in the morning kitchen" sounds.

I remember the smells and sounds of breakfast in my home in Japan. I must be at that age when reminiscing becomes important. By writing this book, I can keep track of the memories. It is also important to me to try to keep the traditional customs of home cooking alive.

My childhood memories of morning kitchen sounds are somewhat different. The first sound I heard was that of washing rice. Washing is the word you would use in English; in Japanese the word used is *togu,* which means the feeling or act of sharpening a knife. We don't say we are washing rice, we say we are polishing it.

Next, kindling was snapped to start the fire under the *kama,* or rice pot. We had a gas stove, but my very traditional mother used only the *kama* for cooking rice. Then I heard the sounds of chopping, as the *tofu* and scallions were cut for *miso* soup. I could tell what kind of *dashijiru* she was using by the smells that drifted from the kitchen.

In traditional Japanese houses, the rooms are separated by paper screens and sliding doors. Aromas from the kitchen easily circulate around the house. The smell of the morning's *ohitashi* (boiled vegetable) blended with the smell of the *dashi.* The smell of *shioyaki* (broiled fish), mixed with the other smells, woke me up enough to be ready when my mother finally called.

After folding and storing our *futons,* my sisters tidied up the house while the boys went outside to tend the garden, the yard, and the section of public road in front of the house. We also took care of the altars. The water for the flowers in the Buddhist altar needed to be changed every day. The Shinto shrine too needed to be dusted and cleaned. Both household shrines were given offerings from the breakfast meal. All of us children lit the incense and the candles and prayed.

About that time, father had finished dressing and was coming down to the breakfast table. In traditional Japanese homes, the father sits down to breakfast first, followed by the rest of the family. No one starts eating before the father.

Just before breakfast my mother would add the *miso* to the morning soup base. Timing was very important. After the *miso* has been added, it loses its flavor if the temperature is raised and lowered, so it is important to put it in last, just before the soup is served. She tried to make sure her soup was timed with father's arrival at the table.

Many of the foods eaten at breakfast, excluding any fish or meat, were first offered at the Buddhist altar. On the Shinto altar, rice, salt, *omiki* (a special herb *sake*), and branches from the *sakaki* plant were offered. Once a month we held a ceremony offering special foods from the mountains and the sea. These memories of my childhood mornings are still fresh and delicious.

I hope that in the U.S. there are the morning sounds of frying bacon, pancakes flipping, the crack of eggs against the frying pan, and the smell of fresh-brewed coffee. It seems everywhere, however, that these customs are being lost, and that restaurants have taken their place.

Originally, breakfast was the family's early morning ceremony, a symbol of unity. Today we are served more often by strangers. Now we have a variety of choices and the luxury of not having to make breakfast ourselves. Today we seem desperate for time. Restaurants advertise free meals if not served in 10 minutes. Time-saving has become more of an issue than the meal itself.

I believe it is important that we learn to MAKE time to spend sharing meals with family and friends.

The media today give a great deal of publicity to the problems associated with raising children. I believe that if families could but eat meals together that alone could diminish many of the problems surfacing today. Any kid returns home when he or she gets hungry. If the kid comes home to an empty kitchen filled with microwaveable boxes, it doesn't do much for them emotionally (not to mention nutritionally).

I was something of a problem kid myself, but whenever I got hungry, I went home. When I returned, even though my mother was angry with me, she fed me. Maybe you can remember from your own experience how important those moments were.

This chapter focuses on basic cooking techniques. But my goal is to not give technical advice only. For each method or food being prepared, I will share the traditional Japanese thoughts and feelings behind each step. I do not want this to be an instant how-to cookbook. I want to introduce you to the traditional joys of cooking. If I can do this, I am confident you will enjoy this book.

Not including the kids, my students at Nippon Kan range in age from 20 to 65. They represent many diverse backgrounds. I sympathize with the men who have been divorced and had little or no experience cooking. Many of my students have watched me cook. I have been surprised by the nature of their questions, realizing how many of them didn't know the most basic methods of preparation. One of my students even remarked while sitting in the Nippon Kan kitchen, "This is the first time I have watched anybody chopping vegetables. It is quite interesting!"

These students are successful businessmen. When they are hungry they go to restaurants. They are well versed in fine dining, but in the kitchen some are not sure what to do with a knife.

Traditional cooking methods can be divided into five major categories:
1) *yaku* — broiling;
2) *niru* — simmering, poaching, braising;
3) *yuderu* — boiling;
4) *musu* — steaming;
5) *itameru* — sautéeing.

In the United States, I have found Japanese cookbooks filled with pictures of beautiful temples and gardens. These books describe exquisite and expensive Japanese dishes. Try to remove these images from your mind. The techniques we will explore here are techniques that have been handed down for generations by the rural farmers, mountain people, and townspeople. They have simple roots and are still simple today. We will discuss these five basic techniques and combinations thereof.

Yaku — Broiling

All meats are either broiled plain or prepared with a marinade. There are two types of broiling in traditional Japanese country cooking. The first is to broil directly over a flame, and the second is pan broiling.

If broiling over a flame (or under, as in an oven broiler), a useful utensil is a *yakiami* or grilling net. To prevent the cooking meats from sticking to the metal bars, wipe the bars with a little vegetable oil just before use. Controlling the flame is very important. If the flame is too high, the outside will scorch before the inside is done and the dripping fat might start a fire. If the fat does catch on fire, the resulting soot will make the meat less than desirable to eat. The best combination is a strong flame from a distance.

The traditional method for broiling meats or fish was to skewer them on sticks that were then stuck into the ground around a fire. This way the melting fat ran down the sticks and didn't catch on fire.

If you are pan broiling, the best skillet to use is an American cast-iron skillet. American cast-iron skillets are the same as Japanese cast iron skillets called *teppan*.

Apply a little bit of oil to the bottom of the pan with a paper towel. If the pan smokes when you first heat it up, it is too hot. To check the temperature of the skillet, sprinkle a few drops of water over it. If the drops dance across the surface, and then evaporate, the skillet has reached a good temperature for cooking.

I know what may be going through your mind: "When I use a cast-iron skillet, the food always sticks." Here is a method to prevent this: Take your cast-iron skillet and heat it until it smokes. Once it has started to smoke, continue heating it for about 10 minutes (make sure the kitchen has good ventilation, or the hood fan is on). Turn off the flame and pour a half cup of vegetable oil in slowly from one corner of the skillet. Tilt and roll the skillet holding the pan by the handle until the bottom has been covered evenly. Let the skillet cool naturally. After it has cooled, pour off the excess oil and wipe the skillet with a paper towel. After following these steps, foods will not stick to the skillet when properly used. After you have finished using the skillet for cooking, do not use dish soap to wash it. A light scrubbing with warm water is sufficient to keep it clean. You can use the skillet seven or eight times without food sticking and you won't have to add much extra oil each time you use the pan.

When using a skillet for pan roasting or pan broiling, put the meat or fish in and cover quickly. This keeps the temperatures hot and even, and allows the foods to be steamed as well as broiled. For those concerned about fat intake, be aware that pan-broiled foods retain more fats, oils, and *aku* than those broiled in a grilling net or skewered and barbecued.

Niru — Simmering, Braising, and Poaching

To cook solid ingredients in a soup stock is called *niru.* The cooking pot is filled with water and the seasonings used to make the soup stock, followed by the vegetables that take the longest to cook. When these ingredients are almost tender, all other solid ingredients are added and brought to a boil. This boiling releases the

brown, white, or grayish *aku* that collects inside the rim of the pot. The *aku* is skimmed off before cooking procedures continue.

There are three methods of flavoring simmered dishes:

1) The first, as just described, is to add the seasonings to the soup stock before meat or fish are added.

2) The second method, used with vegetables, meats, or fish, is to add the seasonings half way through the cooking time.

3) For the third method, as in making a *miso* base stock, the seasonings are added just before serving.

Yuderu — Boiling

This method is mostly used for vegetables. The current trend in the United States is to steam vegetables, but traditionally in Japanese country cooking vegetables are boiled. Vegetables are immersed in boiling water, and *aku,* other impurities, and parasites are removed. This keeps spinach, for example, from tasting gritty. It is very important that you never overcook vegetables. This way they maintain a fresh color and crisp texture.

To boil a certain amount of vegetables, by volume you need twice that amount of water. For every 5 cups of water add 1/4 tsp. of salt. When putting a vegetable that has a root into boiling water, put it in root first because it is harder and will take longer to cook. Do not cover, because the vegetables will begin to steam.

GREEN VEGETABLES, such as green beans, snow peas, zucchini, broccoli, spinach, etc., change to a nice green color as soon as they enter boiling water. Let boil for 30–60 seconds only. For spinach or thinly sliced zucchini, 30 seconds is fine.

When the vegetables have cooked long enough, pour them into a colander and quickly immerse the colander into a bowl of ice water and set aside. By doing this, the vegetables will have a beautiful shiny color and nice texture. It is very important to quickly immerse the vegetables in this ice water. If you have no ice available, running water will do.

In most Japanese country cooking, vegetables are boiled and then served cold. They are served warm only when included in vegetable soups or other dishes.

Perhaps the only other use of warm, boiled vegetables was medicinal. When I was a child, we boiled chrysanthemum leaves and spinach and used the water as a foot wash to kill bacteria and odors. This remedy was taught to me by my mother.

CAULIFLOWER is boiled by adding 1 tsp. of salt and vinegar to the water. Once the water boils, put in bite-size pieces of cauliflower and let boil for 1 to 2 minutes, then quickly immerse in ice water in the same manner as for green vegetables.

DAIKON (Japanese white radish) should be boiled in the water used to wash rice. Using this water removes any hot or bitter taste and makes the *daikon* somewhat whiter in color. All other specifics about water and salt amounts, cooking time, and immersing the *daikon* in ice water are the same as for green vegetables.

GOBO (burdock) and *RENKON* (lotus root) should be soaked in water 10 to 15 minutes before boiling. Add 1 tsp of vinegar per gallon of water used. Bring to a boil, remove *aku*, and continue to cook until tender, with a rich color.

Two important general tips for boiling are that you prepare the bowl of ice water before boiling the vegetables, and that you boil vegetables quickly and never overcook.

Boiled vegetables are used in *ohitashi* and *aemono* (recipes will follow in the breakfast and dinner sections in Chapter 5).

Musu — Steaming

There are different methods for steaming. The first, common in the United States, is to use a steaming utensil over boiling water. This is the method used to make the sticky rice for *mochi*, which is very popular in Japan. Potatoes, fish, and meats are often steamed in this manner. Another method is to combine chicken or fish with vegetables and herbs wrap tightly in leaves, and bury them in ash or rocks around a fire until they steam in their own juices. Fish or meats that are seared and hung away from a flame are basically steamed. (*Teriyaki* is a good example of this.)

In Japan there are many products made from fish paste. Fish paste is made by grinding fish and other ingredients and steaming the pastes into various shapes. *Kamaboko* and *chikuwa* are both popular varieties of steamed fish paste. The imitation crab and lobster available in U.S. supermarkets are produced by these old traditional methods.

Another traditional and popular steamed dish is called *tsukune,* which is hand-rolled balls made from ground chicken meat and bones, mixed with other ingredients and seasonings. *Tsumire* are hand-rolled balls made from mostly white fish (bones included) that are ground, mixed, seasoned, and steamed.

Itameru — Sauteeing

Sauteeing should be done in a heavy cast iron skillet. If you use a thin pan, the temperature drops when you add the ingredients, and instead of sautéeing quickly they simmer instead.

In a heated skillet add 1/2 to 1 tsp. oil. (No oil is necessary if the pan is treated as discussed in the broiling section.) The ingredients are added and quickly sauteed. Finally, flavorings are added to taste. Soy sauce and sugar especially should not be added until the end because they burn easily. By adding the soy sauce at the end, it will retain its nice smell and flavor.

In traditional Japanese country cooking, there are no recipes that call only for sautéed foods. The Japanese do not even have a utensil like the curve-sided sauteing pan used in the United States. Traditionally, meats or vegetables are lightly sauteed, then soup stocks or other flavorings are added, and the meats and vegetables continue to cook by another method.

It comes as a surprise to many people that the Japanese do not use woks for cooking. The wok is a Chinese cooking utensil, specifically designed for a wood or special gas heat source. Since the bottom is curved, a wok does not work well on an electric burner because the surface cannot be evenly heated. The food cannot be cooked as quickly as it should be to ensure the proper taste. The next time you go to a Chinese take-out restaurant, take a look at the woks they are using. The woks may look familiar, but the oil or gas burners being used are much more powerful than the stoves in residential kitchens. A cast-iron skillet with a flat bottom works better on an electric or gas stove.

Choosing Ingredients and Initial Preparation

Shimenawa and Oke.

Yasai — Vegetables

Sometimes when I am cooking, especially when being observed by a child, I get a lot of "why" questions. Even simple answers seem to delight and surprise my audience. Cutting vegetables seems to be especially impressive. "Why do you cut the vegetables this way? It is beautiful" many people have told me. For me, these methods are not unusual. I never paid that much attention to it before; it has always just been the way it is done.

There are many different reasons for the ways we prepare vegetables for cooking. The first, most obvious criterion is to be able to fit them in your mouth! Another reason is that vegetables absorb liquid seasonings more readily when cut certain ways. Vegetables are also cut to prevent them from falling apart while they are cooking. Lastly, vegetables are cut to look beautiful.

Choosing the size into which vegetables are cut depends on how long they are going to be cooked. Vegetables that will be cooked for an extended period should be cut into larger pieces. It is also advisable when cooking for a long time to round the edges with a rolling cut to keep them from falling apart.

Thin slices are better when quickly sautéeing or simmering over a hot flame. There are two different methods for thin slicing. One is to slice with the grain, and the other is to slice perpendicular to the grain. The way in which the vegetables are cut can actually affect their taste. If you want the vegetables to keep their shape, cut with the grain. Think of celery as an example and you can more easily understand these concepts.

The most important factor is to choose vegetables that are very fresh. The next important consideration is the *hocho* (cooking knife) you use. Not surprisingly, the Japanese have a variety of cooking knives for different purposes. When cutting vegetables, a long, thin knife is fine. Today, there are many expensive imported knives available from Japan, but I think that as long as it is sharp, the knife you are used to using daily is best.

A nice, sharp knife produces beautiful-looking vegetables. If you use a cooking knife every day it is best to sharpen it once or twice a week. You have to use more force if your knife is dull, increasing the likelihood of an accident. When cutting you don't push down on the knife, you slice forward away from you.

The cutting board is the knife's counterpart. It "catches the knife." A wood cutting board is best because it offers some resistance. The plastic cutting boards available today are more hygienic but I have found that the vegetables or the knife can slip, damaging the knife or you!

To cut vegetables, place them on the cutting board and hold them in place with your left hand. (Southpaws should use the other hand, but because Japanese cooking knives are sharpened for right-handed use, it is sometimes difficult for a left handed person to use them.) The cooking knife is held so it will work at a 90° angle to the hand holding the vegetables in place. Curve your fingers under, so the knife works next to the second joints of your fingers.

The following illustration displays basic cuts. These techniques are integral to the recipes that follow later in the book.

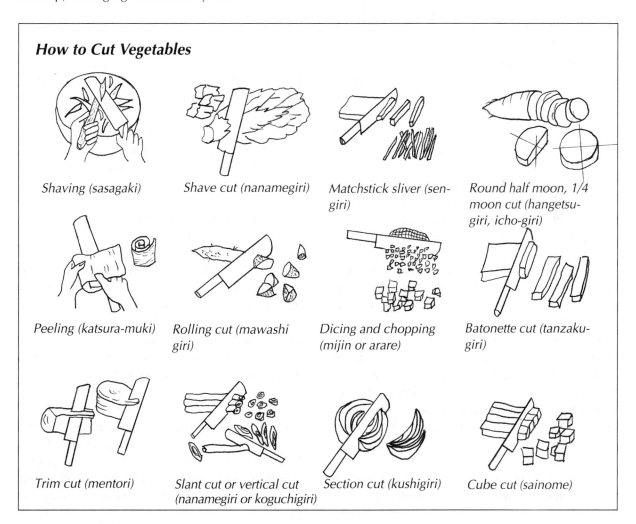

How to Cut Vegetables

Shaving (sasagaki)

Shave cut (nanamegiri)

Matchstick sliver (sen-giri)

Round half moon, 1/4 moon cut (hangetsu-giri, icho-giri)

Peeling (katsura-muki)

Rolling cut (mawashi giri)

Dicing and chopping (mijin or arare)

Batonette cut (tanzaku-giri)

Trim cut (mentori)

Slant cut or vertical cut (nanamegiri or koguchigiri)

Section cut (kushigiri)

Cube cut (sainome)

Sakana — Fish

When I was a kid, fish was a natural part of my daily life. In the markets, the fish section was much larger than the section reserved for meats. I can instinctively tell a fresh fish from a not-so-fresh fish. My American friends have often asked me how I do this. There are many check points, but for me instinct plays the most important role.

In Japan, in the early morning you can still go down to the fisherman's wharf to find live fish flopping in boxes and scattered on nets across the docks. As a kid I was well acquainted with the original colors of the fish delivered at the docks. Japan is a small country. Even landlocked towns have fresh fish caught in the morning, packed in ice, and delivered in time for dinner that same day.

I think the biggest reason people don't like fish is the smell. You might imagine that an open-air fish market is a very smelly place, but actually it is not. The fish in these markets are fresh so they do not smell bad. Strong odors occur only when fish are not so fresh.

Fish spoils easily. For whole fish look for eyes that are bright and rounded, not flat. The belly should have some resilience when you push gently on it. If it doesn't bounce back, or juice appears, don't buy it. Pick up the fish by grabbing the indented area above the tail. If the fish stays stiff it is fresh. If it falls over limply it is not. If you see a fish inside the market display case that has blood collecting around the eyes, gills, fins, or stomach area, it is better not to buy it. I have found fresh fish in Chinatowns, and in Indochinese, Asian, and Italian markets. You can usually find good fish in markets from countries where the diet traditionally includes a great deal of fish. The turnover is high and they know their fish well.

In supermarkets, fish are usually processed for convenience. Remember that precut fish are exposed to more air and can lose their freshness more easily. To check for freshness, examine the piece. The flesh should be firm and there should be a shiny appearance and no discoloration.

Today's world consists of many small families and single people. Whole fish can still be used even by a single person with no waste. For example, take a one-foot-long salmon, cleaned and sliced in half lengthwise, and divide it into three sections. One section can be eaten fresh that day. The second can be marinated in *shoyu* or *miso* for six to seven hours and frozen: this way it is ready to bake and eat any time. The third piece can be seasoned with salt and pepper, rolled in bread crumbs, and deep-fried. Toss it in the freezer, and when you are ready, pop it in the microwave.

If a single person protests that a whole fish or even half a fish is too much, think about the fact that it is cheaper and fresher to buy fish whole, and it can be prepared and saved to fit into your busy schedule. Eating fish fresh the same day it is bought is the best, but if you can't there are ways to prepare for the next day and the next after that. Anyway, it is better than eating frozen dinners.

Frozen fish in Japan is usually deep-sea fish or imported. Imported fish are those that are not available close to Japan's shores or are shoreline fish that have become so rare that they are too expensive to market. These fish then are imported from areas where they are still abundant. Interestingly, over 90% of the fish used to make *sushi* in Japan is now imported. If you visit Japan and go to a *sushi* bar, don't feel a lonely foreign visitor — most of the fish are, too!

Fresh shoreline fish command a higher retail price in Japanese markets because the Japanese value freshness and are willing to pay for it. Frozen fish just don't taste quite as good as fresh fish. Sometimes in the United States, I have seen frozen fish that has been delivered from the

How to clean squid

1. Hold squid and reach inside with your fingers, pull out bones, tenacles, and insides.

2. Remove fins.

3. Peel skin.

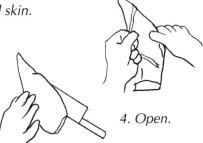

4. Open.

5. Separate the tenacles from the insides.

6. Scrape suction cups from the tenacles.

How to clean fish

1. Remove scales.

2. Place fish with head to the left and cut diagonally at the gills halfway through. Also remove tail.

3. Turn fish over and cut diagonally at the gills, removing the head.

4. Slice the stomach side from the head to the tail.

5. Remove insides and rinse lightly.

6. Cut into steaks or filet by cutting horizontally along the bone; remove bone.

Preparing small fish without using a knife

1. Twist off head.

2. Insert your thumb into the side of the fish, "cut" in both directions.

3. Pull out bones.

wholesaler, defrosted, and displayed in the showcase. If it does not sell in two to three days it is cut and deboned, repackaged, and sold with the frozen fish. This is, I hope, the exception rather than the rule.

This would not work in Japan. The Japanese know their fish too well. An aging fish in the display case is not simply cut up and frozen, but often cooked into a different product altogether. Now maybe you can understand why *sushi* bars serve *tempura!*

When you buy a fish whole, remove the head at the gills and gut the fish. Wash thoroughly, wrap in clear plastic wrap and then store in the refrigerator. Do not put the whole fish in the refrigerator without cleaning it first.

Of course, after cleaning the fish you can continue to prepare the fish for cooking. Basic preparation is demonstrated in the previous illustration.

After you have initially prepared the fish, do not wash it again: it ruins the taste.

Sashimi (thinly sliced raw fish) has become popular these days, due to the "*sushi* boom". I do not recommend that you go to the market to buy *sashimi* to prepare yourself at home. If your local market is very busy and has a high product turnover rate, maybe it is all right. Unfortunately, in the United States there are not yet many supermarkets with fish fresh enough to eat uncooked. I have been invited to *sushi* parties hosted by my American friends, and what was shaped like *sushi* with all good intentions didn't look or smell quite right. I guess eating a piece or two can't kill you. But who knows! Be careful if you are having this kind of party!!

Even if professionally served, *sushi* or *sashimi* can be hazardous. I am concerned not only about *sushi* bars in the United States, but Japanese restaurants with *sushi* counters used mainly to attract customers.

When visiting any restaurant that serves raw fish, check to see if there are a lot of customers at the *sushi* counter. If the fish turnover doesn't look good, you may not get top-quality freshness. If the fish is wrapped in plastic in the cases, this indicates a low turnover. Don't eat tuna if it is very dark, and don't eat any fish if it is not shiny. As a note, there are sprays available on the market that make fish look shiny. Again, be careful.

A *sushi* chef changing frequently might indicate instability either with the restaurant or the chef.

If you have spent a great deal of time (and money) sitting at *sushi* bars studying the fish and how they are prepared, then maybe you can try shopping yourself at the market. It can be difficult to match the quality of the fish found in good restaurants simply because they buy in consistent quantity.

When preparing fish, the Japanese use a special knife called a *deba bocho* which is quite useful. If you don't have one, a heavy knife that will cut through bone will do. Make sure it is sharp. If it is not it will tear the flesh instead of cut it.

Below is a list of the fish most frequently enjoyed in Japan.

Iwashi	Sardine
Karei	Flatfish
Aji	Saurel
Saba	Mackerel
Ayu	Sweetfish
Unagi	Eel
Kisu	Sillaginoid
Ika	Squid
Katsuo	Bonito
Sawara	Spanish mackerel
Tobiuo	Flying fish
Suzuki	Sea bass
Sake	Salmon
Tako	Octopus
Nishin	Herring

Koi	Carp
Tara	Cod
Tai	Porgy or snapper
Samma	Pacific saury
Hirame	Flounder
Buri	Swellfish
Haze	Goby
Maguro	Tuna
Ebi	Shrimp
Asari	Short-neck clam
Shijimi	Corbicula
Hotate	Clam
Kaki	Oyster
Sazae	Turban
Kurage	Jellyfish
Namako	Trepang
Anko	Angler
Namazu	Catfish
Fugu	Pufferfish
Iseebi	Lobster

Niku Rui — Meats

In 1990, the Japanese government issued the results of a market study that indicated that 40% of the beef consumed in Japan is imported. Australia was the biggest supplier, the United States second. American beef is low in fat. Today in Japan, there is a growing focus on health issues, therefore American beef is popular as a health food, due to its low fat content. I find it interesting that presently in the United States, white meats and fish are enjoying more popularity than red meat for the very same reason! In olden times in Japan, specialty meat stores were completely separated from the grocery store. Today there are still many independent meat stores, but packaged meats can now be found in the grocery stores.

Traditionally, meats have been a special food. The butcher prepared them so that the wife or cook just had to use chopsticks to place it in the pan. The butcher removed all the bones and excess and sliced, chopped, or ground the meats for you.

This differs from fish, which you need to prepare yourself. This extra service was an accepted part of the meat's higher price tag.

This relates back to traditional times where it was customary for meats to be handled only by special people. Even today in Japan you cannot buy a large portion of meat to butcher yourself.

Thin-sliced and pretrimmed meats have just recently become fashionable in the United States. Meat in the United States is less expensive than it is in Japan — Americans have had more meat in their diet for generations and have more experience producing them. You probably know better than I how important meats are in this country.

For the recipes in this book it doesn't matter what cut of meat you use. It is not necessary to use the most expensive cuts of meat for the very thin slices and small pieces used in Japanese country cooking. What is important is that these thin slices or small pieces are cooked thoroughly until tender and that the aku is removed.

Using country food recipes, one pound of beef can make a dish that will serve 3 or 4 people. Another 1990 report issued in Japan indicated that the average American consumes 70 pounds of meat a year. This is about six times the annual per capita consumption in Japan. Although meat consumption in Japan is on the rise, it still cannot compare to the consumption of fish. Of course this varies by location. A young, urban wife might find cooking fish too time-consuming. But there is a trade-off for convenience! Four ounces of sliced pork costs about 100 yen. Eight ounces of sirloin steak costs about 1000 yen.

I have been asked by Americans about Japanese beef and, yes, some cows in Japan do drink beer and get massages. This is called Kobe beef and one fillet fetches 6000-7000 yen or more! Although these cows are pampered, I don't think they actually order the beer or request the massages.

The first time Japanese people openly ate beef was during the early part of the Meiji period (1868–1912) when Western culture was being adopted as vogue. "If you do not eat meat, you are not modern" was a popular phrase of the times. During this time the Japanese put Western cultures on a pedestal and welcomed new ways. Many Japanese changed quickly, adopting Western styles. They cut their "*samurai*-styled" hair and wore Western suits with top hats. It was not uncommon to see a gentlemen in a *kimono* and *hakama*, sporting a top hat, leather shoes, and carrying an umbrella. Western foods came with the western fashions.

Before this period, beef was not eaten openly. Even during this cultural revolution, eating a large steak brought on involuntary cultural guilt feelings. To compensate for this, and also for the fact that the Japanese digestive system was not built to handle such large quantities of meat, the meats were sliced very thin and eaten in smaller portions.

When Zen Buddhism was the prominent religion, the *samurai* and nobility classes did not eat four-legged animals. Eventually this belief spread throughout all classes, but the farmers had special days when boar, rabbits, bear, and deer were eaten, but only very little at a time.

People who didn't eat four-legged animals did eat water fowl, mountain birds, and rabbits. The rabbits' long ears look like wings and their back legs are bigger than their front legs, so they are only two-legged. Right? "See, everybody? It's a bird!" Even strong religious taboos had gray areas. Country farmers and mountain people had even more gray areas in their lives to deal with.

Even so, animals were butchered only on special days at certain times by specifically designated people. Still now in my home in Japan, if there is butchering to be done at home, it is done on a special day in a specific location in the house. Knives, bowls, baskets, and the cooking pot used are kept separate from any other utensils.

The origin of this custom came perhaps from the belief in *"ke"* or spirits. But basically, modern theories on culinary hygiene had not been developed — the idea of *ke* was a good reason for adopting certain food preparation procedures.

Historically, illness in Japan was attributed to angry gods. Medical theory was based on religion, and *ke* was designated as the reason for bad luck and illness. To deal with these situations, often whatever the person had been doing before he or she became ill was made taboo. This did serve to isolate some practical causes for illness. In a roundabout way the folklore of the time served its people well.

Toriniku to Yacho — Chicken and Fowl

Traditionally for farmers, fishermen, and mountain people, the domestic chicken was a common sight. When I was young we ate fresh eggs gathered from the yard. On *"hare no hi"* (special days) we would catch one chicken for the day's meal. I think it was probably a pretty special day for the chicken, too!

Those chickens tasted good, but they got a lot of exercise, which resulted in stringy muscles. If you simmered them a long time in *naberyori* (one-pot cooking) they made a nice *dashijiru*. The meat of commercial or young chickens sometimes gets too soft and "mushy."

I remember from childhood hunters catching mountain birds and waterfowl in traditional traps. The most popularly used traps at that time were nets. There were many kinds of nets, each designed for a particular situation. Using these nets successfully required skill and was a competitive match between man's intellect and the animal's instincts.

Before the heavy winter snows fall each year, the sparrows would go to the autumn fields and eat to store for winter. The hunters would go to the fields and yell and scream to startle the sparrows into flight. The birds would follow one leader to the nearest large tree to hide.

The pattern would continue for at least three days. The hunters would go to the fields at the same time each day and yell to start the sparrows into flight. Thousands of startled sparrows would head for the largest tree to wait under cover. The hunters continued the pattern until they were certain of the "emergency tree's" location.

After the birds had returned to their nests the last evening, the hunters set up *kasumiami* (Japanese mist nets) with a network of ropes between the "emergency tree" and the fields. The next morning they would return to the fields and startle the birds again...

They caught a lot of sparrows this way. Animal protection legislation has since made this method of hunting illegal; however, even now, *kansuzume* (wintertime sparrows) can still be found on the menu in some traditional country food restaurants, and the nets can still be purchased.

Friendship ceremony with the Hmong leaders and author Gaku Homma.

When I was a kid, they had another method for catching small birds called *tori mochi*. Tree sap was collected and applied to the end of a long, thin piece of bamboo resembling a fishing pole. They literally "fished" for birds, snagging them with the sticky sap. This method did not kill the birds; it captured them alive. This relates back to the traditional concept of keeping meats from spoiling.

As a kid, I remember the peddlers who came to town toting poles laden with waterfowl and mountain birds. The live birds were hanging upside down by their feet. Ducks, pheasants, and rabbits were hung in front of the *nikuya* (butcher shop). They moved if you went up and touched them. I remember thinking how sad this was.

However sad, these birds and rabbits were bought, taken home, decapitated, drained, plucked, and scorched to remove the tiny down or feathers, cooked, and eaten. These were sights and sounds of late autumn as recently as my own childhood. You cannot find them today.

When I was a curator, I ate a lot of wild game. When the snows began to fall toward the end of October, the *musasabi* (giant flying squirrels) were trapped. They were classified as birds because they "flew," therefore they were considered fair game. With the coming of winter the *musasabi* feasted on nuts, so their meat had a nutty taste.

As I have explained regarding the killing of boar or deer, any butchering was done under the strict guidelines of folk religion. This custom has traditional roots all over Asia. I have evidence of this fact through direct experience in downtown Denver, Colorado.

When I first came to Denver 12 years ago, to supplement my income I worked as an apartment complex manager. This complex housed immigrants fresh from Vietnam, Laos, and Cambodia. There was a Hmong community of about

400 people living in these buildings. I had had experience living with these people, and my Japanese heritage offered a friendly if somewhat distant similarity to their ways. They seemed to accept me, which kept the buildings full.

One early morning the younger Hmongs left in their van. The women waited, sitting on the back stairways in their native sarongs. The youths finally returned carrying something wrapped in plastic so large it took eight people to lift it. They carried it to the elder leader, who lived in a buffet upstairs.

My curiosity aroused, I visited the room. In the center of the room was a large tree stump set up for use as a cutting board. On it sat a lit candle. In front of the group sitting near the stump was an old woman dressed in black. She was the shaman of the group. Full of pride, the young people opened the plastic wrapping to expose the carcass of a cow.

The head was removed from the body and the blood collected on plastic laid down to cover the floor (most of the blood had been drained wherever the cow had been killed). The head was placed in the center of the room. It took the young men only about half an hour to butcher the entire cow. The room was silent, there was no talking. The meat was divided by the men and shared equally. Small bits of meat were stuffed into the intestines and hung like Christmas rope around the ceiling.

This was a living example of true co-op hunting and equal-share compensation. The only difference between this and a more modern version (although this did happen recently) is that now it is co-op buying. Everyone pitches in a few dollars and shares equally.

I was shocked to witness what I had only heard of in stories told to me by village elders. It was happening right before my eyes in Denver, Colorado!

These days, almost all big game in Japan has dwindled to the point these animals are not usually eaten. In some locales, however, horse meat is still enjoyed, either in *nabe* cooking or as *sashimi*. This may seem unappetizing to you, but the French also consider horse meat a delicacy.

In my home town horse meat is called *ketto-bashi,* the word derived partly from "kicking," and it is said to give you strong powers. Many small towns still have specialty horse meat restaurants.

This concludes the explanation of choosing and preparing basic ingredients. The following chapter will focus on cooking and recipes. Don't worry, there are no horse meat recipes. Please keep reading.

Chapter

5

COUNTRY MEALS

Breakfast (Choshoku)

Tofubako and Shiboridai — tofu-making tools.

S etting the Table

I could not begin to count the guests that have visited Nippon Kan. We have had visitors from around the world as well as all kinds of Japanese: students, businessmen fresh from Japan, those who have lived in this country for a long time, even those born here as *issei* or *nisei* (first- or second-generation Japanese-American citizens). We have had visitors from all over Europe, Indochina, and South America, and of course we have had countless American guests.

Usually I begin to prepare for dinner guests one to two days in advance. Japanese guests who were born before WWII have told me that my cooking is rare these days and is not easily found even in Japan. Younger Japanese guests have compared my cooking to that of their grandmothers. Guests from other countries have expressed pleasure over the food even though most of the time they don't know what they are eating. Once

in a while I have a visitor who has had a great deal of experience living in Japan. "This is the real thing," they have said with a smile.

The foods served in Japanese restaurants here in the United States are not what Japanese people typically eat on a daily basis. This book focuses on a country daily diet. For those readers interested in a healthful diet, these recipes can offer guidelines for a balanced, nutritious, and delicious way of eating.

During my time as a curator in Japan, I collected many recipes which I use when serving my guests. The number of individual dishes set at the table indicates the level of formality of the breakfast. If there are many small plates set, you can expect a top-level breakfast.

The most simple breakfast includes *ichihan, inchiju,* and *issai,* which means one bowl of rice, one bowl of soup, and one side dish. This simple breakfast is served during religious training, eaten for four or five days consecutively before a fast, or eaten to change one's diet or to lose weight.

Prior to a fast, this meal is served in less and less quantity until the first day of the fast when *okayu* is served (we will discuss *okayu* later in this chapter). Traditionally, the *ichihan* or *meshi* (cooking rice) used for the breakfast meal is brown rice or barley or 60% white rice mixed with 40% barley. The *ichiju* is either a *kombu*- or *shiitake*-based *miso* soup or a clear soup. The *misoshiru* (*miso* soup) contains a good balance of *tofu* and vegetables. There are many *issai* (called *okazu*), but they can be divided into the following basic categories: *tsukemono* (a variety of vegetables pickled with *miso, salt, shoyu* or *nuka* [rice bran]); *ohitashi* (a variety of vegetables boiled quickly and flavored with *shoyu*); *daizu seihin* (*tofu*, fried *tofu* cutlets, grilled *tofu*, *natto*, and other soybean products); *yakimono* (fish grilled either plain or marinated in *shoyu, miso, sakekasu* [rice wine lees] or *nuka*); and *jobina* (a variety of dishes prepared and stored in the refrigerator to be eaten anytime).

One or more side dishes are selected from these categories, you don't eat them all in one meal! Every morning you can arrange a new combination. Interestingly, as you increase the number of side dishes the portions of each decrease, so that you are always serving the same amount of food. How do we arrive at what the correct amount will be? It is not determined by a calorie count. To understand you need to know more about how to set the Japanese table.

Long ago, Japanese people did not eat sitting around large tables. When sitting around the *irori*, a small tray was placed on the right side of each person. On each tray was a small side dish plate, and an *owan* (the bowl used to eat the food from the large cooking pot).

Wealthier farmers had employees to feed. Each farm worker would bring a *hakozen* to work, which is a box one foot square and about 5 inches deep, with a fitted lid. The *hakozen* contained one set of dishes and a pair of chopsticks. At lunch the workers would remove the lid from their *hakozen* and turn it upside down. In this way the lid served conveniently as a tray. Then they removed the dishes, and placed the tray back on top of the box to make a small eating

table. After the meal, warm water was poured into their rice bowl and they used their chopsticks to clean it. After a sip of the water was taken, it was poured into the soup bowl, swirled around, sipped again, poured into the side dish plate, swirled and drunk. After that, all the dishes were repacked back into the *hakozen*. No washing required! We can conclude from this that the foods being eaten at the time were not oily, as the dishes could be easily cleaned with hot water.

A more modern approach to dining has been to eat on a low dining table called a *chabudai*. In front of each person's place was a drawer, where each person's personal dishes were kept. Except for guests, foods are not served on the individuals' plates. The food is presented in larger bowls and plates, and the individual picks up his or her own foods and places them on the small plate in front of him. A special treatment for a guest would be to arrange his plate beforehand.

Traditionally, the eldest man would serve himself first, followed in order of age by the other men of the family. Then the women would serve themselves oldest first down to the youngest.

The *ozen* (tray) is still used in traditional restaurants in Japan. In traditional *ryokan* (inns), where the rooms are floored with *tatami* mats, *ozen* are always used, never a table. The *owan* and *kozara* vary slightly in size for the adult and the child but are mostly the same.

Like the cafeteria trays you used in school with all the separate sections, there is only a certain amount of room on your *kozara*. For special days, or when guests visited, maybe more than one dish per person was set out, but usually there is only one.

If you put more than one side dish on one plate, the foods must not touch one another. Therefore the amount of food remains the same whether it is one kind or many: the amount of food that goes into your stomach is the same no matter how many dishes you are eating.

The amount of *meshi* served in each *meshiwan* (rice bowl) is usually about one cup. *Tenko meshi* is the term for a *meshiwan* heaped full of rice to form a round dome. *Tenko meshi* is laid before the dead at a funeral ceremony or placed on a Buddhist altar, so it is obviously taboo to serve heaping bowls of rice to guests and family. The rice is gently placed into the center of the bowl with a wooden spatula. To slide the spoon back over the edge of the bowl flattening the rice is bad manners. Fill the bowl only about 60% full and keep it fluffy — don't pack it in. If you soak the *meshibera* (the wooden or bamboo spatula), in water before using it to serve, the rice won't stick to it.

The *shiruwan* and *meshiwan* both hold about one cup. Each dish usually comes with its own lid. If you remove the lid and turn it upside it can be used as a *kozara*. Used this way, the *meshiwan* and *shiruwan* can be the only dishes you need!

Meshi — Rice

The word used on a daily basis for *meshi* is *gohan*. (The Chinese character for *meshi* is pronounced *han*. *Go* or *O* are honorifics frequently used in the Japanese language.) Rice is the most important staple for the Japanese people. Except for a small minority that chooses brown rice or other grains, most family homes and restaurants serve white rice.

Beginning in the Kamakura period (1192–1333), through the end of the Edo period (1603–1867), rice was used as legal tender for collecting taxes. The salaries of the *samurai,* as well as agents of the ruling parties, were paid in rice. Rice is measured in *koku* and the status of a *samurai* determined how much rice he was worth. For example, *samurai* were classed as 10,000 *koku samurai,* 3000 *koku samurai,* etc.

From the beginning, rice was squeezed from the farmers. This was the foundation on which all political and economic systems were built. Today, the government still sets policy, buying rice from the farmers at set prices and distributing to wholesalers for marketing. In this manner the government sets the balance between the producers and the consumers, controlling the economy. Setting the prices for rice naturally affects the prices of other foods and labor, furthering control over the economic system.

Problems arose about 20 years ago when the Japanese began to consume less rice. This caused a three-year stockpile of rice to accumulate. When the market value of this rice dropped to less than the original buying price, it had serious economic effects. Recently the United States has asked Japan to liberalize its rice-buying policies, pressuring the Japanese government to accept United States-grown rice. This combined with the ever-present internal politics of the Japanese government makes for an interesting situation. The point is that rice is an integral part of Japanese life at all levels: not only as the major source of food but economically and politically as well.

For more than eight hundred years rice has fed the people, been used as legal tender, used in spiritual ceremonies, and saved for special celebration. Because rice has a psychological relationship as well as a physical relationship with the Japanese people, it will be interesting to see how new international and political situations are solved. In my opinion, if you study history, any time a country imports its primary crop, it becomes vulnerable in a dangerous way. If rice is imported into Japan and Japanese rice fields are left to seed for even five years, the effects on the soil and its farmers could be devastating. Fields left to seed would fall prey to development, which would eliminate the possibility for future agricultural use. Looking at the big picture, it may be to Japan's best interest on many levels to grow its own rice. What may be important to concentrate on now is restoring a balance between the producers, the government, and the consumers.

Rice grown in California is available in the United States for about 70 cents a pound. In Japan, rice of very similar quality costs about 600 yen. There are certain popular brands of Japanese rice sold in the United States. Occasionally I have seen rice removed from its original packages and sold in "serve yourself" barrels. This is fine, but make sure you ask about the brand used, and make sure it is not a mixture of long grain, mixed grain and/or sticky rice. Japanese rice is short grain. If you have a small family or are single, I recommend you buy smaller packages to ensure freshness. If you are buying brown rice, the short-grain variety is good for Japanese cooking. Make sure that the brown rice you buy has not been mixed with green or very thin rice. This is called *zakkoku* (low-quality rice used as a filler).

Meshi is the word for rice, but is the general term applied to barley, decengrass, foxtail, corn, and beans. For example, *mugi meshi* is barley, and *awa meshi* is foxtail. As we have said, the white rice used in Japanese cooking today is called *gohan*. Sometimes *gohan* is combined with barley or beans. The main part of a Japanese breakfast is white rice or barley or a mixture of the two. In today's world there are rice cookers available that can be preprogrammed to begin cooking your rice for you while you sleep and be ready for breakfast the next morning. A small rice cooker capable of serving two people costs between 30 and 40 dollars. If a warmer is included, the cost is about 120 dollars. Many Japanese appliance companies make rice cookers.

I still think that rice cooked in a *kamado* over a wood fire is the most delicious, but this is becoming increasingly harder to find. If you do not have a rice cooker in your home I will explain in the following chart how to make delicious rice using a regular cooking pot.

If you eat rice every day, it might be helpful to cook a large amount and store individual portions in sealed sandwich bags in the refrigerator.

HOW TO COOK WHITE RICE
(For 5 cups of rice)

1. Before cooking, wash the rice, polishing the grains by grinding them with your hands, and then pour off the water. Repeat three or four times until the rinse water becomes almost clear. In the same amount of water soak the rice for about 30 minutes. If you bite a grain and find it soft, the rice is ready to cook. Drain completely.

   One cup of rice will yield three times the amount when cooked. If you are preparing brown rice, wash the rice in the same manner as the white rice and let it soak in two to three inches standing water for at least 5 hours.

2. The rice should fill the pot only 1/3 full. A heavy pot with a heavy cover that forms a good seal is best.

3. The crucial factor here is the amount of water you use. The volume of water is equal to the volume of rice plus 15% to 25%. If you are cooking a small amount of rice add an extra 25%. If you are cooking a lot of rice 15% more water is enough. Make sure the rice is distributed evenly in the bottom of the pan.

4. Place the covered pot over a strong heat until bubbles begin to escape between the pot and the lid. Turn the heat down 1/3 until the lid stops rattling and no more bubbles come up. If you have an electric stove all the following recipes are the same. Allow for the stove to change temperatures more slowly as they are less responsive to temperature control than gas stoves. NEVER TAKE OFF THE LID. When the steam begins to weaken, lower the heat to low for 5 to 6 minutes. When you cannot see any more steam escaping from between the pot and the lid, reduce heat to the lowest possible and continue to cook for 12 to 15 minutes. Turn off the heat and let the pot sit covered for 7 to 10 minutes to continue steaming on its own.

These individual portions can be reheated in the microwave on high for 1 minute. If you do have a rice cooker, you can prepare your rice

HOW TO COOK BROWN RICE

Brown rice takes longer to cook than white rice. For 5 cups of brown rice, follow all of the same procedures as for white rice. Allow the rice to cool covered until it reaches room temperature. Add **1 cup of water** and cook over a medium heat for 10 minutes. Lower the heat to low and continue cooking for 5 minutes. Turn off the heat and let it continue to steam for 7 to 10 minutes. If you are using a rice cooker, after it has cooked once and cooled, add **1 cup of water** and start the cooker again.

in about 20 minutes, so it is not a major inconvenience.

If you are cooking brown rice, it needs to be cooked twice or pressure-cooked, otherwise, though nutritious, it will be tough and difficult to digest. Fresh brown rice should be soft and fluffy as well as have a nice flavor.

Today in Japan most families have electric rice cookers with warming units capable of keeping the rice warm for 2 to 3 days. Traditionally and presently, after the rice has been cooked, the entire cooking pot is placed in the *ohitsu* (a small wooden tub with a wooden cover). In my home town, which lies in the colder northern regions, there was also an outer casing for the *ohitsu* made out of rice straw to give it more thermal insulation. Traditionally, rice was made for only one meal, so it had to be kept warm for only a short period. The rice's freshness was an important part of the meal's character. The steam from the freshly cooked rice was sometimes even read like tea leaves. It was a religious taboo to let the rice get cold.

Today we use electric warmers to keep the rice warm. This is a modern convenience and saves time, but beneath this concept, through the layers, the original importance of white rice is reflected in the fact that great pains are taken to keep it warm. In Japan you serve cold rice to show dissatisfaction with a person or just to be

mean. This is a blatant hint that you are not pleased with them. When for example someone receives an unfair work assignment, a common comment is, "Oh, it's as bad as if he were served cold rice." It is important to remember to serve your rice warm.

In large families a great deal of rice is cooked for a single meal. Sometimes when the rice is cooking it sticks to the bottom of the *kama* (rice-cooking pot) and burns. This burnt rice is called *koge*. The Japanese have sayings that loosely translate "*koge* has a thousand good points" or "*koge* is the most delicious". For the country folk, there is a tradition of relishing *koge* which reflects the importance of white rice. Honoring this principal concept, everyone volunteers to eat *koge*. *Koge* can be made into rice balls and seasoned with sauteed sesame seed and salt or *miso*. It is a simple, tasty treat. *Koge* can also be grilled on both sides, placed in a rice bowl, and served with hot water or tea poured over it.

In conclusion, remember that the traditional farmer did not eat white rice every day. White rice was held in high regard for spiritual as well as nutritional reasons.

Okayu — Rice Porridge

The traditional farmer ate *gokoku* as a main staple, which you will remember is a mixture of different grains. The amount of water and cooking time is adjusted for the grains that take the longest. An oatmeal-like porridge is made in this way.

This porridge today is called *okayu* or *zosui* and is popularly eaten as a recovery food after surgery or a long-term illness. Temples and *dojos* serve *okayu* as a part of fasting.

Long ago this was the daily staple in Japan. Today it serves as such in many parts of Korea, China, and Indochina. *Okayu* is good for dieting, being low in calories and very filling. If you take plain *okayu* and mix in vegetables, fish, *miso* or *shoyu,* you have *zosui.*

There is an old proverb that says 1 bowl of *zosui* = 2 bowls of *okayu* = 3 bowls of *meshi* = 4 bowls of *sushi* = 5 bowls of *mochi*. What this is referring to is that eating 1 bowl of *zosui* or 5 bowls of *mochi* will result in the same feeling of fullness, so for weight control, eating *okayu* or *zosui* is a healthful way to fill up.

Sometimes people don't find the oatmeal-like texture very appetizing, but served with a tasty side dish, this can be a well-balanced meal.

The simplest *okayu* has no taste, not even *dashijiru* is used as a flavoring. In hospitals, after a patient is taken off an IV, the first solid foods he is given to eat is *omoyu,* which is a very soupy *okayu.* We have different names for *okayu* depending on its thickness. *Okayu* isn't just served to the sick or in hospitals. In my home town, *okayu* was made by mixing rice with decengrass, foxtail, walnuts or chestnuts, and chicken meat or chicken bones. This healthful variety of *okayu* was especially popular before winter.

Morning Side Dishes

Tsukemono — Pickles

Originally *tsukemono* were vegetables pickled in *miso. Miso* was called *"ko"* in earlier times. *Ko no mono* is the old name for pickles. Today there are still *miso* pickles made in Japan but salted pickles are more popular. Pickles are a consistent and important part of the Japanese table. If they are not served, the meal feels incomplete. A person that can make good pickles will be a good chef or sometimes (it is traditionally said) will make a good wife.

For the areas in northern Japan that lie buried under winter snows for five to six months out of the year, *tsukemono* are important. Winter survival bred skillful techniques to create a variety of delicious pickles.

It is difficult to make pickles correctly just by following a set recipe with ingredients and so

---

HOW TO COOK OKAYU

1. Wash **2 cups rice** by polishing the rice with your hand in water, drain, repeat 3 or 4 times, and drain completely. In the same amount of water, soak for 30 minutes until grains feel soft when bitten. Drain again.

2. In a large pot, combine the rice with **6 cups *shiitake, kombu,*** or ***shojin dashijiru*** (refer to *dashijiru,* Chapter 3) and **6 cups water.** You need a liquid-to-rice ratio of 6 to 1. Cover and heat on high until bubbles appear between the lid and the pot. Reduce the heat to the lowest possible and cook for 50 to 60 minutes. Stir occasionally, so it won't stick to the bottom. Serve when it has reached an oatmeal-like consistency.

---

forth. Experience, experimentation, and practice are more valuable. There are different types and methods for making pickles depending on how long they are intended to be stored.

Sokuseki zuke (instant pickles). These pickles are ready to eat after pickling in salt for only two to three hours. They are simple, but the vegetable's fresh taste is enjoyably enhanced. The salt content is 2% to 3% the weight of the vegetables.

Ichiya zuke (overnight pickles). These pickles need one night or seven to 10 hours pickling time. If the pickles are prepared the night before, they are ready the next morning. The salt content is 3% to 4% the weight of the vegetables.

Toza zuke (short-term pickles). These pickles are ready in two to three days and and will keep up to two weeks. The salt content is 3% to 4% the weight of the vegetables.

Hozon zuke (long-term pickles). These pickles need to be pickled for at least one month and can keep for three to five months. To store for longer periods, long-term pickles have a salt content of 5% to 25% the weight of the vegetables.

All pickles fall into these four categories, but there are many different varieties of each. My home town of Akita is famous for its pickles. *Gakko cha* is a popular custom in which a guest that comes for tea and chat brings their own pickles. A guest may bring a colorful arrangement of pickled eggplant, white radish, carrots, cucumber, turnips, cabbage, or gourds. These are enjoyed over a cup of *bancha* (coarse tea). The salt in the pickles compliments the flavor of the bancha tea. Sweet cakes compliment *ryokucha* (green teas) best.

If you are making *sokuseki zuke* or *ichiya zuke,* make only enough for the intended meal. From the time you prepare *toza zuke,* wait two to three days before you begin eating them. Prepare enough so you can enjoy the different tastes that emerge as the pickles change in flavor over a period of a few days.

Traditionally, whole farming families worked very hard to make pickles. As recently as 20 years ago, a creek usually ran in front of the farmer's house. The vegetables were harvested and washed in this clear cold water. I remember watching the farmers do this. Today the beautiful creeks have been paved over and people are reluctant to participate in this cold task — vegetables are washed and prepared in factories. Homemakers don't make their own pickles as often as they used to.

When I was growing up, my mother pickled about 50 large *daikon* and 30 to 40 Chinese cabbage every year. She had a certain farmer's wife come to help, because of her skill at this process. Today in my family's home, that woman's daughter-in-law comes to help make pickles about the same time every year.

Traditionally, the *oke* (pickling tubs) were made of Japanese cedar. The largest was up to 60 gallons. Just before pickling season began,

the tubs would be set outside so they would swell tight with the rain water. The tubs were held tightly together with a strip of braided bamboo called a *taga.* If the *taga* were to break, the whole tub would fall apart. There remains today a kind of proverb that is said in companies and in schools: if control cannot be maintained, the *taga* is loose.

There was a time when the *taga ya* (*taga* repairman) came by the house with his tools and circles of bamboo strips over his shoulder. He came to change or tighten the *taga* on our pickling tubs. I watched him carefully as he braided the bamboo. The strips were very long and he would toss them deftly in the air. Then he would set the *taga* in place and tighten it down with rhythmic strokes of his hammer. Fascinated, it wasn't enough for me to watch him only at my home, I had to follow him to his next job and watch him there, too. I remember getting home late for dinner and the reprimand that followed. Of course, I went to the mountains the next day and cut down some bamboo myself. Although the project was a failure, I did succeed in acquiring numerous cuts on my fingers.

Today, the tubs are usually made of porcelain or plastic so that kind of special craftsman must be supported by the government to keep his craft alive. Although methods are changing, *tsukemono* still plays a vital role in the Japanese sense of taste.

Many of the following recipes will call for a weight to be placed on lid of the *tsukedaru* (large pickling jar). The weight on the lid of the *tsukedaru* serves to compress the pickles. Different pickles, depending on their desired liquid content, require more or less compression. This compression is based on the weight of the ingredients being pickled. For example, the recipe for two pounds of pickled cabbage might call for a weight twice that of the cabbage (four pounds).

Sokuseki Zuke — Instant Pickles

- Kyabetsu zuke — Pickled cabbage

A. Dice enough **cabbage** in 1-inch squares **to fill a 1-gallon bowl. Cut 1 cucumber** in half lengthwise. Random peel and remove seeds with a spoon, slant cut in 1/4-inch sections. Peel and grate **2 oz. carrots.** Soak **1/2 oz. *wakame*** (young kelp) in water until soft, rough chop.

B. Mix A with **1 tsp. salt** and knead by hand until the cabbage changes color and the texture softens. Let stand for 1 to 3 hours, then drain.

C. If you like, squeeze in **1/4 slice lemon or lime.** If you favor a spicy taste, add **1-inch small dried red pepper** (seeds removed), or add **1 tsp. of juice from grated ginger** before you let the pickles stand.

- Kyuri zuke — Pickled cucumber

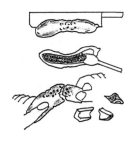

A. Random peel **3 cucumbers,** cut in half lengthwise, and remove seeds with a spoon. Break into bite-sized pieces with your fingers. Peel and grate **2 oz. carrots.** Soak **1/2 oz. *wakame*** (young kelp) in water to soften, rough chop large.

B. In a mixing bowl, mix A with **2 or 3 Tbsp. *shoyu*** and **1 Tbsp. *mirin.*** Knead by hand until juicy. Refrigerate 10 to 15 minutes, and serve. If you like, add **1 red chili** (seeds removed) or **1 tsp. grated ginger.**

How to prepare cucumbers.

- Kyuri to kabu zuke — Pickled cucumber and turnips

A. Random peel **1 cucumber,** cut in half lengthwise, remove seeds with a spoon, and slant cut into 1/4-inch slices. Peel, quarter, and slice **1 fist-sized turnip.** Crush **1 dried red chili,** one inch long (seeds removed). Soak **1 oz. *itokombu*** (thin slivers of *kombu*) in water until soft or soak **1/2-inch squares of *kombu*** (dried kelp) in water until soft and cut into matchstick slivers.

B. In a mixing bowl, mix A with **2 or 3 Tbsp. *shoyu,* 1 Tbsp. *mirin,*** and a few pinches of **salt.** Knead by hand, being careful not to crush the cucumbers. Refrigerate for 1 to 2 hours.

■ Daikon to ninjin zuke — Pickled Japanese white radish and carrots

    A. Cut **3/4 lbs.** *daikon* into 1-inch pieces and slice **2 oz. carrots** into about 1/4-inch pieces. Add **1/2 tsp. salt,** knead by hand until soft, drain. Soak **1 or 2 medium-size** *shiitake* **mushrooms** until soft and slice into wide matchstick slivers (save the soak water to use for *dashijiru*). Crush **1 dried red chili** (seeds removed).

    B. In a heated skillet saute mushrooms and the chili in **2 Tbsp. sesame oil** for 1 to 2 minutes. Turn off the heat. Add **1 Tbsp. sugar, 1 Tbsp.** *shoyu,* and **3 Tbsp. rice vinegar.** Mix with A while still hot. Refrigerate for about 1 hour.

Ichiya Zuke — Overnight Pickles

■ Kabu to kyuri zuke — Pickled turnip and cucumber

    A. Peel, quarter and slice into wide slices **1 fist-sized turnip.** Random peel **1 cucumber,** cut in half lengthwise, remove seeds with a spoon, and break into bite-size pieces. Crush and soak **1-inch square** *kombu,* or soak and use scissors to cut into small pieces. Crush **1 dried red chili** (one inch long, seeds removed).

    B. Mix **1 Tbsp. salt** into A and toss. Place into a *tsukedaru* (a deep, cylindrical-shaped pickle container) and cover with a drop lid or plate that fits fairly tightly inside the container. Place a weight on top of the lid that is twice as heavy as the total weight of all ingredients Serve the next day.

■ Serori zuke — Pickled celery

    A. Remove the leafy parts from **6 ribs of celery** and cut each into 3 sections. Place the total volume of celery in twice the amount of boiling water. Add **1/3 tsp. salt** and boil 3 or 4 minutes. Immediately immerse in cold water. Drain and shake off excess water.

    B. Combine **1 cup** *kombu* or *shiitake dashijiru,* **2 tsp. rice vinegar,** and **3 tsp.** *shoyu.* Fold in celery and it is ready to serve the next day. (If the celery is not totally submerged, you will need to make more liquid.)

■ Burokkori zuke — Pickled broccoli

A. Break **1/2 medium-sized head of broccoli** into bite-size pieces. Place broccoli in boiling water equal to twice the volume of broccoli. Add **1/3 tsp. salt** and boil 1 to 2 minutes. Immediately immerse in cold water, drain, shake off excess water. Soak **1/2 cup *sukikombu*** (sliced, dried kelp in thin sheets), or **1/2-inch square of *kombu*** (dried kelp) until soft.

B. Combine **1 Tbsp. salt, 1/2 sliced lemon or lime,** and **1/2 cup grated carrots** with A and place in the *tsukedaru,* cover with a drop lid or with a tight-fitting flat plate and place a weight on top of the lid twice as heavy as all ingredients. The pickles will be ready to serve the next day.

Toza Zuke — Short-Term Pickles

■ Hakusai zuke — Pickled Chinese cabbage

A. Cut **4 lbs. *hakusai* cabbage** in half lengthwise. Let the cabbage dry (cut side facing up) indoors 1 to 2 days to soften and bring out sweetness (do not let them get completely dry).

B. Sprinkle the bottom of the *tsukedaru* with **1 Tbsp. salt.** Lay the cabbage halves in the *tsukedaru* with the cut side facing up. Pack them tightly together to form one layer. Add layers, sprinkling each with salt. Randomly place **3 or 4 1-inch whole dried red chilis** (seeds removed).

C. Place a weight on top of the lid that is twice as heavy as the total weight of the cabbage before drying. The total amount of salt used should be about 1/3 lbs. This may sound like a great deal of salt, but remember cabbage contains a great deal of water. After 2 or 3 days the salt should dissipate sufficiently. Store at room temperature.

■ Nasu zuke — Pickled eggplant

A. Remove the stems from **8 6-inch Japanese eggplants** and quarter 2/3 of the way up towards the stem end. Place in the *tsukedaru*.

B. Boil **4 Tbsp. salt, 5 cups water,** and if you have it, **1/4 tsp. *yakimyoban*** (burnt alum), stirring until well mixed — let cool.

C. Combine B and A, cover, and place a weight on top of the lid that is twice as heavy as all ingredients. Refrigerate for 2 to 4 days.

Hozon Zuke — Long-Term Pickles

(Before we make long-term pickles we need to produce the marinade, which generally is called called *tsukedoko*. There are many types of *tsukedoko*. The first three steps of the following recipe produce a variety called *nukadoko*, which is made from rice bran. Other *hozon zuke* recipes will call for other varieties of *tsukedoko*.)

■ Nuka zuke — Pickles made with rice bran

A. Combine **4 lbs. *komenuka*** (rice bran or ground husks from brown rice), **4 or 5 slices of white bread** to supply yeast, **1 lb. salt, 5 or 6 one-inch dried red chilis, 1 oz. *kombu*,** and **a few wilted outer leaves from any leafy vegetable,** such as **cabbage** or ***daikon*. Cabbage hearts** can also be used.

B. Place *komenuka* in the *tsukedaru* and mix with **13 to 15 cups of water**. Add the rest of A, pat down flat and cover with gauze. Leaving an air space, cover the *tsukedaru* tightly with plastic wrap, tie, and let sit in a cool area for about 10 hours.

C. The next day stir, folding in air, remove the vegetables and replace with a new batch of wilted outer leaves. Repeat this pattern for 3 or 4 days.

D. Now that you have produced the *nukadoko,* **add one or all of the following vegetables** to equal no more than 1/2 the volume of the *nukadoko*.

Cucumbers (slice in half lengthwise, remove seeds with a spoon); **Japanese eggplant** (remove stem and quarter two-thirds of the way toward stem area, leaving eggplant intact); **Japanese white radish** (cut in half lengthwise); **carrots** (cut in half, if large, lengthwise); **cabbage** (cut in half; if **Chinese cabbage,** leave to partially dry for 1 to 2 days in a shaded area).

Before placing vegetables into the *nukadoko,* wet your hands and rub each piece with salt. Add as many as you wish to equal 1/2 the volume of the *nukadoko*. Place them in the *tsukedaru* at least 24 hours before you wish to eat them. Before serving, remove the vegetables, lightly rinse and cut into 1/4-inch slices.

The *nukadoko,* if stored in a cool area, can be used for up to 2 to 3 months. If the *nukadoko* becomes diluted due to the water contained in the vegetables, add more *komenuka* and salt. Stir well every day and cover tightly.

■ Miso zuke — Pickles made with miso

A. Combine **4 cups *akamiso*** (red *miso*), **1 cup *mirin,*** and **2 1-inch dried red chilis** in the *tsukedaru.* This makes *misodoko.*

B. Prepare vegetables in the same way as in "*Nuka zuke* part D" and set out to partially dry until soft. Wrap each kind of vegetable in gauze and immerse in *misodoko.* Soft vegetables will be ready to eat in one day. Hard vegetables will be ready in two days. After this one- or two-day period, refrigerate. Rinse lightly before serving and slice into 1/4-inch slices.

Miso zuke are commonly served as side dishes with *okayu,* or can be used as the center fillings for rice balls. These long-term pickles can be used for two to three months. If the *misodoko* becomes diluted, add more salt. You can also use this pickling recipe with broccoli, cauliflower, and other vegetables.

■ Kasu zuke — Pickles made with rice wine lees

A. Combine **2 lbs. *sakekasu*** (rice wine lees), **1/2 cup sugar, 1/2 cup *mirin,*** and **1/2 cup *miso*** in the *tsukedaru.* This makes *kasudoko.*

B. Prepare vegetables in the same manner as "*Nuka zuke* part D," let sit indoors for one to two days to partially dry until soft. Mix with *kasudoko.* The vegetables will be ready in about one week. Rinse lightly before serving.

Other Kinds of Pickles

■ Umezuke — Pickled plums

A. Soak **3 lbs. of plums** (hard, slightly unripe) in water overnight. (Apricots can be substituted for plums.) The next day pat the plums completely dry with paper towel and place them in the *tsukedaru.* Mix in **1-1/2 cups salt** and toss. Cover with a drop lid and add a weight equal to the weight of the plums. Let sit for one week. After a week, pour off the resulting pickle juice called *hakubaizu* (white plum vinegar), and save for use in other recipes. Refrigerate *umezuke* in a closed jar.

■ Umeboshi — Pickled, dried plums

A. Place **60 *shiso no ha*** (beef steak leaves) in the *tsukedaru* and add **1 tsp. salt.** Knead by hand until the juices are released. Discard the juice. Add **3 or 4 Tbsp. *hakubaizu*** left over from making *Umezuke* and mix well.

B. Add **3 lbs. *umezuke*** to A and continue to fill the *tsukedaru* with *hakubaizu* until all ingredients are submerged. Cover with a drop lid and place a weight on top of the lid which is the same weight as all ingredients, and let sit in a cool place for about one month.

C. On a very dry, hot day remove B's plums and spread outside on a flat basket for 2 to 3 days until the plums turn light brown and show salt evaporation lines. Do not allow them to dry completely and harden. These plums will keep for a few years if stored in a cool place.

■ Nasu no karashi zuke — Pickled eggplant with mustard

A. Remove the stems from **1 lb. Japanese eggplant** and trim with a rolling cut whole. In an indoor shaded area, lay out to dry for one day. Mix with **1 tsp. salt** and **3 Tbsp. Japanese mustard** and place in the *tsukedaru*.

B. Boil and cool **3 Tbsp. *shoyu*, 1 Tbsp. *mirin*,** and **1 tsp. sugar.** Pour over A. Cover with a drop lid and place a weight on top of the lid which equals the total weight of the ingredients. They are ready in 1 to 2 days.

■ America zuke — Pickles American-style

A. Mix **1 loaf white bread** (shredded), **1 six-pack of beer,** and **1/2 cup salt** and let stand uncovered for 12 hours in the *tsukedaru*.

B. Prepare vegetables the same as "*Nuka zuke* part D" (p. 132) and add to A. Cover and refrigerate. They will be ready in four or five days. Suggested vegetables include **asparagus, celery, cabbage,** and **bell pepper.** Add salt if the pickles are not salty enough for your taste. You can use the base mixture for about one month.

These recipes are only a few examples of traditional pickles. Each locale, each house, has its own special pickle recipes. These recipes were selected because of their simplicity. You can control the amount of salt to suit your taste but remember that the salt acts to soften vegetables and bring out their natural flavors. You simply can't make pickles if you take out too much salt.

Umezuke and *umeboshi* are now readily available in Oriental markets throughout the United States. I have met strict vegetarians who believed that a healthful diet could consist of *genmai* (brown rice) and *umeboshi* alone. It saddened me to note that these people usually had distended stomachs and swollen legs and faces. One can exist on a diet of *okayu* and *umeboshi*, and they themselves are healthy foods, but if they are all one eats there will be vitamin deficiencies and an overabundance of salt, so please take care.

I have never been one to openly criticize another's diet, but I feel there is something wrong with this. If we were all starving and there were only brown rice and pickled plums to eat, then this would be okay — there would be no other choice. But Japan and the United States offer so many more foods that I do not believe limiting one's foods this extensively constitutes a healthy balance of mind and body.

There are a variety of therapies available today for excessive eaters. At the same time those following extremely restrictive diets seem fashionable. I don't understand this. I am more concerned with overall physical and mental health. Maybe this kind of behavior — as the other side of complete health — should be examined as well.

Umeboshi or *umezuke* sometimes turn your mouth red. This is not from beef steak leaves, it is from food coloring. Real top-quality *umeboshi* are expensive, so be careful to read the ingredients when you are shopping for *umeboshi*. Make sure no food coloring or preservatives have been added.

Long ago (and even today) it was a common belief that *umeboshi* was good for stomach aches and head aches. Today our bodies are so used to taking modern drugs that taking a pickled plum for a headache most likely won't work. Long ago however, our bodies were more sensitive to chemicals. Maybe it did work.

Umeboshi are used widely in Japanese country cooking. The recipes for these plums and their juice *(hakubaizu)* have been developed over many generations.

Ohitashi — Boiled Greens

Directly translated, *ohitashi* means boiled greens seasoned with *shoyu*. In country cooking, *ohitashi* takes the place of salads commonly eaten in the United States. When I was a kid, salads were not served at our table. For my mother especially, reflecting the era she was raised in, salads were part of another world's culture.

Modern Japanese foods can be generally divided into two categories by the language in which they are written: *"katakana"* and *"hiragana"* foods. In Japan, foreign words are written using a completely separate set of phonetic symbols called *katakana. Hiragana* is a form of written language used for Japanese words. Today many popular foods are written in *katakana.* These should sound familiar: *sarada, hambargu, furaidochikin, piza, supagetei, yoguruto, chizu, batar, kechappu,* and *mayoneizu* — to name a few. The traditional Japanese language offers no counterparts for these words because they are products that have only recently been introduced to the Japanese culture.

Although foreign *katakana* words were not acceptable during World War II, post-war Japan enjoys many, many *katakana* foods with *katakana* names. All over Japan you can find American pizza parlors, hamburger stands, and convenience stores. I think they are the way of the future.

Before the end of World War II, the foods mostly available were *hiragana* foods, or foods produced in Japan. World War II took place in the Showa period. Preceding the Showa period was the Taisho period. Preceding it was the Meiji period. My mother was born in the Meiji period (1868-1912). She never caught on to the *katakana* foods trend, so I never ate salads as a kid.

Another indicator of how time has changed diet came when I made contact with many first-generation Japanese Americans. I remember one old woman announcing to me one day that we were going to have *seiyo udon* (western noodles). *Udon* is a popular Japanese noodle made from wheat flour. It took me a few minutes to figure out that she meant spaghetti. These first-generation people were raised in the era before World War II so there was no Japanese *katakana* word for western noodles.

Traditionally the Japanese didn't eat salads. When the Japanese did begin to include salad in their regular diet, the mayonaise companies had a lot to do with it. Launching a huge marketing campaign, these companies used many forms of media to promote the healthfulness of salads. Celebrities and doctors endorsed salad as the food that Japan was not eating enough of. Of course, glamorous European and American models were used as slender role models for the young adults. A particular brand used dolls and cartoons to attract youngsters.

For more than 1,000 years raw vegetables were not usually put on the Japanese table. Almost overnight, salad was being served in most households. Western vegetables such as lettuce and celery began to become popular. Although salad has become an important part of the Japanese diet, they survived for generations without it.

The original reason that vegetables were never served raw in Japanese country cooking was that folk religion viewed raw vegetables as still containing bad *ke*. The hygienic foundation for this belief was that raw vegetables harbored parasites. The rule was that vegetables should be boiled before eaten. Today, of course, vegetables are free of parasites, but full of chemicals.

The media bombards us with the "be slim, stay slim, be healthy" campaigns of the '80s and '90s. You've seen it everywhere, heard it everywhere. "In just eight quick weeks, you too can look like this." Many people in Japan joined the salad "boom" trying to emulate the campaign models. Anorexia has become a problem for Japanese youth. Throwing away over 1,000 years of traditional diet, these youths jumped on the bandwagon in a fashion reminiscent of the brown rice and *umeboshi* dieters.

Traditionally, the Japanese serve *ohitashi* every morning as a side dish in place of salad. These side dishes can be made from a variety of vegetables. I remember my mother musing to herself, "What shall I make for tomorrow's *ohitashi*?" She would fret over coming up with a new variation or different combination of vegetables.

Today fresh vegetables are available all year round, but not so long ago, fresh vegetables were rare during winter. The Japanese existed on pickles or stored vegetables such as Chinese cabbage, Japanese white radish, carrot, burdock, and potatoes. These were used to make the morning's *ohitashi*.

Most *ohitashi* are made by boiling vegetables. There are exceptions like *nagaimo* (Chinese yam) that are peeled and finely grated, or sliced into matchstick slivers and eaten raw.

When boiling vegetables, the most important consideration is to not overcook them. We are not trying to make Popeye spinach! The vegetables should be boiled with two to three times the amount of water as vegetables. In other words, if the vegetables fill one inch of a pot, boiled them in three inches of water. Use this method of measuring water whenever boiling is called for. I recommend 1/4 tsp. of salt for every 5 cups of water.

Before boiling, wash the vegetables gently but thoroughly. Spinach and celery especially trap a great deal of dirt so separate the leaves and wash carefully. Before boiling the vegetables, set out a large bowl near the sink and fill it with about the same amount of ice water as you are using to boil the vegetables. Also set out a colander or large-mesh strainer.

When boiling the vegetables place them in root end first, because they are harder at that end and take longer to cook. Although each vegetable is slightly different, average boiling time is 30 seconds to five minutes. Make sure the water is already boiling before you put in the vegetables. After they have cooked, quickly drain into a collander and then immerse them in the bowl of iced water. If you have no ice, cold running water will do. Cooking by this method results in vegetables that have a beautiful shiny color that should last for several hours, and a crisp texture.

This technique requires you to set up your utensils in advance so that once the vegetables begin to cook you can move quickly to each new step.

If you are cooking rooted vegetables remove the roots after they have chilled. Then place them on a *makisu* (small bamboo mat) and roll it tightly to squeeze out any excess water, or squeeze or shake by hand. It is important that your finished *ohitashi* dish not be too watery.

Ohitashi should add a seasonal feel to the table. They should be beautifully arranged on a large plate. Each person picks his own portion and places it on his own small plate. Garnishes are added individually to taste.

Aemono are dishes that have been flavored before they are served. *Aemono* are different from *ohitashi* which are flavored by adding *shoyu* (soy sauce). You should add 1/2 to 1 tsp. of *shoyu* for each half-cup serving of vegetables (water squeezed out). If you have finished eating your *ohitashi* and there is *shoyu* left on the plate, too much was added. If you feel you added too little, just add another drop or two. When I was a kid my parents would be annoyed with me if I left any *shoyu* on my plate.

Garnishes can be set out for added tastes and textures. For a 1/2-cup serving you should use only a three-fingered pinch of each kind.

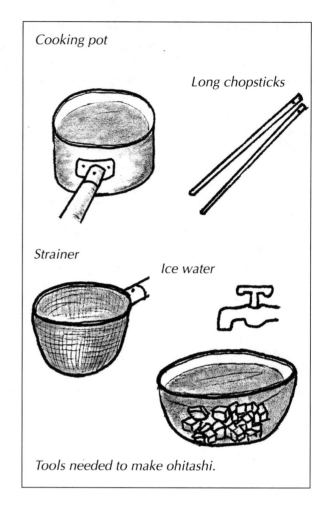

Cooking pot

Long chopsticks

Strainer

Ice water

Tools needed to make ohitashi.

A FEW EXAMPLES OF GARNISHES:	
Kezuribushi — shaved bonito	*Oroshi daikon* — grated Japanese white radish
Kizaminori — shredded laver	*Wasabi* — Japanese green horseradish
Oroshi shoga — grated fresh ginger	*Karashi* — mustard
	Shichimi togarashi — seven-taste pepper

Ohitashi Recipes

The following vegetables are considered surface (as opposed to root) vegetables and require 30 to 60 seconds boiling time: *horenso* (spinach), *shungiku* (chrysanthemum leaves), *nira* (Japanese leeks), *natane* (rapeseed leaf), *seri* (dropwort), *zukini* (zucchini), *moyashi* (soybean sprouts), *kinusaya* (snow peas), *wakegi* (Welsh onion), and *kiku* (chrysanthemum flower).

Other surface vegetables require 1 to 2 minutes boiling time: *asuparagasu* (asparagus), *sayaingen* (green beans), *kyabetsu* (cabbage), *hakusai* (Chinese cabbage), *okura* (okra); and American vegetables such as broccoli, cauliflower, mustard greens, collard greens.

(The following recipes are the same no matter how many vegetables you are cooking.)

■ General surface vegetable guidelines

A. Place the **vegetables** in vigorously boiling, lightly salted water. Prepare the same amount of ice water and set it aside.

B. Boil the vegetables root side down for the appropriate time. Remove, drain in collander, and immediately immerse in ice water. For zucchini, slant-cut or cut into large matchstick slivers before boiling. For broccoli or cauliflower, remove stems and separate into florets before boiling. For snow peas, snap off ends and peel out string.

C. After the vegetables are chilled, drain again and gently sqeeze out excess water with a *makisu* or with your hands. Line them up and cut into about 2-inch sections.

D. Just before serving add **shoyu,** or **vinegar** and *shoyu,* and **garnish to taste.**

Root Vegetables

■ Ninjin — Carrots

Peel **carrots** and cut into 2-inch sections, halve and slant-cut slice, or grate lengthwise into long strips. Boil for about 2 minutes. Continue the procedures for surface vegetables.

■ Daikon — Japanese white radish

A. Peel *daikon,* cut in 2-inch sections, halve, and slice lengthwise. Boil using the **water left over from washing the morning's rice** for about 2 minutes.

B. Soak in fresh cold water then continue the procedures for surface vegetables.

■ Nagaimo — Chinese yam or mountain yam

A. Peel *nagaimo* and cut in 2-inch sections. For each cup of water add **1 Tbsp. vinegar** and let soak for 1 minute. (This keeps the yam from turning brown.) Halve, and slice lengthwise. Watch your fingers, *nagaimo* is sticky.

B. Recommended garnishes include **chopped seaweed** and *wasabi* with **vinegar and shoyu.** The ratio of *shoyu* to vinegar is 1 tsp. to 1/2 tsp.

■ Tororo imo — Ground Chinese yam

A. Peel *nagaimo.* For each cup of water add **1 Tbsp. vinegar** and let soak for 1 minute. Grate or chop finely and grind with mortar and pestle.

B. Garnish with *kizaminori* or *wasabi,* **vinegar,** or *shoyu* to taste.

*How to make
tororo imo.*

Other *Ohitashi*

■ Oroshi daikon — Grated Japanese white radish

Peel *daikon* and grate. Firmly squeeze out any excess water and add *shoyu* to taste. This is an excellent complement to grilled fish.

Oroshi grater.

■ Yaki nasu — Grilled eggplant

A. Broil a **whole Japanese eggplant** about 7 inches from the heat. When the skin blisters, turn it until all sides are toasted. Place the eggplant in ice-cold water and remove quickly. The skin should peel off easily. Remove stem, start quarter slices with a knife, and separate into long sections with your hands.

B. Garnish with freshly grated **ginger,** shaved **bonito,** and *shoyu.* Serve hot.

■ Mushi nasu — Steamed Japanese eggplant

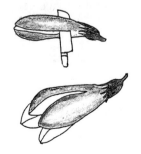

A. Quarter **1 eggplant** two-thirds of the way up leaving the stem intact. Steam in vegetable steamer for 7 to 10 minutes. Remove stem.

B. Garnish with fresh grated **ginger** and *shoyu* to taste. Serve hot.

*How to cut egg-
plant.*

Daizu Seihin — Soybean Products

The Japanese diet includes many foods derived from soybeans and soybean by-products. *Shoyu* and *miso* are the most recognizable seasonings produced but many actual foods are produced as well. Soybean products have a place on the table at virtually every meal in one form or another. They are an integral part of the Japanese food culture.

Tofu (soybean cake), *yuba* (soybean film), and *natto* (fermented soybeans) are all examples of soybean products.

Natto — Fermented Soybeans

Natto is a very popular breakfast food made by stuffing boiled white soybeans into a *tsuto* (casing made from rice-straw) and leaving them to sit in a warm, darkened room. Before they are stored, a natural *natto* fungus is introduced to start the fermentation process. The result is *natto*, which has a sticky "gooey" texture and a pungent odor. Most Americans in my experience turn their noses up at the sight (and smell) of *natto*.

An 80-year-old *issei* (first-generation Japanese immigrant) women I met in Denver made excellent *natto* with a fungus she grew herself from an original batch bought in a local Denver grocery store. She used to share her *natto* with me frequently. When making *natto*, the mixing bowl needs to be completely clean and free from any traces of salt. The *natto* fungus is easily destroyed by salt. Salt is used to preserve most Japanese foods, but *natto* is completely opposite.

There are two kinds of *natto*. The first is called *tsubu* and is made from whole soybeans. The second is called *hikiwari* and is made from slightly crushed soybeans.

Commercially made *natto* can be found in the frozen section at your local Oriental market for about one dollar. There are many different brands to choose from. Defrost the *natto* to room temperature before eating. Making *natto* from scratch involves a fairly complicated procedure. This book will concentrate on how to enjoy commercially produced *natto*.

Tofu — Soybean Cake

Tofu's popularity is increasing rapidly in the United States. It is carried by most major grocery chains. There is a variety of *tofu* available. One brand is sold in a plastic container filled with water and sealed with a plastic wrap cover. Another is vacuum-packed in plastic. Occasion-

---

HOW TO EAT NATTO

1 package *natto* (*tsubu* or *hikiwari*)

Suggested garnishes include chopped **scallion, cilantro, parsley, trefoil, seaweed, Japanese hot mustard, seven-taste-pepper,** and **ginger**

A. If frozen, defrost *natto* at room temperature. Remove from package and put in a bowl. Stir vigorously with chopsticks until sticky. Fold in one or two types of garnishes, 1 tsp. each, and stir vigorously

B. Choose from **1 tsp. shoyu, 2 or 3 pinches of salt,** or **1 tsp. miso.** Add and stir again.

C. If you like it spicy, add **Japanese hot mustard, seven-taste pepper,** or **thin matchstick slivers of gin-** ger to taste. Other garnishes include soaked **sukikombu** and **funori (floating seaweed).**

Follow steps A, B, and C just before meal time.

D. Serve with a bowl of warm white rice. Place about 1 tsp. of *natto* onto your rice and eat them together. The chopsticks used for serving natto are separate from your own chopsticks because the natto is so sticky. Try not to touch your own chopsticks to the natto, touch the rice only. If your chopsticks do touch the natto they will become slippery and other foods will tend to slip. Another method is to use *nori* (dried strips of seaweed) to pick up the *natto* and rice. Place a 2-inch square of *nori* on top of the *natto* and with your chopsticks scoop up a bite of *natto* and rice wrapped in *nori*. This method is the least sticky.

---

ally, I still see *tofu* sold in a container which resembles a Chinese take-out box.

Most brands of *tofu* are made as solid blocks and then packaged. Another brand made by a Japanese company and sold in the United States is made by filling a package with a mixture of soybean milk and a coagulator, and sealing the package shut to let the *tofu* set inside.

Check the expiration date. It is not uncommon to see *tofu* whose plastic covers are bulging from gas, or a *tofu* cake that has turned a light cream color. These are signs the *tofu* is not fresh and should be avoided.

The two types of *tofu* are soft and hard. Traditionally soft *tofu* (*kinugoshi tofu*) was produced by using a very fine cloth as an extra filter during production. This cloth, traditionally silk, was made with a very tight weave which allowed less of the soybean "milk" (made from ground soybeans) to pass through. This made for a softer block with a lower soybean content than hard *tofu*. Hard *tofu* (*momengoshi tofu*) is made using a cotton filter rather than silk. Today, *tofu* is pro-

duced in large factories and the coagulant controls the percentage ratios.

Once a *tofu* package has been opened, change the water immediately, submerging the *tofu*, and refrigerate. Change the water every day. The *tofu* should keep for two to three days. If you find *tofu* in your refrigerator that is a few days old, slice it into 1/2-inch slices and saute in a hot frying pan coated with vegetable oil. Cook until golden brown on both sides. This is called *yaki dofu*. You can also use fresh *tofu* for *yaki dofu*.

We have offered *tofu*-making classes at Nippon Kan. In these classes I don't think the end product, which can be purchased at the grocery store for $1 to $1.50, was as important as the time shared together experiencing part of Japanese culture.

There are many *tofu*-related parables: trying to talk to someone who won't listen is like trying to hammer in a nail with a block of *tofu*.

Instructions for making *tofu* follow these recipes on page 142.

Tofu Recipes

■ Yakko — Soft tofu served chilled

Yakko.

A. Remove 1 **block of soft *tofu*** from packaging, rinse, and place on a flat, woven basket or any flat mesh drainer or paper towel, to drain excess water.

B. Cut into 8 pieces. Place the *tofu* on a serving plate and flavor with **shoyu,** or **vinegar** and **shoyu (1/2 tsp. vinegar** to **1 tsp. shoyu)** to taste.

C. Garnish with **chopped scallions, shaved bonito, chopped nori,** or if you like it spicy, a little **ground ginger** or **a drop of hot sesame oil.** Use 1 Tbsp. of each garnish for a 1/2 block of *tofu*.

■ Yaki dofu — Sauteed tofu

How to drain tofu.

A. Take **1/4 block of *tofu* per person,** rinse, cut in 1/2-inch slices, and place on a fine-mesh drainer or paper towel. Place a weight on top of the *tofu*. A clean cutting board or plate about the same weight of the *tofu* will do. Let drain about 10 minutes.

B. In a heated skillet (cast iron is best), coat the bottom with **1/2 tsp. of sesame oil.** Add *tofu* and cook until golden brown.

C. Cut into bite-size pieces and garnish with **chopped scallions, shaved bonito, chopped nori,** or if you like it spicy, a little **ground ginger** or a drop of **hot sesame oil.** Use **1 Tbsp. of each garnish** for a 1/2 block of *tofu*. Serve warm.

■ Iri dofu — Scrambled tofu

A. Separate **1/2 block hard *tofu*** into large pieces with your fingers. In a heated skillet saute *tofu* in **1 tsp. sesame oil.** As excess water forms, tilt the pan and blot it up with a paper towel.

B. Cut **two *shiitake*** mushrooms left from making *shiitake dashijiru* into matchstick slivers. Soak **1/2 oz. *sukikombu*** in water until soft and slice into matchstick slivers. Soak **1/2 ounce *wakame*** in water until soft and rough-chop. Add to A.

C. Combine **2 Tbsp. *shiitake dashijiru*** and **1 Tbsp. *miso*** and add to A. Continue to saute until all liquid is absorbed. For variety you can add **chopped scallions, tomato,** and **bell pepper to taste.**

HOW TO MAKE TOFU

Ingredients: **2 cups *daizu* (soybeans) and 1/2 tsp. *nigari* (coagulant).**

Utensils: 1) A square box (a plastic *tofu* container with holes poked through the bottom will do). Line the container with a piece of gauze about four times the size of the box; 2) Wooden long-handled spoon; 3) Two-foot-square cotton cloth for straining the "milk" from the mash; 4) Blender; 5) Large strainer; 6) Large mixing bowl; 7) Large cooking pot.

a. Soak the soybeans in three times the amount of water overnight. The beans should triple in size.

b. When soft, drain off the water through a strainer, and pulverize in a blender on high speed for 3 or 4 minutes, until beans are completely pulverized.

c. Add 8 ounces of this mixture to 4 quarts of boiling water.

d. Reduce the heat to medium and cook for 15 minutes, stirring constantly. When it starts to boil up again, do not turn down the heat but add 2 or 3 drops of vegetable oil — this will keep it from boiling over. Continue to cook another 7–10 minutes.

e. Place a wire mesh strainer lined with a cotton cloth in another bowl and pour d. slowly through the lined strainer.

f. This separates the soybean milk from the mash. Pick up the corners of the cloth and gather and twist tight. The mixture is still hot, so using the long-handled wooden spoon, force the remaining liquid into the bowl by pressing repeatedly on the twisted cloth. Be careful to keep a tight hold on the ends of the cloth gathered in your hand as you twist and push with the spoon. If you drop a corner, very hot liquid can spill on you and the *okara* (soybean mash) will escape.

   (The leftover mash is called *okara*. We will discuss *okara* recipes in a further section. The soybean milk is called *tonyu* and can be refrigerated and drunk for a few days if you wish.)

g. Place the *tonyu* in a large cooking pot and keep at about 140° Fahrenheit over low heat. In a separate bowl, mix 5 times the amount of water as the *tonyu* with a two-finger pinch of *nigari* until dissolved. Slowly add 1/2 to the *tonyu*, stirring constantly.

h. After 5 minutes, add the other half of the *nigari* and water slowly and stir. Cover and reduce to lowest possible heat and let simmer for about 15 minutes as the mixture begins to coagulate.

i. After coagulation, scoop the coagulated *tofu* out with your wooden spoon and evenly fill your lined container. Wrap the gauze over the top and let the container sit for 5 minutes to allow extra liquid to drain.

j. Immerse the container in a large mixing bowl filled with cold water, turn it over, gently pull off the container, and remove the gauze.

   Making *tofu* can be an interesting challenge, but be careful not to burn yourself. The price of soybeans and *nigari* is negligible, but making *tofu* does take time and is painstaking. This process has been done by hand for centuries, beginning early each morning. Only someone who has made their own *tofu* knows how delicious the rewards can be.

A. Soak soybeans in water.

B. Grind soybeans in a blender.

C. Add B to boiling water.

D. Simmer over a low flame.

E. Strain through cloth.

F. Squeeze.

G. Separated soybean milk and mash.

H. Add nigari.

I. Pour into box container.

J. Immerse in cold water and remove from container.

Yakimono — Grilled and Broiled Dishes (for breakfast)

The most common breakfast *yakimono* are called *shio yaki,* which means foods that are lightly salted and grilled.

Fish are not usually eaten as *sashimi* (thinly sliced raw fish) for breakfast. There are, instead, many kinds of half-dried salted fish that are grilled or broiled. The following varieties can be found in American Oriental markets: *Shishamo* (half-dried salted smelt,) s*aba no hiraki* (half-dried salted filleted mackerel), and *aji no hiraki* (half-dried salted horse mackerel).

Hiraki is the term for preparing fish in the following manner. First, the fish is cleaned (see basic fish preparation in chapter 4), then laid flat in heavily salted water for half a day, and then dried. When the fish are not dried completely it is called *namaboshi* (half raw, half dried).

Traditionally, fish were hung to dry outside under the eaves of the house for 2 to 3 days. When I was a kid you could find many different kinds of fish hanging to dry under the eaves of most any house. These included *hata hata* (sandfish), *aji* (horse mackerel), *iwashi* (sardine), *saba* (mackerel), *samma* (Spanish mackerel), *karei* (flounder), *tara* (cod), and *ika* (squid).

It is not necessary to dry fish in this manner. Just salt them generously and refrigerate a few days and you can reproduce almost the same taste.

About eight years ago, Nippon Kan went through a period when money was quite scarce. At that time, we had many volunteers arriving from Japan, so it was a challenge to find the money to feed everyone.

A friend of mine at that time owned a *sushi* restaurant and fish market. One day I asked him, "In your fish market you sell salmon — what do you do with the heads?" His reply was, "I save them, but if I can't use them, they just end up

being thrown away." We struck a deal: 5 lbs. of salmon heads for $1. Sometimes I bought 30 or 40 heads at a time. When I got them home I removed the collar area and soaked them in salt, *mirin*, and *sake* for 2 or 3 days in the refrigerator. Grilled, they were delicious and kept the troops fed.

One day I accidentally slipped and told the owner of the fish market how to prepare this salmon collar. It wasn't long before that salmon collar was on the menu at his *sushi* bar, with a price tag of $5 to $6 for a single serving!

That *sushi* bar is a nice place that I enjoy visiting often. Every time I see salmon collar on the menu though, I say to myself, "There's a tribute to your loose tongue."

The first step in making *yakizakana* (broiled or grilled fish) is to use fresh fish. Modern refrigeration makes this possible. In Japan if the fish were not eaten quickly after they were caught, they had to be dried, salted and dried, or pickled. Before pickled fish can be used, they need to be "desalted." This ancient technique is called *shionuki*. To remove excess salt from pickled fish, submerge the fish in water that contains an even higher salt content. This process is called *yobishio*, which literally translates as "calling out the salt." The English equivalent might be "priming the pump." Of course, this method is not only for fish, but for vegetables as well. By immersing the fish in a heavy salt solution the excess salt is drawn out quickly.

If fish are being prepared for the next day's breakfast, salting them the night before is an adequate time period. Another preparation method is to salt the fish just before it is grilled. *Miso, shoyu*, or *sakekasu* can also be used as a marinade. Marinate the fish for 1 to 3 days beforehand.

The portion of *yakizakana* for breakfast is small: 1 lb. of fish can serve two to three people. These are side dishes rather than main dishes.

Yakizakana Recipes

(When using whole fish, **10 to 12 inches per person** is a good size. If the fish has been filleted, the following recipes require 1 to 1 1/2 lbs. Each recipe serves 4 people.)

■ Shio yaki — Salt grill

Yakiami.

How to use a yakiami.

How to use barbecue skewers.

A. Choose from **salmon, trout, flounder, Spanish mackerel, mackerel, smelt,** or **squid.** If the fish are whole, review basic fish preparation, chapter 4. If the fish are small, no preparation is needed.

B. In a large plastic storage bag add **1/2 tsp. salt, 1 tsp.** *mirin* or *sake,* **1 scallion** (lightly crushed), and the fish of your choice. Twist close the bag and gently shake to coat the fish. Marinate 5 to 8 hours in the refrigerator.

C. The next day, remove the fish and place in a *yakiami* (grilling net) and grill or oven-broil. If the fish has been filleted or opened, for ocean fish place the skin side toward the heat, for fresh-water fish place the meat side toward the heat. If oven-broiling, place the fish about 3–4 inches from the heat for 5 to 7 minutes, turn and cook another 5 minutes. Coat the *yakiami* with **vegetable oil** to prevent the fish from sticking.

D. After the fish has been broiled, transfer to serving plate while still hot. Place **1/4 cup of grated, squeezed** *daikon* next to the fish. If the fish taste is too light, add *shoyu* to the *daikon* to taste. Broiled fish and *daikon* is a combination similar to pork chops and apple sauce in the United States.

■ Shoyu zuke yaki — Fish marinated in soy sauce

A. Choose from **shark, tuna, smelt,** or **squid.** If preparing a whole fish, see basic fish preparation, Chapter 4. Even if small, remove head and clean.

B. In a bowl combine **1/2 cup *shoyu*, 3 Tbsp. *mirin*, 1 Tbsp. *sake*, 1 small red dried chili** (seeds removed), and **1 chopped scallion** to make marinade. Mix fish into the marinade 4 to 5 hours before cooking.

How to marinate fish.

C. Remove the fish and place in a *yakiami* (grilling net) and grill or oven-broil. If the fish has been filleted or opened, for ocean fish place the skin side toward the heat, for fresh-water fish place the meat side toward the heat. If oven-broiling, place the fish about 3-4 inches from the heat for 5 to 7 minutes, turn and cook another 5 minutes. Coat the *yakiami* with vegetable oil to prevent the fish from sticking.

D. After the fish has been broiled, transfer to serving plate while still hot. Place **1/4 cup of grated, squeezed *daikon*** next to the fish. If the fish taste is too light, **add *shoyu* to the *daikon* to taste.**

■ Miso zuke yaki — Fish marinated in miso

A. Choose from **tuna, shark, red snapper, butterfish, flounder, salmon,** or **squid.**

B. Combine **1 cup of *miso*** (not necessarily the most expensive), **1 Tbsp. sugar, 2 Tbsp. *mirin*, 1/2 ounce of fresh sliced ginger,** and **1 dried red chili** (seeds removed) to make *misodoko* and marinate fish for 1 to 2 days. Follow procedures in Shio yaki C and D.

■ Kasu zuke yaki — Fish marinated in rice wine lees

Wrapping in gauze.

A. Choose from **tuna, shark, red snapper, butterfish, flounder, salmon,** or **squid.**

B. Combine **1 cup *sakekasu*, 1 Tbsp. *miso*, 1 Tbsp. *shoyu*,** and **1 Tbsp. sugar** to make *kasudoko* (rice wine lees marinade). Pat fish dry with paper towel, wrap in gauze and marinate in the *kasudoko* for 2 to 3 days. Follow procedures in *Shio yaki* C and D.

Marinade.

Jobina — Pre-Prepared Side Dishes

Okazu (side dishes) prepared two to 10 days before serving are called *jobina. Jobi* translates as permanent and *na* means *okazu* or side dish.

These side dishes are not for breakfast only, but can be enjoyed anytime. They are wonderful side dishes for when you don't have time to cook, as appetizers while serving *sake,* or if the fresh vegetable bin is empty.

Jobina dishes are all prepared by slowly cooking vegetables or sometimes meats or fish with *mirin*, sugar, *shoyu*, and *dashijiru* until all the liquid is absorbed. Of the *jobina* group, *tsukudani* is the most popular. There are many different kinds of *jobina.* Traditionally they have been a way to use the parts of vegetables not used in other cooking recipes. Combining parts of the vegetables that would usually be discarded with fish and meats helps economize the food budget. Traditionally, survival meant not wasting food.

Jobina Recipes

■ Kimpira gobo — Sauteed burdock with soy sauce

How to shave gobo.

A. Scrape the skin off **1/4 lb. of burdock** with the dull side of your cooking knife. If the burdock is soft, it is difficult to scrape, so immerse it in water for 1/2 hour until it stiffens.

B. Shave burdock into about one-inch shavings and soak in **3 cups water** and **1 tsp. vinegar.** Remove *aku.*

C. Add **1 tsp. sesame oil** to a heated skillet. Squeeze excess water from the burdock and saute 3 or 4 minutes. Add **2 Tbsp. *mirin* and 2 Tbsp. *shoyu*** and quickly turn off the heat. Continue to stir until *shoyu* reaches a caramel-like consistency. *Shoyu* burns easily so remember to turn off the heat quickly. You can add **1 red chili** (seeds removed) while sauteeing. Garnish with **black sesame seeds to taste.** Hint: you can also mix in **carrots, celery, bell peppers, mushrooms, broccoli stem,** or **green beans,** cut in matchstick slivers. These vegetables do not require soaking to remove *aku.*

- Konnyaku no kimpira — Sauteed yam cake with soy sauce

  A. Drain **1 cup *itokonnyaku*** (yam cake noodles); rough chop, rinse well, and shake off excess water. Or, separate **1 cup *itakonnyaku*** (yam cake) into bite-sized pieces with your fingers. Boil for 5 minutes, immerse in ice water until cool. Drain and shake off excess water.

  B. Add **1 Tbsp. sesame oil** to a heated skillet. Be careful when you put the *konnyaku* in the pan — oil and water tend to flare up. Add *konnyaku* slowly from the side. Slice **3 *shiitake* mushrooms** (from *shiitake dashijiru)* into slivers. Add them and saute 5 to 6 minutes.

  C. Combine **1 Tbsp. *shoyu,* 1 Tbsp. *mirin*** or ***sake,*** and **2 Tbsp. *dashijiru*** into B, stirring over high heat until liquid is absorbed. You can also add **1 dried red chili** (seeds removed). Garnish with **black sesame seeds.**

- Serori no nitsuke — Celery with soy sauce

  A. Remove the leafy ends from **three celery ribs,** cut into 2-inch sections. If the rib is very large, cut sections lengthwise 2 or 3 times. Boil in lightly salted water about 7 minutes, then soak in ice water or cold running water for 10 minutes.

  B. In a cooking pot, combine **2 cups *dashijiru*** (any *dashijiru),* **1/4 cup *shoyu,* 3 Tbsp. *sake,* 2 Tbsp. *mirin,*** and **1 dried red chili** (seeds removed). Bring to a boil. Add A, and bring to a second boil. Cover with a drop lid that fits inside the pan, reduce heat to low, and stir occasionally until liquid is absorbed.

- Serori ha no kimpira — Sauteed celery leaves with soy sauce

  A. Boil **1/2 lb. celery leaves** with **a few pinches of salt** for 1 minute. Immerse in ice water, squeeze tightly to remove excess water, and chop finely.

  B. In a heated skillet combine **1 Tbsp. sesame oil** and **1/2 oz. fresh ginger** cut into matchstick slivers. Mix with A and saute. Add **1/4 cup *dashijiru,* 1 tsp. sugar, 1 tsp. *sake,*** and **1 Tbsp. *shoyu*** and continue to saute until liquid is absorbed. Stir occasionally with chopsticks. Mix in **1 tsp. white sesame seeds** and serve.

- Shimeji no shigureni — Shimeji mushrooms with soy sauce

  A. Remove the stems from **1/2 lb. *shimeji* mushrooms,** shred by hand, wash lightly in salted water, and rinse.

B. In a cooking pot, add **1/4 cup** *shoyu*, **1/4 cup** *sake,* and **1 Tbsp.** *mirin.* Bring to a boil. Add **1/2 oz. fresh ginger** sliced in matchstick slivers and then add A. Bring to a second boil, remove mushrooms, and continue cooking the rest 3 or 4 minutes over a low heat. Turn off heat and return mushrooms to the pan. **Season to taste with seven-taste pepper.**

■ Daikon no ha to sake — Sauteed Japanese white radish leaves and grilled salmon with soy sauce

A. Place **1/2 lb.** *daikon* **leaves** in boiling water. Add a **few pinches of salt** and boil for 10 minutes. Soak in ice water for 10 minutes.

B. Squeeze out excess water, line up the leaves and chop finely. In a heated skillet, combine **1 tsp. sesame oil, 1/2 oz. sliced ginger,** and **2 chopped scallions.** Add A and saute 7 to 8 minutes. After all water has been absorbed, place in strainer and press out any excess water with a wooden spoon. Clean the skillet and reheat. Add **1 tsp. sesame oil,** add all ingredients, and saute.

C. Grill **1/2 lb. salmon** (see *yakimono* section) without salt, and crumble. Slice **3 or 4** *shiitake* **mushrooms** (from *dashijiru*) into slivers. Mix with B. Add **2 Tbsp.** *shoyu,* **2 Tbsp.** *mirin,* and **1 Tbsp.** *sake.* Saute until liquid is absorbed. (Hint: **Chicken** can be used instead of salmon. It is not necessary to grill the chicken beforehand, just chop and saute.)

■ Kiriboshi daikon to ninjin — Shredded or sliced dried Japanese white radish and carrots with soy sauce

A. Soak enough **dried** *daikon* **to equal 2 cups.** Squeeze out excess water. Cut **3 to 4** *shiitake* **mushrooms** (from *dashijiru*) into slivers. Peel and shave **2 oz. carrots.**

B. Add **2 Tbsp. sesame oil** to a heated skillet. Make sure all excess water has been squeezed from the *daikon,* and add *daikon,* carrots, and mushrooms. Saute for 5 minutes. Add **1/2 cup** *dashijiru* and **a few pinches of salt and pepper to taste.** Saute until liquid is absorbed. If the taste is too light add *shoyu.*

■ Kiriboshi daikon to sukikombu — Shredded or sliced dried Japanese white radish and dried sliced kelp with soy sauce

How to cut age.

A. Soak enough **dried *daikon* to equal 2 cups.** Soak enough *sukikombu* **to equal 1 cup.** Place **1 *age* puff** (deep-fried soybean puff) in boiling water for 30 seconds to release oil. Squeeze out excess water and slice into thin matchstick slivers.

B. Add **1 Tbsp. sesame oil** to a heated skillet. Squeeze excess water from A and saute for 5 to 6 minutes. Add **2 Tbsp. *shoyu*, 2 tsp. *mirin*, 1 Tbsp. *sake*,** and **1 cup *dashijiru*.** Lower the heat and cook until all liquid is absorbed. If you wish, add **1 dried red chili** (seeds removed).

■ Shiitake to kombu no tsukudani — Shiitake mushroom and kelp with soy sauce

A. Remove the stems from **10 small to medium *shiitake* mushrooms** (from *shiitake dashijiru*) and slice into 3 or 4 pieces. Cut **1 cup *kombu*** (from *kombu dashijiru*) into 2-inch sections and slice into matchstick slivers.

B. In a cooking pot, combine A with **1/2 cup *dashijiru*** and cook for 5 to 6 minutes. Add **3 Tbsp. *shoyu*, 2 Tbsp. *sake*,** and **2 Tbsp. sugar.** Cook over low heat until all liquid is absorbed.

■ Daizu to kombu no nimono — Cooked soybeans and kelp with soy sauce

A. Wash **1 cup soybeans** in 3 times the amount of water and soak overnight. They should increase 3 times in size. Slice **1 cup *kombu*** (from *kombu dashijiru*) into matchstick slivers.

B. In a cooking pot, add **6 cups boiling water** and cook soybeans until soft. When soft add *kombu,* reduce heat to low, and cook for 2 to 3 hours. If the water is absorbed before ingredients seem completely cooked, add a little more water and continue to cook.

C. Combine **1/3 cup *mirin*, 3 Tbsp. *shoyu*,** and **a few of pinches salt.** Add to B and cook over low heat until the beans have absorbed the *shoyu* taste and the kelp is soft.

■ Nasu no miso ni — Sauteed Japanese eggplant with miso

> A. Remove the stems from **4 5-inch Japanese eggplants** and random peel. Cut in fourths lengthwise and trim each piece with a rolling cut. Soak in lightly salted water for 5 minutes to remove *aku*.
>
> B. Combine **1/3 cup** *miso,* **1/4 cup** *dashijiru,* **1 Tbsp. sugar,** and **1 Tbsp. mirin** in a separate bowl. Add **4 Tbsp. sesame oil** in a heated skillet. Gently squeeze eggplant to remove excess water and saute for 3 to 4 minutes. Add B and turn off heat. Stir until mixed. If you wish, garnish with **black sesame seeds.**

■ Tekkamiso — Sauteed soybeans and burdock with miso

> A. Toast **1/2 cup soybeans** in a heated skillet over a low heat (like popcorn) until they begin to smoke. When toasted, place soybeans in a mortar and crush (don't grind) with pestle, shake mortar, and gently remove skins by blowing on them.
>
> B. Peel and dice **4 oz. burdock** to about the same size as the soybeans. Soak in **1 cup of water** and **1/2 tsp. vinegar** 2 to 3 minutes to remove *aku.* Rinse. Saute briefly in **1 Tbsp. sesame oil** and set aside.
>
> C. Combine **1/2 lb. red** *miso,* **1/2 cup** *sake,* **4 Tbsp. sugar, 1/2 cups mirin,** and **1/2 cup water** in a separate sauce pan and cook over a low heat until melted together. Add burdock and reduce until the texture becomes sticky. Mix in A's soybeans. If you like, add **1 dried red chili** (seeds removed).

It would be difficult to include all the *jobina* recipes — the possibilities are endless. Use your own imagination to create new combinations. For example, if I called for a certain ingredient, try adding another as well, or if the recipe calls for fish try substituting chicken. *Jobina* are dishes that can be stored in your refrigerator and used any time. It is important to understand that all *jobina* recipes use *shoyu, mirin,* sugar, *sake,* or *miso.* These dishes have a concentrated flavor that balances well as a side dish with rice or *okayu.* Only a small portion is needed. The recipes in this section will keep in the refrigerator 7 to 10 days. Aesthetically if the *jobina* dishes you prepare are the same in color, garnishes can help provide a variety of color as well as taste. Sesame seeds, chopped alfalfa sprouts, chopped scallions, and chopped *nori* all add a different look as well as taste. If the taste of the *jobina* is too strong, serve with grated *daikon* on the side. Arrange on small serving plates 3 to 4 inches in diameter. Serve enough *jobina* to cover only 25% to 30% of the surface area of the plate. If you are serving more than one *jobina,* the portion of the plate covered remains the same.

Misoshiru — Soup from Soybean Paste

Misoshiru is an integral part of the traditional Japanese breakfast. Japanese farmers started their work day very early. Traditionally they began their day with a large pot (*nabe*) of grains, cereals, vegetables, and *miso* mixed together to make the porridge like *zosui*. In the last 50 or 60 years the *misoshiru* and rice have been served separately in the traditional Japanese breakfast. Today for special occasions all ingredients are mixed together in dishes like *damako mochi* or *kiritampo*.

Misoshiru and rice are basic foods for the Japanese people. At Nippon Kan we have many visiting business people and students from Japan. Some stay in the United States three months, others up to three years.

Some visitors believe three months abroad is a long time, others have different views. I suppose the definition of "a long time" has many interpretations. The Japanese travelers, while enjoying their visits to the United States, are ecstatic when I serve them *misoshiru*. Even served without any other side dishes except plain rice, they delight in the meal. In Japan they probably would not be so excited about such a simple meal. But so far from home *misoshiru* is always met with smiling gratitude. *Misoshiru* is very much a part of the Japanese food heritage. For myself, if I think about my mother's *misoshiru* I become the most homesick!

In today's modern world, however, with both parents working in most families, instant *misoshiru* has taken mother's place. Even restaurants more and more are relying on instant *misoshiru* soup stocks. For people like you who are interested in books like this, I urge you to explore and enjoy real *misoshiru* made from *dashijiru*.

The most important point to consider when making *misoshiru* is timing. When to add the *miso* is the most critical consideration. Just about when everyone sits down at the table to eat is the time to add the *miso* to the soup. As soon as it starts to boil, remove it from the heat and serve.

The *miso* is mixed in a separate cup with a small amount of *dashijiru* to dissolve it before it is added to the soup. This allows it to blend more easily. It is important not to add the *miso*

too early or the *miso* will lose its taste and smell by over boiling. If the temperature of the soup is raised and lowered repeatedly after the *miso* has been added, the flavor will be lost.

There are two methods for making *misoshiru*. In the first method the *gu* (solid ingredients) is cooked while making the *dashijiru*. In the second method the *misoshiru dashijiru* is made first and poured over individual servings of the *gu* already placed in serving bowls.

Deciding what ingredients go with what are important when choosing the *gu* for your *misoshiru*. Pay attention to the following sample recipes and note which foods have an affinity for one another. Some foods just don't mix well.

Today there are so many kinds and brands of *miso* available on the market it can get confusing. It would be difficult for me to advise you on which *miso* is good. Each different variety has a different balance of salt and *koji*. For this book, white or red *miso* available for about $4 for a 2-lb. package will be used.

When I was the chef at Domo restaurant, I once had an extremely technically informed customer ask me what kind of *miso* I used. I listened patiently to his dissertation on the *miso* varieties and simply asked, "Which kind of *miso* do you like?" This triggered a more involved monologue. My answer to this question is not a technical one: my mother's *miso* is the best. Period.

The most delicious *miso* in my opinion is not made in the finest restaurants of Tokyo and Kyoto, but the simple *miso* made with genuine heart and care at home by the country farmers. Japanese people usually are not aware of the technical differences, they just rely on taste.

It doesn't matter if you use white *miso* or red *miso* or even if you mix them together, what is more important is how the *miso* is used. When making *misoshiru,* make only enough for the meal intended. If you are entertaining guests, make sure you make enough for your guests to have seconds. This is customary. If you are cooking more casually, only make enough for one serving. When serving *misoshiru*, fill the *misoshiru* bowl only two-thirds full, which should equal about 1 cup.

When you are eating *misoshiru* hold the bowl in your left hand, and pick up the *gu* with chopsticks held in your right. It is customary to carry the bowl to your mouth and drink from it. A traditional *misoshiru* bowl has a small stand *(kodai)* on the bottom of the bowl so it will not be too hot to hold in your hand.

Two *gu* ingredients are better than one when preparing *misoshiru*. Choosing ingredients that balance each other is important. After you add the *miso* to the *dashijiru* turn off the heat. To enhance the soup, if the *gu* you use has no green color, garnish with chopped scallion or chrysanthemum leaves. This adds to the flavor and overall appeal of the soup. If the *gu* includes fish or shellfish add a small amount of grated or matchstick-slivered ginger or seven-taste pepper. If the *misoshiru* is plain, you can add shaved *kombu*, called *tororo kombu* or *oboro kombu*.

Many different kinds of *dashijiru* can be combined with different kinds of *miso* — white, red or mixed. One of the joys of making *misoshiru* is experimenting with all of the endless possible combinations. Develop your own personal favorite tastes.

Misoshiru dashijiru — Miso Soup-Base Recipes
(Each recipe serves 4 people)

■ Kombu to shiitake no misoshiru dashijiru — Miso soup-base made from kelp and shiitake mushroom.

A. Wipe a **7 x 6-inch square sheet of *kombu*** clean with a damp towel. Use scissors to make 2 or 3 small cuts around each edge. Soak **4 *shiitake* mushrooms** in 4 1/2 cups water for 30 minutes then place over high heat and cover. When it starts to boil, reduce heat to medium and simmer 15 minutes. If there is time, soak overnight rather than boiling — you won't lose as much flavor.

If you are making only *shiitake dashijiru* you need 6 to 8 medium-sized mushrooms. If you are making only *kombu dashijiru* use a 10 x 10-inch piece.

B. Slice *kombu* and *shiitake* into matchstick slivers. Use some for *misoshiru* or save and use in other dishes or *jobina*.

■ Kombu to katsuobushi no misoshiru dashijiru — Miso soup base made from kelp and shaved bonito

A. Wipe a **7 x 6-inch piece of *kombu*** with a damp towel, use scissors to make 2 or 3 small cuts on each edge, and soak in **4 1/2 cups water** for 30 minutes. Use high heat to bring to first boil, cover, reduce heat to medium, and simmer for 15 minutes. Remove *kombu* and return heat to high, add **1/2 cup shaved bonito** and boil for 30 seconds, turn off heat. Wait for the bonito to sink to the bottom of the pan.

B. Separate the *dashijiru* from the *katsuobushi* through gauze or a mesh strainer and save. The *katsuobushi* can be used in other dishes. Mix **1/2 cup *katsuobushi*, 1/2 tsp. *mirin*,** and **1/2 tsp. *shoyu*.** Use it as a filling for lunchtime rice balls.

■ Niboshi or yakiboshi no misoshiru dashijiru — Dried or dried and grilled sardine (or anchovy) miso soup base

A. Remove the heads and pinch off the stomach areas from **10 to 15 *niboshi* or *yakiboshi*** 1 to 2 inches in length. Soak in **4 1/2 cups water** for 30 minutes. When soft, split in half with your fingers. Bring to a boil over medium heat. Let it boil for 30 seconds, turn off heat, and drain through gauze or mesh strainer. Set the *dashijiru* aside.

B. In a heated skillet add **1 tsp. sesame oil** and ***niboshi* or *yakiboshi*,** saute 2–3 minutes. Mix in **1 Tbsp. *mirin*, 1 Tbsp. *shoyu*,** and **1 tsp. *sake*.** Add **seven-taste pepper to taste.** Stir constantly so it doesn't burn. Save as *jobina*.

Misoshiru Recipes

(Each of the following recipes serves 4 people — 1 cup per person. Use 1 level tablespoon of *miso* per cup. Do not add all of the *miso* at once. Add about 80% and taste. Add more if you wish.)

■ Tofu to wakame — Tofu and strips of young kelp

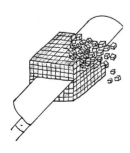

A. Soak **1/2 cup *wakame*** in water till soft and rough chop. Fill a cooking pot with **4 cups *dashijiru*.** In a small side bowl mix **4 Tbsp. *miso*** with a small amount of *dashijiru* until dissolved. Bring *dashijiru* to a boil, add *miso,* and just before second boil add *wakame* and **1/2 block *tofu*** diced into bite-sized cubes.

Serve in individual soup bowls. Garnish with chopped scallion to taste.

How to dice tofu.

■ Wakame to jagaimo — Strips of young kelp and potato

Soak **1/2 cup *wakame*** until soft, rough chop. Peel **1/2 lb. potato,** cut into bite-size pieces, and trim with a rolling cut. In a cooking pot, bring **4 1/2 cups *dashijiru*** and potatoes to a boil over high heat. Boil potatoes until they can easily be pierced with a chopstick. When cooked, add **4 Tbsp. *miso*** dissolved in a **small amount of *dashijiru.*** Just before second boil add *wakame* and turn off heat. Garnish with **chopped parsley** and **scallion.**

How to cut potato.

■ Wakame to shiitake — Strips of young kelp and shiitake mushrooms

Soak **1/2 cup *wakame*** until soft, rough chop. Remove the stems from **4 medium-sized *shiitake* mushrooms** (left from *dashijiru)* and slice into slivers. Place *wakame* and *shiitake* in individual serving bowls. Boil **4 cups *dashijiru*** in a cooking pot. Add **4 Tbsp. *miso*** dissolved in a small amount of *dashijiru.* Just before second boil turn off heat and pour over *shiitake* and *wakame.* Garnish with **alfalfa sprouts to taste.**

■ Sogi tofu to negi — Sliced tofu and Japanese leeks

Cut **3 oz. Japanese scallion** (leeks are fine) into 1-inch lengths and slant-cut slice lengthwise. Boil **4 cups *dashijiru*** in a cooking pot. Add **4 Tbsp. *miso*** dissolved in **a small amount of *dashijiru*** and **1/2 block *tofu*** sliced horizontally into 1/4-inch slices. Turn off heat just before second boil. Place Japanese scallion slices in individual serving bowls and cover with soup. Garnish with **seven-taste pepper.**

How to slice tofu.

*How to cut scal-
lion.*

■ Kuzushi tofu to horenso — Mashed tofu with spinach

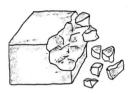

How to separate tofu with your fingers.

Wash **8 to 10 leaves of spinach (parsley, chrysanthemum leaves,** or **trefoil** will also do), tear into bite-size pieces, and shake off excess water. Boil **4 cups *dashijiru*** in a cooking pot. Add **4 Tbsp. *miso*** dissolved in a small amount of *dashijiru.* Just before the second boil, break **1/2 block *tofu*** into bite-size pieces and add. Turn off heat. Pour over spinach leaves already placed in individual serving bowls.

■ Kyabetsu to age — Cabbage with deep-fried tofu puff

Boil **4 1/2 cups *dashijiru*** in a small cooking pot. Chop **4 cabbage leaves** into bite-size pieces, add to *dashijiru,* and continue to boil about 5 minutes. Dissolve **4 Tbsp. *miso*** in a small amount of *dashijiru.* Turn off heat before it reaches a second boil. In a separate pot, boil water and dip **1 *age* soybean puff** for 30 seconds to remove excess oil. Remove, squeeze out excess water, and cut into matchstick slivers. Place in serving bowls and cover with **cabbage** and ***dashijiru.***

■ Moyashi to age — Soybean sprouts with deep-fried tofu puff

Dip **1 *age* puff** in boiling water for 30 seconds to remove excess oil. Squeeze out excess water and tear apart with your fingers into bite-size pieces. Place **1 cup soybean sprouts** in boiling water for 30 seconds then completely shake off excess water. Boil **4 1/2 cups *dashijiru*** in a cooking pot. Add **4 Tbsp. *miso*** dissolved in a small amount of *dashijiru.* Just before the second boil turn off heat. Pour over soybean sprouts and soybean puff already set in individual serving bowls. Garnish with **seven-taste pepper.**

■ Kinusaya to age — Snow peas with deep-fried tofu puff

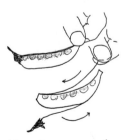

How to snap ends and peel out string.

Dip **1 *age* puff** in boiling water for 30 seconds to remove excess oil. Squeeze out excess water and cut into matchstick slivers. Boil **4 cups *dashijiru*** in a cooking pot. Add **4 Tbsp. *miso*** dissolved in a **small amount of *dashijiru*** and **12 snow peas** after snapping off both ends and removing the strings. Turn off the heat just before the second boil. Pour over *age* already set in individual serving bowls. .

■ Daikon to ninjin — Japanese white radish and carrots

Peel and grate **1/2 lb. *daikon*** and **2 oz. carrots.** Soak in water for 5 minutes, shake off excess water. In a small cooking pot, boil **4 1/2 cups *dashijiru,*** *daikon,* and carrots. After reaching first boil continue to boil 3 to 4 minutes. Add **4 Tbsp. *miso*** dissolved in **a small amount of *dashijiru.*** Turn off heat just before reaching a second boil. Garnish with **seven-taste pepper.**

■ Tamanegi to jagaimo — Onion and potato

Peel **1/2 lb. potato** and cut into bite-size pieces. Slant-cut **2 oz. onion** lengthwise. Boil **4 1/2 cups *dashijiru*** in a cooking pot. Add vegetables and continue boiling until potatoes are soft. Add **4 Tbsp. *miso*** dissolved in **a small amount of *dashijiru*** and turn off heat just before reaching a second boil.

How to slice onion.

■ Kabocha — Japanese pumpkin

Intermittently peel **1/2 lb. *kabocha*** (if you peel it completely it will fall apart while cooking). Cut into 8 pieces. Boil **4 1/2 cups *dashijiru*** in a cooking pot. Add pumpkin and cook until soft. Add **4 Tbsp. *miso*** dissolved in **a small amount of *dashijiru*** and turn off heat just before second boil. Garnish with **seven-taste pepper** or **chopped scallion** to taste.

■ Satsumaimo — Sweet potato

Intermittently peel **1/2 lb. sweet potatos.** Cut into 16 pieces and trim with a rolling cut. Boil **4 1/2 cups *dashijiru*** in a cooking pot. Add sweet potato and continue to boil until soft. Add **4 Tbsp. *miso*** dissolved in **a small amount of *dashijiru.*** Turn off heat just before second boil. Garnish with **seven-taste pepper** or **chopped scallion** to taste.

■ Asari or hamaguri — Short-neck clam (or regular clam)

A. Take **2 to 3 short-neck clams** or **small regular clams** for each serving. Soak in salted water for 3 to 4 hours until the clams open, releasing excess sand. Be careful if the shells are open when you buy them, this means the clams are already dead. Boil **4 1/2 cups *dashijiru*** in a cooking pot and add clams. Boil for about 2 minutes. Add **4 Tbsp. *miso*** dissolved in **a small amount of *dashijiru.*** Turn off heat just before second boil. Garnish with **1/3 tsp. fresh grated ginger** per serving. Be careful not to pour in all the soup stock as there may be sand in the bottom of the pan.

This concludes our breakfast section. It may seem like a lot of recipes, but remember that we eat breakfast 365 days a year. Different combinations each day make for a varied breakfast menu.

The illustration below displays how the breakfast tray is set. Remember that the side dishes are served on plates 3 to 4 inches in diameter and that each portion should cover only 25% to 30% of its plate.

HOW TO SET THE BREAKFAST TRAY

1

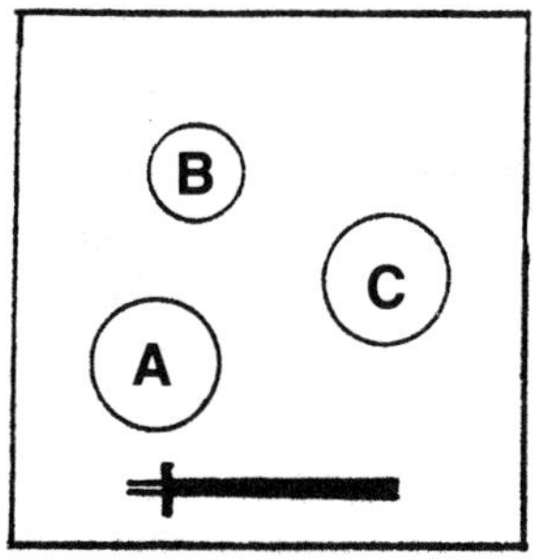

A. Okayu.
B. Tsukemono.
C. Jobina (1 to 2).

2

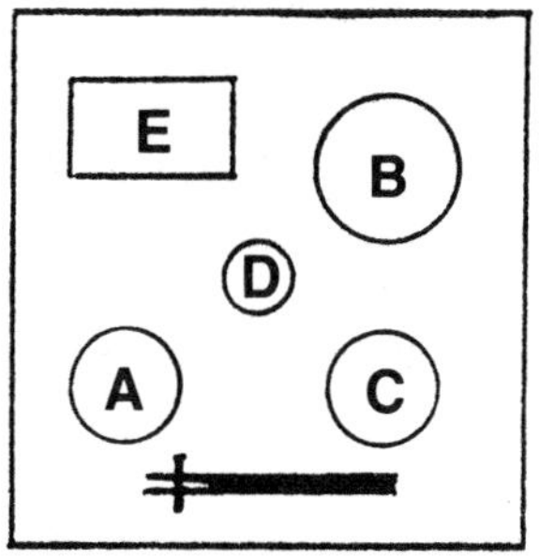

A. Okayu.
B. Jobina (1 to 3).
C. Ohitashi (1 to 2).
D. Tsukemono.
E. Yakizakana.

3

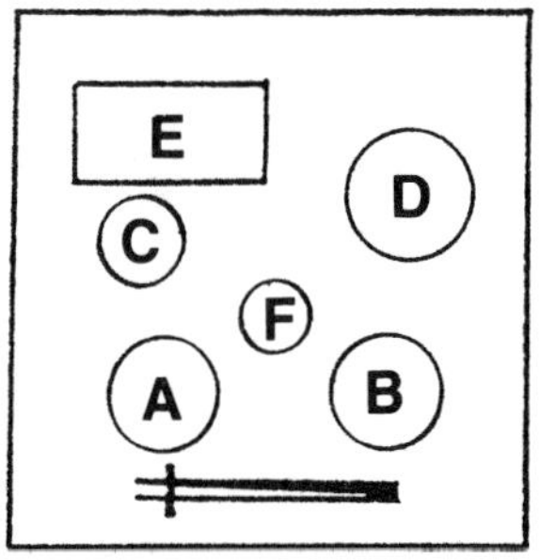

A. Gohan.
B. Misoshiru.
C. Ohitashi (1 to 2).
D. Jobina (1 to 2)
E. Yakizakana.
F. Tsukemono.

Lunch (Chushoku)

Noshiita and Noshibo — soba-making tools.

This book is based on the lives of the Japanese farmers, fishermen, and mountain people. These people had no time to return home from their daily chores to enjoy a leisurely lunch. During the hard winter months, everyone spent their daily hours indoors, but during spring, summer, and fall, long days were spent in the fields, in the mountains, or at sea with no time for long lunch breaks. The overriding consideration in preparing lunch was how to use leftover breakfast foods, and how to make them easy to carry and eat.

Omusubi (rice balls) are as common in Japan as sandwiches are in the United States. Traditionally, of course, white rice was saved for special occasions only, so rice balls were made from other grains steamed and rolled into balls, or from flour ground from other grains. *Dango* and *mochi* are both made from grain flour. *Omusubi* were wrapped in bamboo, oak, butterbur, or lotus leaves, tied with rice-straw rope, and hung from one's belt. In certain historic villages, these *dango* and *mochi* balls can still be purchased as souvenirs.

One day in Denver, I went to the Korean market to buy Oriental vegetables. Next to the cash register I was surprised to find a stack of what looked like fresh *mochi*.

Upon inquiry, I found out they were made fresh from California rice. The owner of the store gave me two as a gift. When I was a kid, I delighted in white rice flour *mochi* cakes filled with crushed sweet red beans. These were lightly grilled and called *oyaki*. It surprised me to think that such a traditional Japanese treat could be found at the foot of the Rocky Mountains.

Omusubi — Rice Balls

Twice a year in spring and autumn, most rural Japanese elementary and junior high schools take major field trips to the beach or mountains. There are also field trips to more urban settings, such as factories or museums, but these outdoor outings are special. When I was a student, each kid was set a certain budget for how much he could spend on snacks for the day. Every year there was a class clown who filled his canteen with a juice-flavored liquid instead of water, which was against the budget rules.

My mother, being the oldest mother in my peer group, was very strict and traditional. It was important to her that we abide by the rules to the letter. I tried to convince her that other kids put instant juice flavoring in their canteens. I had to settle for *bancha* (sauteed coarse tea).

Her justification was that the juice flavorings are not as healthful as the *bancha*. Her concerns remind me of the health-conscious mothers of today. In the mornings my mother would wrap my *omusubi* in bamboo leaves rather than aluminum foil. Although aluminum foil was available at the time, she believed bamboo was a better and more natural way to wrap rice balls.

Like kids everywhere, we traded our rice balls amongst ourselves at lunch time. Needless to say, the one you traded for was by far more delicious than the one you brought from home! I remember making my mother fret by telling her all of the stuff other kids got in their rice balls. Traditional mothers like mine made their rice balls the old way.

Younger mothers of the time were trying new approaches. Sometimes the fillings were different. Some kids had triangle-shaped *omusubi* and mine were round. That was a big difference to a kid. My mother completely covered the rice ball with *nori* (seaweed) while other kids had their triangle-shaped *omusubi* with only one strip of *nori* around it. To top it off, theirs had *dembu* (sauteed, sweetened salmon) crumbled over the top. I was shocked. Theirs were completely different!

I remember my mother's worry the night I left to visit with Morehei Ueshiba for the first time. He lived then in Akita City, which was about a 12-hour train ride. "Here," she said. "This will make everything okay" as she handed me eight neatly wrapped *omusubi*.

When I began my job as the curator, I had my first experience living with traditional farmers. We ate a great deal of *omusubi*. One of the reasons we could eat so many was that the white rice metabolized quickly with the amount of

work we did. I was lucky to participate in *tawue* (rice planting) and *inekari* (rice harvesting).

Today it is all done by machine, but then entire families, neighbors, and relatives pitched in to help in the fields. *Omusubi* were plentiful during the noon hour. In the early morning a huge rice cooking pot was used to make more than 200 *omusubi*. It took more than 10 people working in the kitchen to prepare lunch. Today, professional catering businesses visit the fields to deliver lunch boxes. It is easier for the farmer today, but lost is the happy, busy time in the kitchen the farmers' families spent making *omusubi*. I think it a sad loss.

For the first few years I was in the United States, I couldn't eat sandwiches or hamburgers. I tried, but I just couldn't eat them. Whenever I went on an outing, I would take a few rice balls with me. I usually snuck off and ate them by myself. Now that Japanese foods are more popular I am more comfortable eating them in public.

My Denver *Aikido dojo* has a branch *dojo* in the ski resort town of Vail, which I visit frequently. On one trip, we combined *Aikido* practice with a ski day. The ski area provides outside picnic tables, where we set up our lunch. Amidst white snow and blue sky we set out a large pile of *omusubi*, which resembled a stack of black tennis balls. I am sure this was somewhat of a curious sight to our fellow patrons. One fellow skier cried out good-naturedly, "That sure is big *sushi!*" Skiing makes you hungry, and my American friends made no complaints as they devoured them.

I have a friend in Denver who is the son of a wealthy, established family in Tokyo. Whenever we go skiing or hiking together, he always reminds me not to forget the *omusubi*! *Omusubi*, like *miso* soup, was always a direct reflection on the taste and style of one's mother. Anyone growing up in Japan, whether it be in Tokyo or in the country, has the same experience with and affinity for *omusubi*. That is why the honorific "O" is added to *musubi* to make it *omusubi*. Similarly, *nigiri* is called *onigiri*.

The word *musubi* can be found in ancient history books. It is used frequently by the elders of all areas, but especially the northeast. The word has its origin in Shintoism.

Literally, it means to bring your hands together in front of you, touching them together in a clap. The left hand symbolizes *Izanagi* (the male god), while the right hand symbolizes *Izanami* (the female god). The joining of the gods is symbolized in ritual hand clapping. When making *omusubi,* we bring our hands together in the same action.

Shinto is the basis of all *hare no hi* (special days) and during religious events anything white, especially white rice, has *Shinto* origins. In this case the position and action of the hands is also *Shinto*.

HOW TO MAKE OMUSUBI

See the breakfast section for information on how to prepare white rice. If you are using brown rice, add a little more water and cook twice as explained for breakfasts. Cool the rice until you can hold in your hand. Wet your hands (shake off excess water) so the rice won't stick to you. When packing the finished rice balls, wrap them individually in aluminum foil lightly coated with vegetable oil so they won't stick together. You can apply the oil with a paper towel.

■ Nori musubi — Rice balls with seaweed wrapping

A. In a slightly moistened rice bowl, add **about 1 cup of rice** and make a depression in the center for the filling. Add filling. Put the rice bowl in your right hand and cover it with your left hand. Turn it over quickly to drop the rice into your left hand. Remove the bowl, return the rice and filling to your right hand "face up," fold and tuck the rice over the center filling, completely covering it, and shape into a flattened ball.

B. Wrap the rice ball with **1/8-inch-wide strips of *nori*** (sheets of dried seaweed) until completely covered. (If your hands are not wet, the *nori* will stick to you, not to the rice ball.) *Nori* shrinks as it dries so if any rice is exposed the ball will shrink unevenly and break apart. Wrap the balls as directed at the beginning of these recipes.

■ Yaki musubi — Grilled rice balls

A. Follow the steps in "*Nori musubi* A and B."

B. Gently place the balls in a *yakiami* (grilling net). In a broiler or toaster oven, grill until golden brown on both sides. Dip the seared sides of the riceballs in *shoyu.* (The sides not grilled will absorb too much *shoyu* and the rice ball will fall apart.) Wrap the balls as directed at the beginning of these recipes.

■ Miso yaki musubi — Grilled rice balls with *miso*

A. Follow the steps in "*Nori musubi* A and B." (above)

B. Place about **1 tsp. of *miso*** in the palm of your hand and smear it over a **rice ball.** Repeat for each rice ball.

C. Place the rice balls in a *yakiami* and in a broiler or toaster oven-grill until the *miso* starts to toast on both sides. Wrap the balls as directed at the beginning of these recipes.

■ Maze musubi — Mixed rice balls

A. For each rice ball, combine **1 *umezuke*** (remove seed and chop), **1 tsp. shaved *bonito,*** **1/3 tsp. white sauteed sesame seeds** (be careful when sauteeing — they burn easily), and **1 cup of rice.** Follow the steps for "*Nori musubi* A and B," but do not add a center filling. You can cover the balls with *nori* if you wish. Wrap the balls as directed at the beginning of these recipes.

HOW TO MAKE OMUSUBI NO GU — CENTER FILLINGS FOR RICE BALLS

■ Shiozake — Lightly salted and grilled salmon

Sprinkle **1 salmon steak or fillet** with **1/2 teaspoon salt** and refrigerate overnight. Broil the salmon five inches from heat for five to nine minutes on one side, five minutes on the other. Let cool, remove skin and small bones, crumble, and salt to taste. The skin can be broiled again until crispy, chopped, and mixed in. Add about **1 tsp**. or less depending on size of rice ball. If there are leftovers, you can freeze and save.

■ Okaka — Shaved bonito

One cup shaved bonito (you can also use bonito left from making *dashijiru*), **1/2 tsp.** *shoyu,* **1/3 tsp.** *mirin.* Mix, then squeeze out excess *shoyu* with your fingers. Use **1/2 tsp. filling** per rice ball.

■ Tarako — Grilled pollack eggs

Grill **pollack** until skin turns light brown. Chop into bite-size pieces. Add **one bite-size piece per rice ball** as the center filling.

■ Umeboshi or umezuke — Dried pickled plum or pickled plum

Use ***umeboshi*** or ***umezuke*** about the size of a quarter. Remove the seed so you don't break a tooth! **Add one per rice ball.**

■ Miso zuke — Pickles made with *miso*

Rinse the miso from **miso zuke** (see breakfast section, *tsukemono* recipes), mince, and squeeze out excess water. Add about **1 tsp**. per rice ball.

■ Tsukemono — Pickles

Use **long-term pickles** (those with a high salt content). Mince and squeeze out excess water. Add **1 tsp**. per rice ball.

■ Niboshi or yakiboshi no tsukudani — Dried sardines, dried broiled sardines, or anchovies cooked with soy sauce

A. Save **niboshi** or **yakiboshi** left over from making *dashijiru*. Squeeze out excess water and save in the freezer until you collect about **2 oz.** then defrost. Saute in a skillet over a low heat until they snap easily.

B. In a small cooking pot add **1/3 cup *dashijiru,* 3 Tbsp.** *shoyu,* **2 Tbsp. sugar,** and **2 Tbsp.** *mirin.* Bring slowly to a boil. Remove the dried skins from A and add to B. Mix with chopsticks over low heat until all liquid is absorbed. This can also be used as a *jobina* side dish. Add about **1 tsp**. per rice ball.

■ Shiitake no tsukudani — *Shiitake* mushrooms cooked with soy sauce

Cut **7 or 8 medium-sized *shiitake*** mushrooms (left from making *dashijiru*) into slivers. Bring **1 cup** *dashijiru,* **1 Tbsp.** *shoyu,* **1 tsp. sugar,** and **3 tsp.** *mirin* to a boil. Add *shiitake* mushrooms, reduce heat to low, and cook until liquid is absorbed, stirring occasionally. This also makes a good *jobina* side dish. Add about **1 tsp**. per rice ball.

■ Kombu no tsukudani — Kelp cooked with soy sauce

Cut **1 cup *kombu*** (left from making *dashijiru*) into matchstick slivers. In a cooking pot, combine **2 cups water** (twice the amount of water as solid ingredients) with *kombu* and cook over medium heat until soft. When soft, pour off excess water leaving just enough to cover the *kombu*. Add **3 Tbsp.** *shoyu,* **1 tsp. sugar,** and **2 tsp.** *mirin.* Cook over low heat, stirring occasionally until liquid is absorbed. This also makes a good *jobina* side dish. Add **1 tsp**. per rice ball.

Soba to Udon — Buckwheat and Wheat Flour Noodles

We discussed *soba* and *udon* briefly in previous chapters. These noodles are eaten primarily at lunch time. Traditionally, noodles were called *nagamono,* which translates as "things that are long," and were eaten on *hare no hi* (special days) and when planting and harvesting rice.

If you visit Japan, you will find that noodle stands can be found in every city and town. The saying "I need a bowl of noodles" is similar to saying "I need a snack" in the United States.

Northeastern Morioka City is famous for a tournament it holds during *hare no hi* festivals. This tournament is called "*Wanko soba*" and is conducted by having participants see how many bowls of *soba* they can eat in a certain time, while an attendant fills the bowl a couple of bites at a time. Even though there is only a bite or so in each bowl, my limit was a mere 38 bowls! To give you an idea how I ranked, many contestants finished more than 100 bowls.

Udon is sometimes called *chikara udon* (power *udon*). After a hard day's work it is a popular dish meant to restore one's energy (or, if nothing else, one's spirits).

Most Japanese train stations that have attendants also usually have snack and noodle stands. If there is not one directly inside the station you can bet there is one very close by. Most major local train stations are known for their own special *ekiben* (train station box lunches). People are known to plan their lunch time around the arrival time into a station with a particular *ekiben.*

There is more than one reason why train stations serve noodles. For one, they can be quickly prepared. Precooked noodles are placed in a strainer and dipped in boiling water to reheat them. Pour *dashijiru* over the noodles (and occasionally add an egg or *tempura*) and you have a hot meal ready in less than a minute. In the U.S. there are restaurants that give you your lunch free if it is not served in 10 minutes. These noodle stands serve lunches much faster than that! The noodles are also consumed very rapidly. People eat standing up, adding their own garnishes of chopped scallion and pepper. Their bowls are usually empty in under five minutes. A familiar scene in the cold northern areas is a small noodle stand crowded with men and women of all ages, slurping noodles as the steam billows out from under the canopies.

Although the primary reason noodles are eaten in train stations is speed, there are more historical reasons based on folk religion. The first Japanese railroad was completed in 1872. The line first established in the Tohoku area in northeastern Japan wasn't completed until 1924. At that time riding the train brought a lot of status to its passengers.

Simple farmers and common people did not ride the train. There was a distinct socio-economic dividing line between those who rode the trains and those who didn't. The train's passing was an event in every town. Kids clamored to the tracks to feel the train's power and watch it go by. As a kid, I also used to hang from train bridges and make play knives by placing nails on the tracks just before the train went by. I spent a lot of time as a kid hanging around the train tracks. I developed quite an affinity for them. These were trains powered by steam engines. Although modern trains are considered noise polluters, it used to be an important status symbol to have the railroad tracks running through your property.

When I was a curator I collected many amusing stories about those first days in locomotive history. One 92-year-old woman told me the story about the first time she rode on a train. Her husband was a town leader and had been summoned to an important meeting in Tokyo. At that time it was extremely rare for a woman to accompany her husband on business, but this time she was invited to come along. She looked forward with great anticipation to viewing the imperial gardens (from outside the gates, of course) and paying her distant respects to the Emperor.

This being her first train experience, they started out on foot early in the morning to reach the station in time for departure. They arrived four hours early, to make sure they weren't late. They were both dressed from top to bottom in brand-new clothes. Her husband, in a suit that reminded her of Charlie Chaplin, looked amusing to her. She wore a fine new *kimono*. The thought running through both their minds was that if they left the village they might not ever return again. The day before their departure the entire family gathered for a send-off celebration. Before they left for the station special prayers were said at the *Shinto* and Buddhist altars.

At that time the country people were mostly rice farmers who lived a very settled existence. Generation after generation would stay in one location. For this small village couple, taking a 15-hour train ride to a big, strange city was a very new experience. Today you can complete the same journey by plane in about one hour.

When they arrived at the train station with time to spare, they went to a restaurant near the station to eat. Her husband ate *soba* and drank *sake* while she ate *udon*. At the station there is a point beyond which only passengers are allowed. This was to them a fairly ominous point. It was a religious gesture according to folk religion to eat *soba* and *udon* on any auspicious occasion. This custom has continued in the stations to today.

The train finally arrived and the town leader and his wife were astounded by the gigantic, clean, and beautiful passenger car. This was the first time they had been so close to a train. They were impressed. They abided by the custom they were familiar with when entering one's home.

They removed their *zori* (sandals) and left them on the platform before entering the car! The train conductor, having had a lot of experience with this sort of reaction, piled the shoes (not only theirs) onto the floor of the car.

Every local station's noodle stand has its own recipe for the *dashijiru* served with the noodles. These recipes also vary by region. Certain stations famous for their noodles entice passengers with even the briefest of stops to jump off and grab a quick bowl.

Suiton is made from the same wheat flour as *udon* but instead of being made into noodles, the dough is torn into bite-size chunks, boiled, and served with soup broth. *Suiton* is very easy to make but historically for religious reasons "long foods" are better. For formal occasions, the shape was always long.

In this chapter I will explain how to make homemade *soba* and *udon*, and provide recipes for serving them. Dry *soba* and *udon* are readily available in Oriental markets, so in the interest of efficiency the following recipes call for dry *soba* and *udon*.

HOW TO MAKE SOBA

(serves 4 people)

A. Dissolve **1 Tbsp. salt** in **1/3 cup warm water** and mix in **1/2 to 2/3 cup grated mountain yam.**

B. Put **1 lb. buckwheat flour** into a large bowl. Add part of A to the center of the flour and mix to make dough. Add a **little more water** and knead until you have dough the consistency of an ear lobe.

C. After the dough is ready, set it in a bowl and cover tightly with plastic wrap. Let set for 1 hour, then knead, wrap, and let sit for an additional 30 minutes.

D. Dust a large cutting board with flour and roll out the dough with a rolling pin to about 1/4 inch in thickness. Dust with flour and fold in half. If still too large to work with, dust again and fold. Cut into 1/4-inch strips. Boil the noodles in a large kettle for 10 to 20 minutes, until tender. Drain and rinse gently in cold running water. Drain again and shake until all excess water is removed.

E. Using a *miso* soup bowl as a measure, divide the noodles into 4 individual portions and transfer them to sandwich bags for storage or place them in *donburi* (large bowls) to serve with *kakejiru* (soup broth) and garnishes.

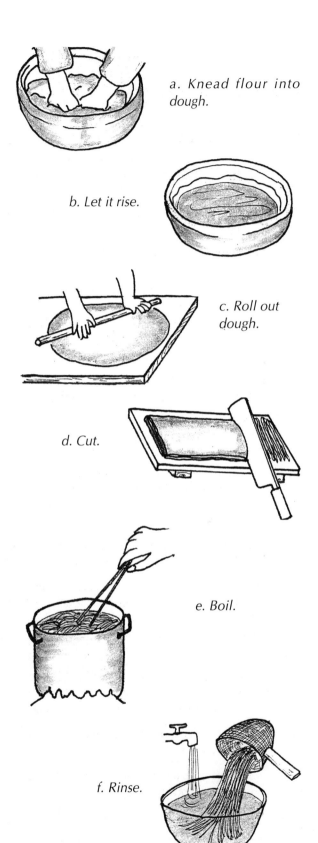

a. *Knead flour into dough.*

b. *Let it rise.*

c. *Roll out dough.*

d. *Cut.*

e. *Boil.*

g. *Drain.*

f. *Rinse.*

HOW TO COOK DRIED SOBA
(serves 4 people)

A. Boil **one gallon water** with **1 Tbsp. salt,** add **1 lb. dried *soba,*** separate and stir with chopsticks to avoid sticking. When it starts to boil again quickly add about **1/2 cup cold water** (this ensures even cooking). As it starts to boil again, test a noodle by biting it; if it is soft all the way through it is done. If it is still hard, add another **1/2 cup cold water** and continue to cook. Be careful not to overcook.

B. Have **two gallons of ice water** prepared and set aside. Drain *soba* in mesh strainer and quickly submerge, strainer and all, in the ice water and then rinse under cold running water.

C. Shake off excess water completely and divide into 4 individual portions. If refrigerated it should keep 3 to 4 days.

HOW TO MAKE SOBA KAKEJIRU AND TSUKEJIRU — SOBA SOUP BROTH AND DIP SAUCE
(serves 4 people)

■ Kombu to kezuribushi no soba kakejiru — Soup broth made from kelp and shaved bonito

A. In a large sauce pan, soak one **4 x 5-inch piece of *kombu*** in **6 cups of water** for 4 hours, then place over high heat. Just before boiling, remove *kombu*. Reduce heat to low and add **1 cup shaved bonito,** cook 2 to 3 minutes, and turn off heat. Strain through a fine strainer to remove bonito. This makes your basic *dashijiru.*

B. In a cooking pot, add **1/2 cup *mirin*** and **8 Tbsp. *shoyu.*** Bring to a boil and add the *dashijiru* from A. Continue to heat until almost boiling and turn off heat. This makes your *soba kakejiru* (*soba* soup broth).

C. To make *tsukejiru* (dip sauce), mix **1/2 cup *mirin,*** **1/2 cup *shoyu,*** and **2 cups of A's *dashijiru.*** Heat over a high heat until just before boiling. Serve in individual small serving bowls.

■ Niboshi or yakiboshi no soba kakejiru — Soba soup broth made from dried or broiled and dried sardines or anchovies

A. Snap the heads and stomach areas off of **30 to 45 *niboshi* or *yakiboshi.*** Saute over low heat for 3 minutes to remove fish smell. Add **6 cups of water,** turn up heat to high, and boil for 15 minutes. Strain to remove fish (save the broth!). This makes your basic *dashijiru.*

B. Add **1/2 cup *mirin,*** **8 Tbsp. *shoyu*** to A's *dashijiru* when it almost reaches a second boil, then turn off heat. This makes your *soba kakejiru* (*soba* soup broth).

C. If making *tsukejiru* (dip sauce), mix **1/2 cup *mirin,*** **1/2 cup *shoyu,*** and **2 cups of A's *dashijiru.*** Heat over high heat until just before boiling. Serve in individual small serving bowls.

Soba Recipes
(Each recipe serves 4 people)

- Kake soba — Plain soba with soup broth

    A. Bring **3 times the amount of water than soba** to a boil. In a separate cooking pot, heat **6 to 7 cups** *kakejiru* (do not boil).

    B. Place precooked *soba* (see page 168) in a strainer smaller than the pot of boiling water. Place s*oba* and strainer in boiling water for 1 minute, and shake noodles to heat evenly. Remove, shake off excess water, place in a *donburi* bowl. Fill bowl with broth until noodles are covered.

    C. Garnish with chopped **scallions,** chopped *nori,* **alfalfa sprouts,** or *kaiware* (*daikon* **sprouts**) to taste. If you like it hot, add **seven-taste pepper** to taste.

- Yasai soba — Vegetables and soba with soup broth

    A. Follow A&B in *kake soba* (above), then **see breakfast *ohitashi* recipes for vegetable preparations.** Using any vegetables you may have on hand, add to *donburi* with *soba* and broth in a decorative arrangement with the vegetables placed on top of the noodles.

    B. Garnish with chopped **scallion,** chopped *nori,* and a **wedge of lime or lemon.**

- Sankai soba — Seaweed, vegetables, and soba with soup broth

    A. **Four medium-sized *shiitake* mushrooms** or **1 1/2 oz. oyster mushrooms.** If dried, soak in water until soft. Slice *shiitake* mushrooms into bite-size pieces; tear oyster mushrooms lengthwise with your fingers.

    B. In cooking pot, combine **3 Tbsp.** *mirin,* **3 Tbsp.** *shoyu,* and **1 cup** *dashijiru* and bring to a boil. Add A, reduce heat, and simmer until about 1/2 cup of liquid remains.

    C. Bring *soba* to a boil in three times the amount of water. In a separate cooking pot heat **6 to 7 cups** *kakejiru* but do not boil. Place precooked *soba* in a strainer smaller than the pot of boiling water and submerge both the *soba* and strainer in the water for 1 minute. Shake noodles to heat evenly. Remove, shake off water, and place in a *donburi* bowl. Cover noodles with broth. Top with mushrooms and sprinkle with **1/2 oz. soaked and chopped** *wakame,* **1/2 oz. soaked** *sukikombu,* and **1/2 oz. soaked** *funori.*

D. For garnish, take your pick among chopped **scallions,** chopped **tre-foil, cilantro,** or **nori and seven-taste pepper** to taste. **Any ohitashi** can be substituted for the mushrooms in this recipe. You can also make *tsukejiru* (dip sauce) instead of *kakejiru* (soup broth) by mixing **2 cups of dashijiru** with **1/2 cup mirin** and **1/2 cup shoyu.**

■ Tororo soba — Grated Chinese yam and soba with soup broth

Mortar and pestle.

A. Peel, grate, and grind **1 lb. of mountain yam** (use mortar and pestle). Grate **1 lb. daikon,** squeeze out excess water with your hand, and mix with mountain yam.

B. Follow A&B in *kake soba* (above), top with A's mountain yam and *daikon.* Garnish with chopped **nori** and **kaiware** to taste. Add **wasabi** (Japanese green horseradish) to taste if you want. Just before serving squeeze in a little **fresh lime juice.** The soup should be eaten hot. (Instead of mountain yam try **3 oz. of natto** stirred until sticky. This is called *natto soba.*)

■ Zaru soba — Soba served on a woven basket plate with dip sauce

Zaru soba.

Place pre-cooked *soba* in a strainer and run under cold water to loosen. Shake off excess water. Place *soba* on a *sobazaru* (traditional flat woven-bamboo basket) and place another plate underneath to catch any excess water that leaks through. If you do not have one, just completely drain and place on a plate. Just before serving, top with **1/4 sheet chopped nori** per person. Serve with individual bowls of dip sauce, two-thirds cup per person. Arrange a garnish plate of **wasabi,** chopped **scallion,** and, if you like, **raw quail eggs.** To eat, mix garnishes and dip sauce individually to taste.

■ Maki soba — Soba roll

How to roll soba.

A. Place about **one filled miso bowl of cooked soba** in *donburi* bowl. Heat **3 Tbsp. vinegar, 1 Tbsp. mirin,** and **1 Tbsp. sugar** in cooking pot until the sugar melts. Add to individual servings of *soba.* (Make sure you have poured off any excess vinegar.) Arrange *gu* (solid ingredients) on a platter. Optionally, add slivered **cucumber, kaiware,** sliced **avocado,** and boiled **crab** or **shrimp** (shelled). Pick the amounts of each to suit your taste. Set the platter aside.

B. Place a sheet of **nori** (dried seaweed) on a *makisu* (bamboo roller used to make *sushi* rolls). Line up *soba* to cover *nori* evenly. Arrange *gu* in an orderly fashion on top of the *soba* — be careful to leave about one inch of *nori* exposed on the front end so when it is rolled the roll will stick to the front end piece of *nori.* Cut into 2 to 4 sections, serve with dip sauce.

■ Ume dofu soba — Soba with pickled plum tofu dressing

How to rinse soba.

A. Pit **4 or 5 large *umezuke.*** Drain **1/2 block soft *tofu*** on paper towel by putting a weight equal to the *tofu* on top of the block for 10 minutes. Grind *umeboshi* and *tofu* in a mortar with pestle until thoroughly mixed.

B. Take precooked *soba*, run under cold water, rinse, shake off excess water, and place on *sobazaru*. Add **sliced red cabbage, any seaweed** (***wakame, sukikombu,*** or ***nori***), **alfalfa sprouts,** or ***kaiware*** and serve with ***umetofu* dressing** on the side. It makes a beautifully color-balanced arrangement.

HOW TO MAKE UDON
(serves 4 people)

A. Dissolve **1 Tbsp. salt** in **2/3 to 1 cup warm water.** In large mixing bowl add **1 lb. wheat flour** a little at a time, mix, and knead until soft (if still hard add a little more water).

B. Cover tightly with plastic wrap for 1 hour. Knead again, cover, and let sit for another 30 minutes.

C. Dust a large cutting board with **flour,** and roll out the dough with a rolling pin to about 1/4 inch in thickness. Dust with flour and fold in half. If still too large in size, dust again and fold. Cut into 1/4-inch strips. In **5 times the volume of water,** boil for 10 to 20 minutes, until tender. Drain and rinse gently in cold running water. Drain again and shake off excess water.

D. Using a *miso* soup bowl as a measure, divide the noodles into 4 individual portions and transfer them to sandwich bags for storage or place them in *donburi* (noodle bowls) to serve with **kakejiru** (soup broth) and garnishes.

HOW TO COOK DRIED UDON
(serves 4 people)

A. Add **1 lb. dried *udon*** to **1 gallon boiling water** with **1 Tbsp. salt.** Add *udon* separately and stir with chopsticks to prevent sticking. When it starts to boil, quickly add **1/2 cup cold water.** This ensures even cooking. As it starts to boil again, test a noodle by biting; if it is soft all the way through it is done. If it is still hard, add another **1/2 cup water** and continue to cook. Be careful not to overcook.

B. Have **2 gallons of ice water** prepared and set aside. Drain *udon* in strainer and quickly submerge, strainer and all, in the ice water and rinse under cold running water.

C. Shake off excess water and divide into 4 individual portions and store in sandwich bags. If refrigerated, it should keep 3 to 4 days.

HOW TO MAKE UDON KAKEJIRU — UDON SOUP BROTH
(serves 4 people)

■ Kombu to kezuribushi no udon kakejiru — Soup broth made from kelp and shaved bonito

A. In a large sauce pan, soak one **4 x 5-inch piece of** *kombu* in **6 cups of water** for 4 hours, then place over high heat. Just before boiling, remove *kombu*. Reduce heat to low and add **1 cup shaved bonito,** cook 2 to 3 minutes, and turn off heat. Strain through fine strainer to remove bonito. This makes your basic *dashijiru.*

B. In a cooking pot, add **1/2 cup** *mirin* and **8 Tbsp.** *shoyu.* Bring to a boil and add A's *dashijiru.* Continue to heat until almost boiling, and turn off heat. This makes your *udon kakejiru* (*udon* soup broth).

■ Niboshi or yakiboshi no udon kakejiru — Soup broth made from dried or broiled and dried sardines or anchovies

A. Snap the heads and stomach areas off of **30 to 45** *niboshi* **or** *yakiboshi.* Saute over low heat for 3 minutes to remove fish smell. Add **6 cups of water,** turn up heat to high and boil for 15 minutes. Strain to remove fish (save the broth!). This makes your basic *dashijiru.*

B. Add **1/2 cup** *mirin,* **8 Tbsp.** *shoyu* to A when it almost reaches a second boil, then turn off heat. This makes your *udon kakejiru* (*udon* soup broth).

Udon Recipes
(Each recipe serves 4 people.)

■ Kake udon — Plain udon with soup broth

A. In a pot, add **6 cups** *udon dashijiru,* **5 Tbsp.** *shoyu,* and **5 Tbsp.** *mirin.* Bring to a boil, then lower heat to low to keep warm. This makes *udon kakejiru.*

B. In a separate cooking pot, in about **3 times the amount boiling water as** *udon,* place *udon* in a strainer, and immerse in boiling water for about 1 minute. Shake off excess water, place in *donburi* bowls and cover with soup broth. Garnish with chopped **scallion** and **seven-taste pepper** to taste.

■ Niku yasai udon — Meat, vegetables, and udon with soup broth

Niku yasai udon.

A. Take your pick of **1 cup sliced cabbage, spinach, onion, zucchini, broccoli, Chinese cabbage, scallion, leek, bell pepper, or carrots** (a few different kinds make for a nice color balance). Skin, debone, and cut into bite-size pieces **one chicken thigh** or sliver-cut **1/2 lb. pork** or slice **1/2 lb. beef** against the grain.

B. In a heated skillet add **1 Tbsp. sesame oil** and **1 clove crushed garlic.** Saute meat quickly for 2 minutes, add vegetables, and continue sauteing for 1 minute. Add **7 cups** *dashijiru,* and continue to cook for 5 minutes. Remove *aku* then add **5 Tbsp.** *shoyu,* **4 Tbsp.** *mirin,* and **1/4 tsp. salt.**

C. Move these ingredients to the side of the pot and add **4 servings of udon.** In individual *donburi* bowls first place noodles, top with meat and vegetables, and cover with broth. Garnish with chopped **scallion** and **seven-taste pepper** to taste. If you use only vegetables, reduce *shoyu* by 1 Tbsp.

■ Shabushabu udon — Cooked sliced beef and udon served chilled

A. Thinly slice **1/3 lb. beef.** Quickly wave each slice through boiling water until color changes to brown, then quickly immerse in ice water. Shake off excess water. Boil **3 oz. spinach** and immerse it in ice water (see breakfast recipes — any leafy vegetable can be substituted). Squeeze out excess water. Add **1/2 Tbsp. vinegar, 1/2 Tbsp.** *sake,* **1/2 Tbsp.** *shoyu,* and mix in with spinach.

B. In cooking pot, add **4 cups** *dashijiru,* **2 Tbsp.** *shoyu,* and **1/2 tsp. salt.** Bring to a boil and chill for soup broth. Place *udon* in strainer and run under cold water to loosen. Shake off excess water and place in individual *donburi* bowls.

C. Top with beef and vegetables and cover with soup broth, garnish with **1/2 cup grated** *daikon* squeezed of excess water.

■ Sankai udon — Seaweed, vegetables, and udon with soup broth

A. Slice **4 medium-sized** *shiitake* **mushrooms** into bite-sized pieces, or tear **1 1/2 oz. oyster mushrooms** lengthwise. If the mushrooms are dried, soak them in water until they soften. In a cooking pot, boil **3 Tbsp.** *mirin,* **3 Tbsp.** *shoyu,* and **1 cup** *dashijiru.* Reduce heat, add mushrooms, and simmer until about 1/2 cup of liquid remains.

B. In cooking pot add **6 cups** *dashijiru,* **4 Tbsp.** *shoyu,* and **4 Tbsp.** *mirin.* Bring to a boil to make *udon kakejiru* (soup broth). Add *udon* and bring to second boil, turn off heat. Serve in individual *donburi* bowls.

C. Top with mushrooms from A and sprinkle with **1/2 oz. soaked and chopped** *wakame,* **1/2 oz. soaked** *sukikombu,* **1/2 oz. soaked** *funori.*

D. Garnish with chopped **scallion,** chopped **trefoil, cilantro,** or *nori* and **seven-taste pepper** to taste.

■ Sukiyaki udon — Sukiyaki with udon

A. Thinly slice **1/2 lb. beef** and shred **1/2 block** *tofu* into bite-size pieces. Soak **4 medium-size** *shiitake* **mushrooms** until soft, cut each into 4 or 5 slices. Take **3 oz. leeks,** remove tough outer skin and slant cut. Soak **1/2 cup sliced bamboo shoots** in **3 times the amount of water** for 15 minutes. Cut **6 (about 1 oz.) chrysanthemum leaves** into 2-inch strips. Rough chop **1 cup yam cake noodles**, then soak in water 15 minutes.

B. In a heated skillet, add **1/2 cup** *shoyu,* **1/2 cup** *mirin,* and **3 Tbsp. sugar.** Bring to a boil. When it boils, add sliced beef one piece at a time opened up flat. Then push each to the side and add another until all are cooked. Then add yam cake noodles, carrots, bamboo shoots, mushrooms, and tofu. Add **1/2 cup** *udon dashijiru.* Move above ingredients to the side and add precooked udon. Bring to a boil then add chrysanthemum leaves for color and turn off heat. Serve in the pan. Let individuals serve themselves. Garnish with **seven-taste pepper** to taste.

■ Yaki udon — Sauteed udon and vegetables

A. Chop **4 fist-size cabbage leaves** into bite-size pieces. Slant-cut **2 oz. onion.** Peel and grate **2 oz. carrots.** Slant-cut **3 oz. zucchini.** Slant-cut **2 oz. bell pepper** into large slices. Wash and drain **1 cup bean sprouts.** Skin, debone, and dice **1 oz. chicken.**

B. In a heated skillet, saute chicken and carrots in **2 Tbsp. sesame oil** for 1–2 minutes. Then add other vegetables and quickly saute. Take precooked *udon,* rinse in running water to separate, shake off excess water, and add to pan. Completely mix and saute. Add **1/2 cup** *dashijiru,* **1/3 tsp. salt, 1 Tbsp.** *sake,* **2 Tbsp.** *mirin,* and cook until all liquid is absorbed.

C. Arrange on individual plates and top with **1/2 sheet of shredded** *nori* per person. Garnish with pitted **umeboshi** or **umezuke.**

Soba and *udon* recipes both follow a very set pattern. The important point to remember is to have all the utensils and ingredients prepared before you start cooking. Set out the *udon* or *soba,* boiling pot of water, ice water, strainers, solid ingredients, broth, and garnishes. Then, when everything is ready, cook quickly.

These recipes are very basic in nature and offer opportunities for experimentation on your own. Feel free to add different ingredients or mix them to make your own delicious noodle recipes. If you visit a Japanese restaurant and have leftover *tempura,* bring it home in a "doggie bag" and use it to make *tempura udon.* It is best to pour the soup broth over the noodles just before serving time so the noodles do not get mushy. Other interesting garnishes that are not traditionally Japanese include chopped jalapeno peppers or cilantro. Again feel free to experiment. There are other Japanese noodles, such as *somen* or *hiyamugi.* Basically these noodles are prepared as you would prepare *udon.*

Somen is a noodle that is eaten during Zen training in Japanese temples. The height of summer is what is called *O-Zeeshin* (the peak of the training schedule). The completion of *O-Zeeshin* is celebrated with *udon kuyo* (the *udon* ceremony). I have participated in both the training and the celebration. The ceremony is called *udon kuyo* but what we ate was *somen.* The priests call *somen "udon."* At that time the *unsui* (priests in training) were allowed to eat huge portions of *somen.* In gallon-sized bowls they ate *somen* with *kombudashi no tsukejiru* (dip sauce), garnished with grated *daikon,* chopped scallion, grated ginger, chopped beef steak leaf, sesame seeds, and chopped seaweed.

Inside the temple the only time the training priests were allowed to make any noise at all was during morning cleanup and during these special *udon kuyo.* It was great fun to make loud slurping noises while enjoying the noodles.

During the summer months when the weather is hot and the appetite is small, chilled *somen* is a refreshing dish. It is also healthful: easily digestible and high in carbohydrates.

If you are worried about salt intake you can ease up on the *shoyu.* If by doing so, you find the taste somewhat lacking, use *umezuke* or sour fruits as a garnish, or make your *dashijiru* stronger to deepen the flavor. *Jobina* can be added as a side dish to balance the flavor of the meal.

Traditionally during *hare no hi* or special days *shojin dashijiru* or *niboshi dashijiru* were not usually used. Instead, chicken or pork were used as base flavors for *nabe* (one-pot cooking). Chicken or pork, vegetables, *tofu,* and finally *udon* were added to one large pot. *Shojin dashijiru* with simple *gu* ingredients were eaten during religious training or on *kegare no hi* (bad luck days).

The traditional Japanese farmer made and ate noodles according to religious mandates. Today *soba* and *udon* are used as a practical base ingredient for a variety of dishes enjoyed at any time.

Today in Japan, foods from all over the world are served at all times of the day or night. *Omusubi* and *soba* and *udon* as well are not restricted to lunch time only but can be enjoyed any time. Traditionally these were lunch foods, and since this book focuses on the traditional diet of Japanese farmers and mountain people, they have been included in this section.

Dinner (Yushoku)

A child at dinner.

Unlike modern society in which our lives are dictated by the hands of a clock, the traditional farmer's life revolved around the rising and setting of the sun. I can remember these times — this way of life belongs to the not-so-distant past.

Meal times for the farmers were dictated by their work schedule, subtly changing to follow the rhythm of the chores day by day and season by season. Even today the busy planting and harvest seasons bring back these age-old patterns.

I don't know which is the most natural or healthy way — to have one's life ruled by the clock or by the sun. It is a question worth asking. Intrinsically, I think our bodies yearn to be in sync with the rising and setting of the sun.

My students sometimes ask about my daily routine. As a martial arts instructor some people think my life must be very special and mysterious. Basically my daily life is no different from other people's. Only my schedule may be different from those who hold 9-to-5 jobs. Nippon Kan offers classes in Aikido and other cultural activities in the evenings after most people have finished their regular working day. These classes run until 9:00 p.m. Other special classes and seminars are held on weekends. My working time therefore begins when most people's end.

After morning training I eat breakfast at 9 or 10 a.m. I eat a light lunch at about 3 p.m., and dinner at about 9:30 p.m. after classes are finished. People have asked me if it is good to eat so late in the evening, but since I usually go to sleep at midnight it is a balanced schedule.

It is important for me to share meals with my students in the evenings. This custom began with the conception of Nippon Kan and continues today. A nice change from the old days is that the refrigerator is not as empty as it once was. Maybe my life is finally getting more "normal." This basic foundation of enjoying meals together, the communication and sense of sharing, is what Nippon Kan has been built upon. This concept can be traced to the traditional beliefs of Japanese folk religion. The pattern of life at Nippon Kan and that of the traditional Japanese farmer are very similar, to which I attribute to Nippon Kan's success. Sharing meals provides a common method of communication for people of different ages, nationalities, and backgrounds. During one seminar held at Nippon Kan more than 50 people at one time found places to sit on the wooden floors of our Japanese rooms and shared *miso* soup, brown rice, and various side dishes. Watching this, my conviction was reinforced that the first way to break any cultural or communication gap between people is to share food.

One of my most gratifying times was after cooking for a party of 300 people. Even with all the hard work — and staring at the clean-up to follow — to see all of the food eaten was a joy to me. The following section will focus on dinner recipes, but remember they don't have to be eaten only in the evenings. These recipes will include traditional daily recipes and also recipes served on *hare no hi* as well. Ingredients varied for foods served on special days depending on the purpose of the special event.

I have also included in these recipes those vegetables readily available in the United States, blending them with traditional Japanese cooking methods and flavors.

The amounts given for the flavorings are suggested — please keep in mind there is room for flexibility according to your tastes. If one teaspoon of a flavoring is suggested, start with half the amount and taste it, then add more if it suits your taste. The same holds true for the amount of *dashijiru*. If the dish tastes too strong to you, add *dashijiru* to dilute to taste. Use your own imagination and creativity to experiment substituting different vegetables or combinations of vegetables.

Aemono — Side Dishes Dressed with Various Sauces

Aemono are vegetables boiled quickly in the same manner as *ohitashi* (see breakfast recipes). Sea vegetables, seafoods, or meats are cooked individually or combined and flavored with a variety of seasonings, such as *shoyu, miso,* salt, sesame seeds, ginger, mustard, *umezuke,* lime, lemon, and nuts. These seasonings, individually or mixed, create dishes varying in flavor and balanced for color. All *aemono* ingredients are chosen specifically for color balance and taste, and mixed to flavor just before serving time. This prevents them from becoming watery.

Aemono Recipes
(Each recipe serves 4; a small portion is enough for each person.)

- Shiraae — vegetables and tofu flavored with miso

A. Peel **3 oz. carrots** and cut into one-inch sections. Boil vigorously to soften slightly. Soak **2 medium-size *shiitake* mushrooms.** Dip **1/2 *age* puff** in boiling water to remove excess oil. Squeeze out excess water. Boil **1/4 block *itakonnyaku*** for 2 to 3 minutes. Soak **1/2 oz. *kikurage*** (black mushrooms). Cut all of the above into matchstick slivers.

B. In a cooking pot combine **1/2 cup *dashijiru,* 2 tsp. *mirin,* 1 tsp. sugar,** and **1 Tbsp. *shoyu.*** Cook with A for 2 to 3 minutes. Use your hands to separate **1 block hard *tofu*** into large pieces and boil separately for 5 minutes. Place the boiled *tofu* on a large cloth, gather up the corners, twist and squeeze. Push out excess water by pressing gently with a wooden spoon.

C. In a bowl combine **3 Tbsp. white sesame seeds, 1 Tbsp. white *miso*, 2 tsp. sugar,** and **1/3 tsp. salt** with *tofu*, grind in mortar with pestle, and return to bowl. Mix with 2 Tbsp. of the juice produced from B. Then add the *gu* (solid ingredients) from B.

■ Kaiso no ume shiraae — Sea vegetables and tofu flavored with miso and pickled plum

A. Peel **3 oz. carrots** and cut into 1-inch matchstick slivers. Boil **3 oz. spinach** for 1 minute, immerse in ice water, remove, and squeeze out excess water. Soak **1/2 oz. *wakame*, 1/2 oz. *sukikombu*,** and **1/2 oz. *funori*,** soaking each separately.

B. Use your hands to separate **1 block hard *tofu*** into large pieces and boil separately for 5 minutes. Place the boiled *tofu* on a large cloth, gather up the corners, twist and squeeze. Push out excess water by pressing gently with a wooden spoon.

C. Use a mortar and pestle to grind together **3 Tbsp. white sesame seeds, 1 Tbsp. white *miso*, 2 tsp. sugar, 1/3 tsp. salt, 3 pitted *umezuke*,** and B's *tofu*.

D. Drain the water completely from A, fold into B, and gently mix with chopsticks.

■ Burokkori no shiraae — Broccoli and tofu flavored with miso and pickled plum

How to cut broccoli

A. Use your hands to separate **1/2 block hard *tofu*** into large pieces and boil separately for 5 minutes. Place the boiled *tofu* on a large cloth, gather up the corners, twist and squeeze. Push out excess water by pressing gently with a wooden spoon.

B. Remove the stems from **1/2 lb. broccoli.** Start to cut florettes at the stem and pull apart into bite-size pieces, boil 2 to 3 minutes. Immerse in iced water, drain quickly. Soak **1/2 oz. *wakame*** until soft and chop. Soak **1/2 oz. *funori*.** Peel and grate **1 oz. carrots.**

C. Use a mortar and pestle to grind the *tofu* together with **2 Tbsp. white *miso*, 3 pitted *umezuke*,** and **1/2 cup *dashijiru*.** Add B and mix gently with chopsticks.

- Nanohana no ume shiraae — Rapeseed leaves and tofu flavored with miso and pickled plum.

    A. Boil **1/2 lb. rapeseed leaves** for 1 to 2 minutes. Squeeze out excess water, rough chop into 1-inch bite-size pieces. Mix in **1 tsp. *shoyu.***

    B. Use your hands to separate **1/2 block hard *tofu*** into large pieces and boil separately for 5 minutes. Place the boiled *tofu* on a large cloth, gather up the corners, twist and squeeze. Push out excess water by pressing gently with a wooden spoon.

    C. Use a mortar and pestle to grind the *tofu* together with **2 tsp. white sesame seeds, 2 Tbsp. white *miso*, 1 Tbsp. sugar,** and a few pinches of **salt,** to taste. Fold in A already squeezed to remove excess *shoyu* and mix gently with chopsticks. (Spinach or chrysanthemum leaves can be substituted for rapeseed leaves.)

- Sayaingen no goma misoae — Green beans flavored with miso and sesame seeds

    A. Snap the ends off **1/2 lb. green beans,** break into 2 to 3 pieces, and boil 1 to 2 minutes. Immerse in ice water and drain. Add a few pinches of salt and set aside.

    B. Saute **3 Tbsp. white sesame seeds** over very low heat, being careful not to burn. Grind with mortar and pestle. Separately, mix and grind **1/4 lb. red *miso*, 1 Tbsp. sugar, 3 Tbsp. *mirin*,** and **1 Tbsp. *sake*.** Add sesame seeds. This makes *gomamiso.*

    C. Mix A with B just before serving. You can save *gomamiso* in the refrigerator and use with any vegetable (**asparagus, broccoli,** or **carrots,** for example).

- Karifurawa to karado gurin no katsuobushiae — Cauliflower and collard greens flavored with shaved bonito and soy sauce

    A. Remove the stems from **1/2 lb. cauliflower** and cut into bite-size pieces. Boil 2 to 3 minutes and immerse in ice water, drain. Boil 5 collard green leaves for 2 to 3 minutes and immerse in iced water. Drain and rough chop. Grate **2 oz. carrots** into matchstick slivers.

    B. Just before serving, mix **1 cup bonito, 4 Tbsp. *shoyu*,** and **2 tsp. fresh ginger juice** with A making sure A is completely drained. Then grab loosely in your hands and shake off excess *shoyu* and serve.

■ Horenso no goma shoyuae — Spinach flavored with soy sauce and sesame seeds

    A. Wash **1 lb. spinach** including stem end. Place in boiling water, stem end first. Boil for 1 or 2 minutes, then immerse in ice water, remove, and squeeze out excess water. Cut into 1-inch pieces, discarding stem area. Add **2 Tbsp.** *shoyu* and toss.

    B. In a heated skillet, saute **5 Tbsp. white sesame seeds** over very low heat, then grind completely with mortar and pestle. Add **3 Tbsp.** *dashijiru,* **2 tsp.** *mirin,* and **2 tsp.** *shoyu,* mix, and grind again.

    C. Squeeze out excess *shoyu* completely from A and mix with B with sticks. You can substitute **chrysanthemum leaves, mustard greens, collard greens, broccoli,** or **leeks.**

■ Sayaingen no kurumiae — Green beans and walnuts flavored with soy sauce

    A. Shell and skin **3 oz. walnuts.** Combine with **2 Tbsp.** *mirin,* **1 Tbsp.** *shoyu,* **1 Tbsp.** *dashijiru,* and grind with a mortar and pestle.

    B. Snap the ends off **1/2 lb. green beans** and put in boiling water for 1 to 2 minutes. Immerse in ice water and drain. Remove the stems from **4 oz.** *enoki* **mushrooms,** put in boiling water for 30 seconds. Immerse in ice water and drain. In a bowl, combine **2 Tbsp.** *dashijiru,* **1 Tbsp.** *shoyu,* and **2 tsp.** *mirin* and let sit 5 to 6 minutes. Just before serving, gently squeeze out excess liquid from beans and mushrooms and add A. Mix all ingredients with chopsticks.

Plain vegetables or *aemono* mixed with a vinegar dressing are called *sunomono.*

Sunomono Recipes
(Each recipe serves 4; a small portion is enough for each person.)

■ Sasami to negi no karashi sumiso — Chicken breast and scallion with vinegar-mustard-miso dressing.

A. Skin and debone **4 chicken breasts.** Boil for 3 minutes and shred. In a bowl, combine **2 Tbsp.** *shoyu* with **1 Tbsp.** *mirin* and marinate chicken for 5 minutes. Cut **1/2 lb. scallions** into 2-inch-long pieces (white part only). Halve lengthwise, put in boiling water for 1 minute. Soak **2 oz.** *wakame* until soft, drain, and rough chop. Marinate vegetables in **1 tsp.** *shoyu* and **1 tsp. vinegar.**

B. In a cooking pot combine **3 oz.** white *miso,* **1 oz.** red *miso,* **1 Tbsp.** *mirin,* **2 Tbsp. sugar, 1 cup** *dashijiru,* and **1 Tbsp.** *sake.* Stir over low heat until the mixture thickens. Turn off heat. In a separate bowl combine **1 Tbsp. Japanese hot mustard** (premixed from powder) and **2 Tbsp. vinegar mix** to make *sumiso.*

C. Just before serving, squeeze marinade out of A and mix with B. Fresh **tuna** can be used as well only don't boil it, raw is best. *Sumiso* can be refrigerated and used any time.

■ Jagaimo no shogazu — Potato with vinegar-ginger dressing

A. Combine **6 Tbsp. vinegar, 1 Tbsp.** *shoyu,* **2 Tbsp.** *mirin,* **2 Tbsp.** *dashijiru,* and **1 tsp. fresh ginger juice** to make *shogazu.*

B. Peel and slice **1 lb. potatoes.** Soak in water and remove *aku.* Place in mesh strainer and put in boiling water for 2 minutes. Place strainer and potatoes in ice water, rinse and drain. Put potatoes in a large bowl and marinate with 3 Tbsp. of A's *shogazu.* Separately marinate **3 oz. cooked crab meat in 1 Tbsp.** *shogazu.* Cut **5 trefoil stems** in 1/2-inch sections. Mix A and B just before serving.

■ Kaiso no shogazu — Sea vegetables with vinegar-ginger dressing

A. Soak **1 oz.** *wakame* until soft. Rough chop, and drain. Soak **1 oz.** *sukikombu* until soft. Drain, place into boiling water for 30 seconds. Immerse in iced water, drain.

B. Mix **1 tsp. fresh ginger juice, 2 Tbsp.** *mirin,* **3 Tbsp. vinegar,** and **2 Tbsp.** *dashijiru* to make *shogazu.*

C. Squeeze water completely from A and, in a serving bowl, add B. Soak **1 oz.** *funori* until soft and sprinkle on mixture for decoration.

■ Itokonnyaku no karashizuae — Yam cake noodles with vinegar-mustard dressing

A. Rough chop **1/2 cup yam cake noodles** and put in boiling water for 5 minutes. Immerse in iced water and drain. Place **2 to 3 cups bean sprouts** in boiling water for 30 seconds. Immerse in iced water and drain. Soak **1 oz.** *sukikombu* until soft, then drain.

B. In a separate bowl, combine **1 tsp. Japanese mustard** (premixed from powder), **3 tsp.** *mirin,* **3 Tbsp. vinegar, 1 tsp. sesame oil, 2 tsp.** *shoyu,* and a **few pinches salt** to make *karashizu.*

C. Just before serving squeeze out excess water from yam cake noodles and combine A with B. Mix with chopsticks.

■ Age to moyashi no gomazuae — Deep-fried soybean puff and bean sprouts with vinegar-sesame dressing

A. Put **2 to 3 cups bean sprouts** in boiling water for 30 seconds. Immerse in ice water and drain. Dip **1** *age* **puff** in boiling water for 30 seconds to release excess oil, and squeeze out excess water. Cut *age* and **4 oz. bell pepper** into matchstick slivers.

B. In a heated skillet saute **3 Tbsp. white sesame seeds** over low heat, being careful not to burn. Grind with mortar and pestle. Return to skillet and add **2 Tbsp.** *mirin,* **1 Tbsp. vinegar, 1 tsp.** *shoyu,* and **2 Tbsp.** *dashijiru.* Cook over low heat until thick to make *gomazu.*

C. Soak **1 oz.** *funori* to soften, then drain. Mix with A. Just before serving mix with B's *gomazu.*

■ Ebi no raimuae — Shrimp with lime juice

A. Leaving the tails of **12 jumbo shrimp** intact, remove the rest of the shell and de-vein. Mix **1 tsp. *sake*** and **1/4 tsp. salt** with the shrimp, and steam shrimp in a steamer. Chill in the refrigerator.

B. Cut **1 rib celery** into 1-inch sections. Peel **2 oz. carrots,** cut into 1-inch sections, and cut both into matchstick slivers. Cut **2 or 3 leaves red cabbage** into matchstick slivers and immerse in iced water for about 10 minutes until crunchy.

C. In a separate bowl, mix juice from **1 lime,** a few pinches **salt, 2 tsp. *mirin*** and **1 Tbsp. sesame oil.** Arrange A and B on individual plates in decorative patterns and cover with C. Garnish with **one slice of lime** per serving.

■ Asuparagasu to sukikombu no bainikuae — Asparagus and dried, sliced kelp with pickled plum dressing

How to cut asparagus.

A. Remove the hard portions of the stems from **1/2 lb. asparagus.** Trim with a long rolling cut. Boil 1 to 2 minutes. Immerse in ice water and drain. Soak **1 oz. *sukikombu*** until soft and drain.

B. Pit **5 *umezuke*** and grind with mortar and pestle. Add **1/8 block soft *tofu*** and continue to grind. In a separate bowl combine A and B gently with chopsticks.

■ Hakusai no sujyoyu — Chinese cabbage with vinegar-soy sauce dressing

A. Boil **1/2 lb. Chinese cabbage** for 4 to 5 minutes. Immerse in iced water, drain, and cut into 1- to 2-inch-long sections.

B. Place A in a bowl and mix in **2 Tbsp. vinegar, 3 Tbsp. *shoyu,*** and **1/2 tsp. Japanese mustard** (premixed).

■ Daikon no namasu — Japanese white radish with vinegar dressing

A. Peel and grate **3/4 lb. *daikon*** and **3 oz. carrots** into long slices with a grater.

B. In separate bowls add **1/3 tsp. salt** to the *daikon*, and add a few pinches of salt to the carrots. Mix each separately and let sit for 1 hour.

C. In a separate bowl, combine **3 Tbsp. vinegar, 2 Tbsp.** *mirin,* **1 tsp. sugar,** and **1/4 tsp. salt.**

D. Completely drain excess water from B and mix with C. Refrigerate covered for 5 hours. This dish will keep 2 to 3 days.

■ Kyuri momi — Cucumber slices with vinegar dressing

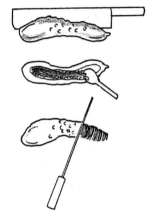

A. Random-peel **1 lb. cucumber.** Cut in half lengthwise, remove seeds, and slice into thin 1/2-moon slices with a grater. Add **1/3 tsp. salt** and mix with your hands. Completely squeeze out excess water.

B. Combine cucumber with **3 Tbsp. vinegar, 2 tsp.** *mirin,* **1 Tbsp. sugar,** and **1/4 tsp. salt.** It is the most delicious if refrigerated for 1 hour.

How to cut cucumber.

■ Sankai namasu — Seafood and vegetables with vinegar dressing

A. Shell and de-vein **8 jumbo shrimp,** leaving tails intact. Skewer on a *yakitori* stick lengthwise to keep them straight. Place in boiling water 2 to 3 minutes. Immerse in iced water, remove sticks, and then drain. Soak **1 oz.** *wakame* and **1 oz.** *funori* separately until soft, then drain. Rough chop *wakame.* Cut **1/4 lb. cucumber** in half lengthwise. Remove seeds and cut into thin 1/2-moon slices with a grater. Add a few pinches of **salt,** mix in, and knead with your hands. Squeeze out excess water. Peel **3 oz.** *daikon* and cut into matchstick slivers with the grater. Add a few pinches of salt, knead by hand, and squeeze out excess water.

B. Arrange A in beautiful patterns on individual serving dishes. In a separate bowl combine **3 Tbsp. vinegar, 2 tsp.** *mirin,* **1 tsp. sugar,** and **1/4 tsp. salt** and spoon over A.

Nimono are dishes using a variety of ingredients and flavorings that are cooked with a broth in a *nabe* (cooking pot). *Nimono* dishes are delicious both when served immediately and when saved for the next day when the flavors have developed. Note that heavier pots are better for cooking *nimono* dishes.

Nimono Recipes
(Each serves 4 people.)

Yasai — Vegetables

■ Yuba to kikurage — Soy milk film with black mushroom

A. Soak **2 oz. *yuba*** and cut into 1-inch pieces. Soak **1 oz. black mushrooms** and tear into bite-size pieces. Peel **3 oz. carrots,** cut into 1-inch sections, and trim with a rolling cut. Add **5 collard green leaves** to boiling water for 2 to 3 minutes. Immerse in iced water, drain, and rough chop into large pieces. Slice **1/2 block hard *tofu*** horizontally into 1/4-inch slices.

B. Place *yuba,* black mushrooms, and carrots into a cooking pot. Cover with ***dashijiru.*** Cover and bring to boil over high heat. When it boils, add **6 Tbsp. *shoyu*** and **3 Tbsp. *mirin.*** Reduce the heat to medium and cook uncovered for 7 to 10 minutes. When it boils again, add *tofu* and collard greens and turn off heat.

■ Kiriboshi daikon — Braised, sliced, or shredded daikon

A. Wash **2 oz. dried *daikon*** in cold water, pour off, and use clean water to soak until soft. Squeeze out excess water. Dip **1 *age* puff** in boiling water for 30 seconds to release excess oil, squeeze out excess water. Cut into matchstick slivers.

B. In a cooking pot combine **2 cups *dashijiru,*** dried *daikon,* and *age.* Bring to a boil over high heat. Reduce heat to medium and cook for 2 to 3 minutes. Add **4 Tbsp. *shoyu,*** **2 Tbsp. *sake,*** and **3 Tbsp. *mirin*** and continue to cook for 6 to 7 minutes. Mix in **1/2 cup shaved bonito** and turn off heat.

■ Hijiki or arame — Dried hijiki or arame seaweed

A. Rinse **2 oz. *hijiki*** in a fine-mesh strainer under cold running water. In 3 times the amount of warm water, soak for 10 to 15 minutes. Remove *hijiki* with a tea strainer. (Sand and pebbles will sink to the bottom of the bowl.) Return to fine-mesh strainer and drain off excess water. Grate **2 oz. carrots** into matchstick slivers. Dip **1 *age* puff** for 30 seconds in boiling water to release excess oil. Immerse in iced water, squeeze out excess water, and cut into matchstick slivers. Place **1/3 block hard *tofu*** in a heated skillet and mash with a spatula. Let it simmer in its own water until reduced to small crumbs. Snap the ends off **5 green beans** and place in boiling water for 1 to 2 minutes. Immerse in iced water, drain, and cut into 1/2-inch-long pieces.

B. In a heated skillet, saute **2 Tbsp. sesame oil,** *hijiki,* carrots, *age,* and *tofu* (all completely drained of water). When ingredients have acquired a shiny appearance, add **1 cup *dashijiru*, 3 Tbsp. *shoyu*, 2 Tbsp. *sake*,** and **2 Tbsp. *mirin*.** Reduce heat to low and cook, stirring frequently, until liquid has been absorbed. Turn off heat and add green beans.

C. Place B in a serving dish, sprinkle with **1 tsp. lightly sauteed white sesame seeds.** If you like, add **seven-taste pepper** to taste.

■ Okara — Soybean mash

A. Place **1 lb. *okara*** in a cloth sack with a tight weave. Place in a bowl and slowly allow cold water to flow through the bag for about 30 minutes. Completely wring out the bag to remove all excess water. Peel **2 oz. burdock,** shave with a grater, and soak to remove *aku.* Peel and dice **2 oz. carrots.** Soak **2 oz. *shiitake*** **mushrooms** until soft, squeeze out excess water, remove stems and cut into matchstick slivers (save the water to use as *dashijiru*). Cut **3 oz. chicken breast** into 1/2-inch squares and marinate with **1/2 tsp. sesame oil.**

B. In a heated skillet, saute burdock and carrots with **2 Tbsp. sesame oil** until soft and add the chicken. Continue to saute 1 to 2 minutes. Add the *okara* (water completely squeezed out) and *shiitake* mushrooms and saute for an additional 1 to 2 minutes. Add **1 cup *dashijiru*** and cook for about 5 minutes. Add **3 Tbsp. *mirin*, 1 tsp. sugar,** and **3 Tbsp. *shoyu*** and mix.

C. Lower the heat to low and cook until all liquid is absorbed. Turn off heat. Add **4 chopped scallions** and **1 Tbsp. white sesame seeds.** Mix and serve.

■ Hijiki to daizu — Dried hijiki and soybeans

A. Wash **1 cup soybeans** 2 to 3 times and soak in 3 times the amount of water overnight and drain. In a cooking pot, add soybeans and 3 times the amount fresh water. Bring to a boil over high heat. When it reaches a boil reduce the heat to medium, and let simmer until soft. Save the cooking water. Rinse **1 oz. *hijiki*** in a fine-mesh strainer under cold running water. Soak in 3 times the amount of warm water for 10 to 15 minutes. Remove *hijiki* with a fine-mesh strainer (sand and pebbles will sink to the bottom of the bowl). Return to fine-mesh strainer and drain off excess water. Dip **1 *age* puff** in boiling water for 30 seconds to release oil. Immerse in iced water, squeeze out excess water, and cut into matchstick slivers. Soak **4 *shiitake* mushrooms** until soft and cut into slivers (save the water for *dashijiru*).

B. In a heated skillet over high heat add **2 Tbsp. vegetable oil.** Saute *hijiki* until shiny in appearance. Add *shiitake* and saute 2 to 3 minutes. If you like, you can add **diced chicken** to this recipe.

C. In a cooking pot, boil **1 1/2 cups of the water used to cook the soybeans, 4 Tbsp. *shoyu,* 2 Tbsp. sugar,** and **2 Tbsp. *mirin.*** When boiling, add soybeans, reduce heat, and cook 15 minutes over very low heat.

■ Konnyaku to gobo — Yam cake and burdock

A. In a cooking pot, place **1 cup *itokonnyaku*** (yam cake noodles) into cold water and bring to a boil, then remove. Rough chop and shake off excess water. Peel and shave **3 oz. burdock** with a grater, soak for 10 minutes to remove *aku* and drain.

B. In a heated skillet add **1 Tbsp. sesame oil** and saute A over high heat for 3 minutes. Add **3 Tbsp. *shoyu,* 2 Tbsp. *mirin,*** and **1 Tbsp. sugar.** Reduce heat to low and continue to cook until all liquid is absorbed. Turn off heat.

C. Mix in **1 Tbsp. sauteed white sesame seeds.** If you like it spicy, flavor the sesame seeds with **seven-taste pepper** while they are sauteing.

■ Kabu no yawarakani — Soft cooked turnips

A. Peel **1 lb. (tangerine size) turnip.** In a cooking pot, immerse in water and boil for 15 minutes. In another pot place **1/2 oz. *dashikombu*** on the bottom of the pan and add **2 1/2 cups *dashijiru,* 2 Tbsp. sake, 1 Tbsp. *mirin,* 1 tsp. sugar, 2 tsp. *shoyu,*** and **1/4 tsp. salt.** Add turnips, cover, and cook over medium heat until they can easily be pierced with a chopstick.

B. Serve in individual dishes. Garnish with **1/3 tsp. (premixed) Japanese mustard** for each serving. The *kombu* can be sliced and served as a side dish.

■ Nasu no misoni — Eggplant flavored with miso

A. Random-peel **1/2 lb. Japanese eggplant** and with a fork or toothpick poke about 20 holes in each. Remove stems, cut into fourths, and cut each section into bite-sized triangular pieces. Deep-fry eggplant for 2 minutes in a deep pan of **vegetable oil** heated to 210° Fahrenheit. Remove with mesh strainer and drain on paper towel.

B. In a separate bowl mix **1/2 cup *dashijiru*, 3 Tbsp. *mirin*, 1 tsp. sugar, 1/3 cup *miso*** until dissolved.

C. Add **1 tsp. sesame oil** to a heated skillet. Add A & B. Reduce heat and slowly saute until the *miso* sauce completely coats the eggplant. Serve on individual plates. Garnish with sauteed **black sesame seeds** to taste.

■ Koyadofu no tamagoni — Freeze-dried tofu with soft scrambled egg

How to prepare freeze-dried tofu.

A. Cover **2 pieces of freeze-dried *tofu*** in a bowl with hot water (150° Fahrenheit). Place a plate that fits inside the bowl over the *tofu* to keep it from floating to the top, and soak until soft. Squeeze out excess water by compressing the *tofu* with your hands like a sponge. Repeat 3 or 4 times.

B. Cut *tofu* in half horizontally then cut into matchstick slivers. In a heated skillet combine **1 1/2 cups *dashijiru*, 2 tsp. sugar, 1/2 tsp. salt,** and **2 tsp. *shoyu*.** Heat over high heat. Just before boiling, add *tofu*, cover with a lid that fits inside the pan. Reduce heat to medium and cook for 5 minutes. Add **2 beaten eggs.** Poke with chopsticks to make sure the egg reaches the bottom and gets cooked. Sprinkle with **1/2 oz. *funori*** (dried not soaked) and about **10 *kaiware* (Japanese daikon sprouts).**

Drop lid.

C. Reduce heat to very low and cover with a regular lid to steam until the egg is cooked. Place the entire pan in cold water so that the bottom is covered. As long as it is not burned this will prevent sticking (don't let the water run into the pan!). Cut into bite-sized pieces in the pan and remove with chopsticks.

■ Niyakko tofu — Soft scrambled eggs with tofu, spinach, and mushrooms

A. Dice **3/4 block soft** *tofu.* Remove the stems from **3 oz.** *shimeji* **mushrooms** and tear into bite-size pieces. Wash **7 or 8 chrysanthemum leaves or spinach leaves** and cut into 1-inch pieces. Chop **1 scallion.**

B. In a heated skillet, combine **2 cups** *dashijiru,* **3 Tbsp.** *shoyu,* **2 Tbsp.** *mirin,* and **1 tsp. sugar.** Cook over high heat until almost boiling. Just before reaching a boil, add *shimeji* mushrooms and *tofu.* Just before it reaches a second boil, add spinach. Pour **2 beaten eggs** over the mixture. Cook until egg is done but not hard.

C. Serve in individual dishes and garnish with chopped scallion and **1/4 sheet of shredded** *nori* to taste.

■ Age no fukuroni — Stuffed deep-fried tofu puffs

How to cut age puff.

A. Dip **4** *age* **puffs** in boiling water for 30 seconds to remove excess oil, squeeze out excess water, and cut in half horizontally. Gently lift cut edge open to make a pouch. Place **1/2 block hard** *tofu* in a heated skillet, mash and cook in its own water until all water is absorbed. Turn off heat. Boil **1 cup bean sprouts** in water for 30 seconds. Immerse in iced water and drain. Peel **2 oz. carrots** and cut into matchstick slivers with a grater. Soak **1 oz.** *sukikombu* until soft and drain.

B. Mix *tofu, sukikombu,* bean sprouts, and carrots with **1 tsp.** *shoyu* and stuff the pouches. Close pouches by fastening them shut with a toothpick.

How to fill age puff.

C. In a separate bowl, combine **2 cups** *dashijiru,* **2 Tbsp.** *shoyu,* a **few pinches salt, 3 Tbsp.** *mirin,* and **1 Tbsp.** *sake* and pour into cooking pot. Over a strong heat, add B and bring to a boil. Reduce heat to medium and cook 10 to 15 minutes.

■ Iridofu — Scrambled tofu flavored with miso

A. Soak **1 oz. black mushrooms** and cut into matchstick slivers. Soak **two** *shiitake* **mushrooms** and cut into slivers. Soak **1 oz.** *sukikombu.* Snap the tips off **4 green beans** and chop. Sliver-cut **1 oz. carrot** with grater.

B. In a heated skillet, add **1 tsp. sesame oil, 1/2 block hard** *tofu,* mash and saute over high heat until all water is absorbed. Add the rest of A (completely drained of water).

C. In a separate bowl, combine **2 Tbsp.** *mirin,* **1 Tbsp.** *miso,* **1/2 tsp.** *shoyu,* **1/2 cup** *dashijiru* and add to B and saute until all liquid is absorbed.

Tori niku — Chicken

■ Tori no terini — Chicken with vegetables

How to slice shiitake mushrooms.

A. Skin and debone **1/2 lb. chicken,** cut into bite-sized pieces. In a cooking pot place **1/2 block yam cake** into cold water and bring to a boil. Continue to boil 2 to 3 minutes, remove and dice. Soak **4** *shiitake* **mushrooms,** slant-cut slice horizontally. Peel and dice **3 oz. carrots.** Chop **3 oz. burdock** into 1/4-inch slices and soak for 10 minutes to remove *aku.* Snap the ends off **6 green beans,** place in boiling water 1 to 2 minutes. Immerse in iced water, drain, and slant cut.

B. In a heated skillet saute chicken in **2 tsp. sesame oil** over high heat. Add yam cake, *shiitake* mushrooms, burdock, and carrots, and continue to saute until completely shiny in appearance (coated with oil). Add **1 cup water** and bring to a boil. Remove *aku* and continue cooking 3 to 4 minutes. If you like you can add **1 clove of crushed garlic** or **1 dried red chili** (seeds removed) while cooking.

C. Add **5 Tbsp.** *shoyu,* **1 Tbsp. sugar, 1 Tbsp.** *mirin,* and **1 Tbsp.** *sake* to B. Cover, reduce heat to low, and continue to cook for 15 minutes. When all ingredients are soft, return heat to high and continue to cook until liquid is almost absorbed. Be careful not to burn it. Shake the pan occasionally. Turn off heat and add green beans.

■ Tori to zenmai no nitsuke — Poached chicken and dried osmond

A. Skin and debone **1/2 lb. chicken,** and cut into bite-sized pieces. Boil **2 oz. dried** *zenmai* (dried osmond) in twice the amount of water until soft. Turn off heat. Let cool naturally. When cool, rinse and drain, rough chop into large pieces. Briefly soak **2 pieces freeze-dried** *tofu* in a bowl of hot water (150° Fahrenheit) and squeeze like a sponge 2 to 3 times. Bring **1/2 block yam cake** to a boil from cold water and continue to boil 3 to 4 minutes. Remove and slice into thin strips. Peel **3 oz. carrots** and slice lengthwise into matchstick slivers.

B. In a heated skillet, add **2 Tbsp. sesame oil,** saute chicken, then add zenmai, yam cake, and carrots and continue to saute 3 to 4 minutes. Add enough water to cover ingredients. Then add **3 Tbsp.** *shoyu,* **2 Tbsp.** *sake,* and **2 tsp.** *mirin,* and bring to a second boil. Add freeze-dried *tofu* and simmer for 15 minutes over medium heat.

■ Tori no tsukuneni — Braised ground chicken croquettes

A. Skin, debone and mince (like hamburger) **1/2 lb. chicken.** Grind with mortar and pestle by pushing down (it won't grind if you push around in circles).

B. In a separate bowl, combine **2 Tbsp. flour, 1 tsp.** *shoyu,* and **1 Tbsp. fresh ginger juice** with A. Fold in **2 soaked and chopped** *shiitake* **mushrooms** and **2 chopped scallions.**

C. Coat your hands with a **small amount of vegetable oil** and make golf-ball-sized balls. Place in steamer and steam approximately 10 minutes until insides are cooked. Place in cooking pot with **1/2 cup** *dashijiru,* **2 Tbsp.** *sake,* **2 Tbsp.** *mirin,* **2 tsp.** *shoyu,* and **1 tsp. sugar.** Cook over medium heat for 10 minutes, shaking the pan occasionally. For the last few minutes add enough **asparagus** for color and flavor balance.

■ Tori to tofu no ageni — Fried and simmered chicken with tofu

A. Skin and debone **1/2 lb. chicken.** Add to boiling water for 30 seconds until it turns white. Remove and chop into bite-size pieces. In another pot over medium heat combine **1 cup water, 4 Tbsp.** *sake,* **1 tsp.** *mirin,* and **2 tsp.** *shoyu.* Add chicken, cook covered for 20 minutes. Place **1/2 block hard** *tofu* on flat woven drainer or paper towel to drain. (Place a weight equal to the weight of the *tofu* on top to facilitate draining.) Cut into 1-inch squares.

B. Remove chicken and drain. Mix **2 Tbsp. flour** and **2 Tbsp. cornstarch** and dust chicken with a brush. Combine **1/2 egg beaten, 2 Tbsp. cornstarch,** and **2 Tbsp. water** to make a batter. Coat chicken, and deep-fry in a deep skillet containing enough oil to completely cover the chicken (230° to 240° Fahrenheit). Premix **1 Tbsp. Japanese hot mustard.** Poke a hole in each piece of *tofu* with a chopstick and fill with mustard. Mix **2 Tbsp. flour** and **2 Tbsp. cornstarch** and use a brush to dust *tofu.* Deep-fry in oil 230° to 240° Fahrenheit until crunchy on the outside, light and crispy, golden in color. Drain on a paper towel.

C. In a cooking pot, add the water used to cook A's chicken plus enough additional water to equal 1 1/2 cups. Combine with **2 tsp. sugar, 2 Tbsp.** *shoyu,* **1 Tbsp.** *mirin,* and a few pinches of **salt** and bring to a boil. Add B's chicken and *tofu* and cook over medium heat for 3 to 4 minutes. Add **one handful of spinach** and cook for 1 minute. Place on individual plates. Serve the spinach on the side for color balance. Spoon a little cooking juice over all. Garnish with **chopped scallion** and **seven-taste pepper.**

■ Tori to shiitake no umeshuni — Simmered chicken and shiitake mushroom with plum wine sauce

Roll chicken...

...and serve.

A. Skin and debone **4 chicken thighs.** Pierce with a fork, and salt and pepper. Roll each piece into a roll skin side facing outward and tie with thread. Soak **8 *shiitake* mushrooms,** remove stems, and slant cut into 2 or 3 sections.

B. In a cooking pot, bring **1/2 cup plum wine** to a boil. Add chicken and *shiitake* mushrooms. When chicken turns white, add enough water to cover chicken, bring to a second boil, reduce heat to low, and cook until chicken can be easily pierced with a bamboo skewer. When cooked, add **3 Tbsp. *shoyu*** and continue to cook 2 to 3 minutes.

C. Let cool. Remove thread from chicken and slice into 1/2-inch sections. Place on individual plates with equal portions of *shiitake* mushrooms arranged decoratively. Spoon cooking juice over all.

■ Tori no hakusai maki — Chicken rolled in Chinese cabbage

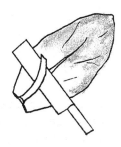

Remove center...

...add filling...

...roll and fasten.

A. Skin, debone, and mince **1/2 lb. chicken.** Boil **4 large Chinese cabbage leaves** for 7 to 8 minutes. Immerse in iced water and drain. Cut out the center hard stem section of each leaf.

B. Grate **1/2 oz. fresh ginger** and mix with A's chicken. Lay out Chinese cabbage leaves and add a spoonful of chicken mixture on each. Roll and fasten each with a toothpick.

C. In a cooking pot combine **2 cups *dashijiru*, 2 Tbsp. *shoyu*, 1/4 tsp. salt, 3 Tbsp. *mirin*,** and cabbage leaves. Cover and cook over high heat for 15 minutes.

Gyu niku — Beef

- Niku jaga — Simmered beef with potatoes

    A. Cut **1/2 lb. sliced beef** into bite-size pieces. Peel **1 lb. potato** and cut into bite-size pieces and soak. Peel **1/2 lb. carrots,** cut into 1-inch sections, and trim with a rolling cut. Rough chop **1/4 lb. onion.** Bring **1/2 lb. yam cake noodles** to a boil from cold water and continue to boil 3 to 4 minutes. Rinse and rough chop.

    B. In a heated cooking pot, saute beef in **2 1/2 Tbsp. sesame oil** until the beef changes to a brown color. Add onions, potatoes, and carrots. Saute 5 minutes. Cover with enough hot water to submerge all ingredients and bring to a boil. Reduce heat to low and cook to release *aku.* Remove *aku* and add **6 Tbsp. *shoyu,* 2 1/2 Tbsp. sugar, 1 Tbsp. *mirin,*** and **1 Tbsp. *sake.*** Continue to cook 15 to 20 minutes. If you wish, add **1 clove of crushed garlic** or **1 dried chili** (seeds removed) while sauteing.

- Gyuniku no yasai maki — Simmered beef and vegetable rolls

    A. Slice **1/2 lb. beef** and marinate in **1 Tbsp. *sake,* 1 tsp. *mirin,*** and a **pinch of salt and pepper** for 10 minutes to create an undertaste. Peel **1/4 lb. carrots,** cut into 2-inch sections, and quarter lengthwise. Cut **1 medium-sized bell pepper** in half, remove seeds, and cut lengthwise into 1/2-inch-wide slivers.

Add vegetables...

    B. Lay out beef slices. Place carrots and bell pepper horizontally at one end and roll. Fasten with a toothpick. Brush with **cornstarch** and pat off excess. Heat **5 Tbsp. vegetable oil** in a skillet over high heat. Add the rolls, being careful not to burn them. Roll them until cornstarch batter becomes crunchy. Drain on paper towels.

...roll and fasten.

    C. In another cooking pot combine **4 Tbsp. *shoyu,* 5 Tbsp. *mirin,* 1/2 cup *dashijiru,*** and **1 dried red chili,** crushed (seeds removed). Bring to a boil. Add B and bring to a second boil. Reduce heat to medium and cover. Shake pan occasionally. Cook for 6 to 7 minutes. Serve on individual plates, cut each roll in half horizontally, and stand the pieces on end.

- Gyuniku to goboni — Braised beef with burdock

    A. Peel **1/4 lb. burdock** and cut into thin slant-cut slices. Soak 10 minutes to remove *aku.* Thin slice **1/2 oz. ginger.** Slice **1/2 lb. beef** and cut into matchstick slivers. Marinate beef in **2 Tbsp. *sake*** for 10 minutes.

    B. Drain the burdock and boil in just enough fresh water to cover. Boil until soft. When soft, add A's ginger with **1 Tbsp.** *sake,* **5 Tbsp.** *shoyu,* and **2 Tbsp. sugar.** Return to a boil. Add beef, reduce heat to low, and continue cooking until liquid is absorbed (be careful not to burn).

C. Serve on individual plates. Garnish with **1 tsp. sauteed white sesame seeds or chopped scallion,** and **seven-taste pepper.**

Buta niku — Pork

- Gomoku mame — Simmered pork with diced vegetables and soybeans

    A. Wash **2/3 cup soybeans** 2 to 3 times. In 3 times the amount of water, soak overnight and drain. In a cooking pot, boil the soybeans over low heat until soft and drain.

    B. Cut **1/4 lb. pork** into bite-sized pieces. Marinate in **1 Tbsp.** *shoyu* for a few minutes. Peel and dice **2 oz. carrots.** Peel, dice, and soak **2 oz. burdock.** Dice **1/2 block yam cake.**

    C. Combine B and A with **2 Tbsp.** *shoyu,* **1 Tbsp. sugar,** and **2 Tbsp.** *mirin.* Cook over medium heat until soft. If you wish, you can add **1 clove of fresh crushed garlic.**

- Buta to daikon no nikomi — Pork sauteed and simmered with Japanese white radish

    A. Dice **1/2 lb. pork** and marinate in **1 Tbsp.** *shoyu* and **1 Tbsp.** *sake.* Peel **1 lb.** *daikon,* cut into bite-size pieces, and trim with a rolling cut. Slice **4 scallions** into 1-inch-long pieces. Slice **1 oz. ginger** into matchstick slivers.

    B. In a heated skillet, saute scallions and ginger in **2 Tbsp. sesame oil** for 30 seconds, add pork and saute until color changes, then add *daikon* and saute 3 minutes.

    C. In a separate bowl mix **1 Tbsp.** *shoyu,* **1 Tbsp. sugar,** and **1 Tbsp.** *miso* and add to B. Continue to saute for 2 to 3 minutes. Then add **1 cup of hot water** and a **few pinches of pepper.** Cover and simmer over medium heat until *daikon* is soft. (If the liquid is absorbed before *daikon* is soft, add a little more hot water.) Cook for about 15 minutes.

■ Buta no shoyuni — Simmered pork and quail egg flavored with soy sauce

A. Dice **1 lb. pork,** place in cooking pot with **4 cups water,** and bring to a boil. When it reaches a boil, lower the heat to low, remove *aku* and cook until tender. Soak **5 *shiitake* mushrooms** and slice diagonally. Boil and peel **8 quail eggs.** (Chicken eggs can be substituted. Cook whole but section before serving.)

B. When pork is tender, add **1/2 cup *shoyu*, 1 Tbsp. *sake*, 2 Tbsp. *mirin*,** *shiitake* mushrooms, and quail eggs. Simmer over low heat for another 15 minutes. Shake the pan occasionally.

Sakana — Fish

■ Saba no misoni — Poached mackerel flavored with miso

How to remove fish smell

A. Rinse **1 mackerel (about 12 inches in length),** filet, and cut into 3 sections (see basic fish preparations in Chapter 4), remove small bones. Score the skin side once or twice with a knife. Arrange on *zaru* (basket plate) or any flat drainer skin side up. Lightly sprinkle with salt and let sit for 10 minutes. Pour boiling water over the fish followed immediately by cold water to rid the fish of any "fishy" odor.

B. In a flat-bottomed cooking pot boil **1 cup *dashijiru*, 2 Tbsp. *sake*, 2 Tbsp. sugar, 1 Tbsp. *mirin*,** and **2 tsp. vinegar.** Add the fish, being careful not to overlap the pieces. Sprinkle with **1 oz. fresh ginger** cut into matchstick slivers. Cover with drop lid that fits inside pot and lower the heat.

C. In a separate bowl mix **4 Tbsp. red *miso*,** 4 tsp. sugar, and **1/2 cup cooking broth** from B until dissolved. Add to B. Simmer over a low heat for 10 to 15 minutes, covered with a drop lid. Serve on individual plates. Spoon juice over all and garnish with **1 to 2 Tbsp. grated, squeezed *daikon*.**

■ Karei no nitsuke — Poached sole

A. Place **1 lb. (4 pieces) sole** on *zaru* (or any flat drainer), lightly sprinkle with salt, and let sit 10 minutes. Pour boiling water over fish followed immediately by cold water to rid the fish of any "fishy" odor.

B. In a flat-bottomed deep skillet boil **9 Tbsp. *dashijiru*, 3 Tbsp. *mirin*, 1 Tbsp. *sake*, 1 Tbsp. sugar,** and **3 Tbsp. *shoyu*.** Add the fish, laying each piece flat (be careful not to overlap). Sprinkle with **1 oz. sliced fresh ginger** cut into matchstick slivers. Bring to a second boil and reduce heat to medium. Cook 5 to 6 minutes, add **1 Tbsp. *shoyu*,** and continue to cook 5 to 6 more minutes.

C. Serve on individual plates. Arrange the fish with **a variety of *ohitashi*.** (For example **spinach** or **zucchini, snow peas, asparagus,** etc.) **One Tbsp. grated, squeezed *daikon*** can also be added to the side to balance color and taste. Any **white fish, snapper, butterfish, flounder,** etc., can be used in the recipe.

■ Samma no umeboshini — Poached Spanish mackerel flavored with pickled plum

A. Remove the heads from **4 whole 10-inch Spanish mackerel,** clean and rinse well, and cut in half. Slice **1 oz. fresh ginger** into matchstick slivers.

B. In a flat-bottomed skillet boil **5 Tbsp. *shoyu*, 2 Tbsp. *mirin*, 2 Tbsp. *sake*,** and **2 Tbsp. sugar.** Add fish, being careful not to overlap.

Preparing samma.

C. Add **1 cup *bancha* tea** (1 Tbsp. *bancha* or Japanese coarse brown tea will make 1 cup of brewed tea) to B and bring to a second boil. Reduce heat to low. Add **4 large, pitted *umezuke* (pickled plums).** Continue to poach fish, basting occasionally, for about 10 minutes until liquid is almost absorbed. Serve on individual plates. Arrange the *umezuke* and the fish with **1 Tbsp. grated, squeezed *daikon*** as a garnish on the side. Large sardines or small regular mackerel can be used for this recipe as well.

■ Tai rui no ageni — Deep-fried and poached snapper

A. Debone **1 lb. snapper** and cut into 1 x 2-inch pieces with skin on (scales removed). Dust with **flour** and tap off excess. In a heated skillet saute fish in **4 Tbsp. vegetable oil** on both sides until crunchy. Drain on paper towel.

B. In another cooking pot boil **3 Tbsp. *dashijiru*, 3 Tbsp. *shoyu*, 1 Tbsp. sugar, 1 Tbsp. *sake*,** and **1 Tbsp. *mirin*.** Add A and **1 oz. fresh ginger** sliced and cut into matchstick slivers. Reduce heat to medium and simmer 4 to 5 minutes.

C. Serve on individual plates, arranging the fish with any *ohitashi* and/or **grated, squeezed *daikon*.**

■ Ika no shoyuni — Poached squid flavored with soy sauce

A. Pull the legs out of **8 squid** (6 inches long) and wash thoroughly. Remove head and bones, but leave skin intact. Peel **2/3 lb. *daikon*,** halve lengthwise, and cut into half-moon slices 1/2-inch wide. In a cooking pot, add twice the amount of water as volume of the *daikon* (water used to wash rice is recommended but plain water will suffice). Boil the *daikon,* until it can be easily pierced with a chopstick. Drain and let sit in fresh water for 10 minutes.

B. In a cooking pot boil **1 Tbsp. *shoyu*, 1/2 cup *dashijiru*, 1 Tbsp. *mirin*,** and **1 Tbsp. sugar.** Add *daikon* and continue to boil for 2 to 3 minutes. Add squid and **1 oz. fresh ginger,** sliced and cut into matchstick slivers. Continue to cook 5 to 6 minutes.

C. Serve on individual plates, spooning cooking juice over all.

■ Maguro no yudoshi — Fresh tuna flavored with vinegar

A. Cut **1/2 lb. red tuna** into 1-inch squares. Peel **2 oz. *daikon*** and **2 oz. carrots** and cut into long matchstick slivers. Cut **4 scallions** into 1-inch pieces. Crush **one small dried red chili** (seeds removed).

B. In a cooking pot, combine **2 Tbsp. *shoyu*, 3 Tbsp. vinegar, 1/2 tsp. salt,** and **4 Tbsp. vegetable oil** and bring to boil over low heat. Then add *daikon,* carrots, and red chili. Stir, turn off heat, and let sit for 10 minutes.

C. In a separate pot add tuna to boiling water until it changes to white (about 1 minute). Drain on *zaru* (or any flat drainer) and add to B. Marinate for 5 to 6 minutes. (The tuna does not necessarily have to be completely cooked.)

Yakimono — Grilled Dishes (for dinner)

When I was chef at Domo Country Foods Restaurant, the most popular grilled dish on the menu was *teriyaki.* For Domo's *teriyaki* dishes I used marinades flavored with *shoyu, miso,* or *sakekasu* to create a variety of tastes with chicken, pork, beef, shrimp, clams, and fish. Because we have already discussed *teriyaki* in previous chapters, this chapter's explanation will be short.

Sometimes in Japanese restaurants here in the United States the chicken used in *teriyaki* is pre-boiled. When a customer places his order, the chicken is grilled just long enough to make grill lines on the outside. Marinades heavy with cornstarch, sugar, and *shoyu* are poured on top. Unfortunately, this is frequently the way of American-style *teriyaki* chicken. True *teriyaki* cannot be made so quickly. *Teriyaki* must marinate for half a day at least (one day is preferred). The meat is then seared on both sides and hung away from the heat to grill slowly for an additional two to three hours.

"*Teri*" means shiny. Foods cooked in this manner naturally have a shiny, glazed appearance. A gourmet magazine highlighted Domo's *teriyaki* as being authentic, cooked by original Japanese country cooking methods.

Yakimono cooking methods are the simplest and oldest form of cooking. For these recipes, a grilling net or skillet is used for convenience. Traditionally, however more time-consuming, meats were skewered on barbeque sticks and grilled slowly over an open fire. This is by far the most delicious. The outside is shiny and excess fats drip away. The following recipes follow a two-step procedure. First the marinade, followed by the cooking method. Once you understand the basic marinade, it can be adapted to suit many different recipes and ingredients.

If you have a busy schedule, you will find these *yakimono* recipes quick, easy, and health-ful. These dishes can be cooked by oven-broiling or over an open barbeque. If you are using your oven broiler, preheat the broiler for 5 to 6 minutes until hot and place the grilling net or broiler rack 3 to 4 inches from the heat. In some instances the distance varies and I will specify these cases individually.

If you are using a charcoal barbeque the heat's intensity is not controlled by using more or less charcoal. The distance between the coals and the grill is the most important factor. Using a strong fire at a distance is more desirable. When grilling, the juice can drip into the coals and ignite. Place the coals on one side and grill the meat over the empty space on the other side. Timing is very important. Time the rest of the dishes being served and coordinate the cooking durations appropriately.

Yakimono Recipes
(Each recipe serves 4 people)

Tori niku — Chicken

■ Tori no teriyaki — Chicken teriyaki

    A. Skin and debone **4 chicken thighs.** Grate **1/2 oz. fresh ginger.** In a bowl, combine **3 tsp. *mirin*, 1 Tbsp. *sake*, 2 Tbsp. *shoyu*,** and **chicken.** Marinate for 4 to 5 hours. If you like it hot, add **one dried red chili** (seeds removed).

    B. Oven broil method: Preheat broiler. Place marinated chicken in grilling net, meat side closest to the heat, and broil 3 to 4 inches away for 10 to 12 minutes. Turn and continue to broil the other side 7 to 8 minutes.

    C. Place the chicken in a heated skillet, cover with the marinade left over from A mixed with **1 Tbsp. *shoyu*, 1 tsp. *mirin*,** and **1/2 tsp. sugar,** and quickly turn off heat. Shake pan to coat the chicken. Serve on individual plates.

■ Tori no nabeteri — Pan-fried teriyaki chicken

A. Skin and debone **4 chicken thighs.** Score skin side, by making an X with a knife. Grate **1/2 oz. fresh ginger.**

B. In a heated skillet, rub one of the chicken skins over the bottom of the pan to oil it. Add chicken meat side down (do not overlap them). Cook covered on high heat for 5 minutes. Turn chicken and continue to cook covered for 7 to 8 minutes. Check to see if chicken is done by cutting with a knife and checking the inside. When done, blot excess fat with a paper towel.

C. In a small cup, combine **3 tsp. *mirin*, 1 Tbsp. *sake*, 3 Tbsp. *shoyu*, 1 tsp. sugar,** and **1/2 oz. ginger.** Add to B and quickly turn off heat. Shake pan to coat the chicken and serve on individual plates.

■ Tori no shottsuru yaki — Grilled chicken with fish sauce marinade

A. Skin **4 chicken thighs.** Make a slit in the flesh next to the bone but leave the bone intact. Score the other side (skin side) with 2 or 3 cuts. In a large bowl, mix **3 Tbsp. fish sauce, 2 Tbsp. lime juice, 1/3 tsp. pepper** and marinate chicken 4 to 5 hours.

B. Oven broil method: Preheat broiler. Place chicken in grilling net, skin side closest to the heat. Broil 3 to 4 inches from heat for 10 to 12 minutes. Turn and continue broiling 7 to 8 minutes.

C. With a mortar and pestle, crush **1 clove garlic, 2 small dried red chilis** (seeds removed), **2 chopped scallions, 2 Tbsp. lime juice,** and **2 Tbsp. fish sauce.** Use as a dip sauce. This sauce will keep refrigerated for one week.

■ Tori no miso zuke yaki — Grilled chicken with miso marinade

A. Skin and debone **4 chicken thighs.** Mix **1 lb. white *miso*, 4 Tbsp. *mirin*,** and **5 Tbsp. *sake*** and marinate chicken 1 to 3 days. Wrap chicken individually in gauze.

B. Remove chicken from marinade and remove gauze. Rinse chicken in **4 Tbsp. *mirin*, 4 Tbsp. *sake*,** and **2 Tbsp. *shoyu*** to remove excess *miso.*

C. Oven broil method: Preheat broiler, place chicken in grilling net, skin side closest to the heat and broil 3 to 4 inches from heat for 10 to 12 minutes. Turn and continue to broil 7 to 8 minutes. When cooked, cut into bite-sized pieces and serve on individual plates. A's *miso* can be re-used 3 to 4 times.

Gyu niku — Beef

- Usu giri gyuniku no teriyaki — Sliced beef teriyaki

    A. Thinly slice **1 lb. beef** (it is easier to cut if slightly frozen).

    B. Mix **3 Tbsp.** *sake*, **2 Tbsp.** *mirin*, **1 Tbsp. sugar**, **3 Tbsp.** *shoyu*, **1 Tbsp. sesame oil**, and **1 tsp. grated garlic** and marinate beef for 7 to 8 hours.

    C. In a separate bowl combine **1/2 cup** *shoyu*, **5 Tbsp.** *mirin*, **4 Tbsp.** *sake*, **1 clove of garlic** (crushed), and **1/2 tsp. grated fresh ginger.** If you like a sweeter taste add **1 Tbsp. sugar.** Pour into a small heated cooking pot, stir and quickly remove from heat. This makes a *teriyaki* sauce. Add **a few drops of sesame oil** to a heated skillet and saute beef one piece at a time (laid flat) front and back and move to the side of the pan until all slices are cooked.

    D. Spoon *teriyaki* sauce over the meat and serve on individual plates.

- Gyuniku no miso zuke yaki — Grilled beef with miso marinade

    A. Cut **1 lb. beef** into 1/2-inch-wide slices or prepare whole as one steak. Marinate for 15 minutes in **4 Tbsp.** *sake.*

    B. In a large bowl combine **1 lb. red** *miso*, **1 Tbsp. sugar**, **4 Tbsp.** *mirin*, **3 Tbsp.** *sake*, and **1 crushed and dried red chili** (seeds removed). Add beef wrapped in gauze and marinate for 2 to 3 days.

    C. Oven broil method: Remove beef and unwrap gauze. Place beef in grilling net. Preheat broiler and broil each side 3 to 4 minutes 3 to 4 inches from the heat. If the steak is cooked whole, slice thin and serve on individual plates.

    Miso marinade can be reused 3 or 4 times. Store in the refrigerator.

- Gyuniku no nabeteri — Pan-fried beef teriyaki

    A. Salt and pepper both sides of **4 beef steaks** and marinate in **2 Tbsp.** *sake* for 10 minutes. In a separate bowl combine **2 Tbsp.** *shoyu*, **2 Tbsp.** *mirin*, and **1 Tbsp.** *sake* for each steak.

    B. In a heated skillet saute **one crushed and chopped clove of garlic** in a **few drops of sesame oil.** Move garlic to the side of the pan and add beef. Saute on both sides to your taste (rare, medium rare, etc.). Cover with A's juice, turn off heat, shake pan to coat the beef, and remove. Be careful not to burn.

■ Gyuniku no teriyaki — Beef teriyaki

A. Marinate **4 beef steaks** in **2 Tbsp.** *sake,* **1 Tbsp.** *shoyu,* **1 Tbsp.** *mirin,* and **1/4 tsp. pepper** for each steak. Marinate for 10 minutes.

B. Oven broil method: Preheat broiler. Place steak in a grilling net and broil 3 to 4 inches from the heat for 5 to 6 minutes per side to suit your taste.

C. In a separate bowl, mix **2 Tbsp.** *shoyu,* **2 Tbsp.** *mirin,* **1 Tbsp.** *sake,* **1/2 tsp. fresh grated ginger,** and **1/3 tsp. grated garlic** (optional). In a heated skillet, combine beef with mixture. Turn off heat and shake pan to coat the beef.

Serve on individual plates.

Variety of teriyaki.

Buta niku — Pork

■ Butaniku no nabeteri — Pan-fried pork teriyaki

    A. Score the fat on **4 pork chops** and marinate in **2 tsp.** *sake* for 10 minutes.

    B. In a separate bowl mix **3 Tbsp.** *shoyu,* **3 Tbsp.** *mirin,* **1 Tbsp.** *sake,* and **1 Tbsp. grated ginger.**

    C. In a heated skillet, brown pork chops on both sides in **2 tsp. vegetable oil.** Test by making a small slit with a knife and checking inside. When cooked, add B, turn off heat, and shake pan to coat the pork chops. Be careful not to burn.

    Serve on individual plates.

■ Butaniku no miso zuke yaki — Grilled pork with miso marinade

    A. Cut **4 pork chops** into 1/2-inch-wide slices or prepare whole as single chops. Marinate in **4 Tbsp.** *sake* for 15 minutes. In a large bowl combine **1 lb. red** *miso,* **1 Tbsp. sugar, 4 Tbsp.** *mirin,* **3 Tbsp.** *sake,* and **1 crushed and dried red chili** (seeds removed). Place pork wrapped in gauze in the marinade, cover, and refrigerate for 2 to 4 days.

    B. Oven broil method: Preheat broiler. Remove pork from *miso* and place in grilling net. Broil 3 to 4 inches from the heat, the first side 6 to 7 minutes, turn and continue to broil 4 to 5 minutes. Make sure the pork chops are well done.

■ Butaniku no karashiyaki — Grilled pork with mustard marinade

    A. Score the fat on **4 pork chops** and marinate in **2 Tbsp.** *sake,* **3 Tbsp.** *shoyu,* and **1 tsp. premixed Japanese mustard** for 15 minutes.

    B. Oven broil method: Broil pork chops 3 to 4 inches from heat in grilling net 6 to 7 minutes on the first side, 4 to 5 minutes on the other (depending on size). Make sure they are well done.

Gyokai rui — Fish and Shellfish

■ Ika no shioyaki — Grilled salted squid

Remove head and legs.

A. Remove the heads, legs, and bones from **8 squid** (about 10 inches in length) and wash well. Peel skin, salt lightly, and let sit 15 to 20 minutes. Blot excess water from squid with a paper towel.

B. Place in a heated skillet lightly greased with **sesame oil.** Sprinkle again with salt. When squid shrinks to half the size, turn off heat. Quickly add **1/3 tsp. fresh grated ginger** and **1/2 tsp. lime juice,** and serve on individual plates.

■ Ika no misoyaki — Grilled squid with miso marinade

A. Remove the heads, legs, and bones from **8 squid** (about 10 inches in length) and wash well. Peel skin, salt lightly, and let sit 15 to 20 minutes. In a separate bowl mix **1/2 lb. red *miso,* 3 Tbsp. *mirin,*** and **4 Tbsp. *sake*** to make marinade.

Place squid wrapped in gauze in the marinade, cover, and refrigerate for 1 to 3 days.

B. Remove squid from marinade and remove the gauze. Cook the squid in a heated skillet lightly greased with **sesame oil** over high heat until the squid shrinks to half its size. Turn off heat and serve on individual plates.

■ Ika no sakekasuyaki — Grilled squid with rice wine lees marinade

A. Remove the heads, legs, and bones from **8 squid** (about 10 inches in length) and wash well. Peel skin, salt lightly, and let sit 15 to 20 minutes. In a bowl mix **1/2 lb. rice wine lees, 3 oz. *miso,*** and **2 Tbsp. *shoyu*** to make marinade. Wrap squid in gauze and marinate for 2 to 3 days.

B. Remove squid from marinade and remove the gauze. Cook the squid in a heated skillet lightly greased with **sesame oil** over high heat until squid shrinks to half its size. Turn off heat and serve on individual plates.

■ Ika no tsumeyake — Grilled stuffed squid

A. Remove the heads, legs, and bones from **8 squid** (about 10 inches in length) and wash well. Peel skin, salt lightly, and let sit 15 to 20 minutes. Blot excess water with paper towel.

B. In a bowl mix **1 chopped scallion, 1/2 oz. finely chopped walnuts, 4 Tbsp. *miso,* and 1 Tbsp. sugar.** Separate into 8 equal portions and stuff squid 50% full. Fasten each with a toothpick.

C. In a heated skillet lightly greased with **sesame oil,** roll stuffed squid while cooking over high heat until the squid shrinks to 1 half its size. Drain on paper towel. Cut each piece in half diagonally and serve on individual plates.

■ Sake no teriyaki — Salmon teriyaki

A. Select **2 salmon steaks** or **4 salmon fillets.** (If you choose salmon steaks cut each in half and remove center bone.)

B. In a bowl, mix **4 Tbsp. *shoyu,* 2 Tbsp. *mirin,*** and **2 Tbsp. *sake.*** Add salmon and marinate for 2 to 3 hours. Turn a couple of times.

C. Preheat broiler. Place salmon in a grilling net and grill 3 to 4 inches from heat 7 to 8 minutes on one side, 5 to 6 minutes on the other. In a heated skillet combine B's leftover marinade with — premixed in a separate cup — **2 Tbsp. *shoyu,* 1 Tbsp. *mirin,* 1 Tbsp. *sake,*** and cook until it thickens. Place salmon on individual plates and spoon over with sauce. **Yellowtail or tuna** may also be used for this recipe.

■ Sake no misoyaki — Grilled salmon with miso marinade

A. Select **2 salmon steaks** or **4 salmon fillets.** (If you choose salmon steaks cut each in half and remove center bone.) In a bowl combine **1 lb. white *miso,* 1 Tbsp. sugar, 4 Tbsp. *mirin,* 2 Tbsp. *sake,*** and **1 dried red chili** (seeds removed). Wrap fillets in gauze and marinate skin side down for 1 to 3 days.

B. Remove salmon from *miso* marinade and remove the gauze. In a preheated broiler, place salmon in a grilling net (meat side out if fillets) and broil 3 to 4 inches from heat 7 to 8 minutes on one side, 5 to 6 minutes on the other. **Yellowtail or tuna** will also work for this recipe.

■ Sake no kasu zuke yaki — Grilled salmon with rice wine lees marinade

    A. Select **2 salmon steaks** or **4 salmon fillets.** (If you choose salmon steaks cut each in half and remove center bone.) In a bowl mix **1/2 lb. rice wine lees, 3 oz.** *miso,* and **2 Tbsp.** *shoyu* to make marinade. Wrap salmon in gauze and place skin side down in marinade for 2 to 4 days.

    B. Remove salmon from marinade and remove the gauze. Preheat broiler. Place salmon in a grilling net meat side out (if fillets) and broil 3 to 4 inches from heat 7 to 8 minutes on the first side. Turn and continue to broil 5 to 6 minutes. **Yellowtail** or **tuna** will also work for this recipe.

■ Sake no shioyaki — Grilled salted salmon

    A. Select **2 salmon steaks** or **4 salmon fillets.** (If you choose salmon steaks cut each in half and remove center bone.) Place in ziplock bags with **1/2 tsp. salt.** Shake and refrigerate for 1 to 2 days.

    B. Preheat broiler. Place salmon in a grilling net, meat side out, but do not rinse off salt. Broil 3 to 4 inches from the heat for 7 to 8 minutes, turn and continue to broil 5 to 6 minutes. If the taste requires more salt, add to taste. Serve individually with **1 Tbsp. grated squeezed** *daikon* flavored with a few drops of *shoyu* served on the side.

■ Ebi no teriyaki — Shrimp teriyaki

    A. Shell and de-vein **8 jumbo shrimp,** leaving tails intact.

    B. Place shrimp in grilling net and hold the handles tightly so the shrimp don't curl while cooking. Preheat broiler and broil 3 to 4 inches from heat on both sides 1 to 2 minutes.

    C. Mix **2 Tbsp.** *shoyu,* **2 Tbsp.** *mirin,* **1 tsp. sugar, 1 Tbsp.** *sake* to make a *teriyaki* sauce. Combine shrimp and sauce in a heated skillet. Shake pan to coat the shrimp and turn off heat. Serve on individual plates and sprinkle with **seven-taste pepper** (optional).

■ Ebi no shioyaki — Grilled salted shrimp

    A. Shell and de-vein **8 jumbo shrimp,** leaving tails intact.

    B. Place in a grilling net, hold the handles tightly so the shrimp don't curl while cooking, and sprinkle with salt. Preheat broiler and broil shrimp 3 to 4 inches from the heat for 1 to 2 minutes on each side.

    C. Serve on individual plates, garnished with a squeeze of lime.

■ Ebi no gyunikumaki — Beef roll with shrimp

A. Shell and de-vein **8 jumbo shrimp,** leaving tails intact.

B. Roll shrimp inside **8 thin slices of beef** and fasten with a toothpick. In a separate bowl, combine **1/2 oz. fresh ginger** cut into matchstick slivers, **2 Tbsp.** *shoyu,* **2 Tbsp.** *mirin,* **1 Tbsp.** *sake,* and **1 tsp. sugar.**

C. In a heated skillet, saute ginger in **1 tsp. sesame oil** and add beef and shrimp rolls. Saute 4 to 5 minutes (shaking the pan). Add B's sauce and turn off heat. Continue to shake the pan to coat the rolls. Serve on individual plates.

■ Hotate no teriyaki — Scallop teriyaki

A. Rinse and drain **16 large scallops.**

B. In a heated skillet, add scallops, cover and steam.

C. In a separate bowl, mix **2 Tbsp.** *shoyu,* **3 Tbsp.** *mirin,* **1 Tbsp.** *sake,* and **1 tsp. sugar.** Add to B and turn off heat. Shake pan to coat the scallops. Serve on individual plates.

Shell cooking.

■ Murugai teriyaki — Green-lipped mussel teriyaki

A. Soak **16 unopened mussels** in lightly salted water 1 to 2 minutes. The sand will be released naturally. (You may also use half-shelled frozen green-lipped mussels.) When the mussels open, remove them from the shell by cutting the adductor.

B. In a heated skillet, brush mussels (without shells) with **sesame oil** and saute. In a separate bowl, premix **2 Tbsp.** *shoyu,* **3 Tbsp.** *mirin,* **1 Tbsp.** *sake,* and **1 tsp. sugar.** Add sauce and turn off heat. Shake pan to coat the mussels. Be careful not to burn. On individual plates, arrange original mussel shells and replace seasoned mussels. Spoon sauce over all.

■ Maguro no teriyaki — Red tuna teriyaki

A. Cut **1 lb. fresh red tuna** into 4 pieces (1/4 lb. per serving). For each piece, mix **1 tsp.** *shoyu,* **1 tsp.** *sake,* and **1 tsp.** *mirin,* add tuna and let marinate for 10 minutes. In a separate bowl, mix **2 Tbsp.** *shoyu,* **3 Tbsp.** *mirin,* **1 Tbsp.** *sake,* and **1 tsp. sugar.**

B. Preheat broiler. Place tuna in a grilling net and broil 3 to 4 inches from the heat for 4 to 5 minutes. Turn and continue to broil 2 to 3 minutes.

C. In a heated skillet combine tuna and A's sauce. Turn off heat. Shake pan to coat the tuna and serve on individual plates. If the tuna is fresh, it is all right to serve rare.

■ Maguro no suyaki — Pan-fried red tuna

A. Cut **1 lb. fresh red tuna** into 4 pieces (1/4 lb. per serving), **salt** and **pepper** both sides and roll in **cornstarch.** Pat off excess.

B. Grill the tuna in a heated skillet with **1 tsp. vegetable oil** on both sides for 30 seconds to 1 minute. If the tuna is fresh, rare is fine.

C. In a separate bowl mix **4 Tbsp.** *shoyu,* **3 Tbsp. lime juice,** and **2 Tbsp.** *mirin* to make a dip sauce. Serve on individual plates.

■ Masu no tsutsumiyaki — Wrapped baked trout

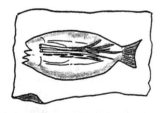

Fish wrapped for baking.

A. Clean **4 fresh trout** (see basic fish preparation in Chapter 4.) Marinate in **1 tsp. (per fish) fish sauce** for 10 to 20 minutes. Lightly crush **8 scallions** (by hitting). Slice **1/2 oz. fresh ginger** into matchstick slivers.

B. Open trout and lay in 2 scallions per fish and ginger. Close fish and wrap in aluminum foil, lightly greased with **vegetable oil.** Preheat broiler and place wrapped fish 15 inches from the heat for 15 to 20 minutes.

C. Serve on individual plates, cover with cooking juice and garnish with a squeeze of **lime.**

■ Tako no shogayaki — Grilled octopus with ginger marinade

    A. Cut **1/2 lb. octopus** into bite-size pieces and trim with a rolling cut. In a bowl mix **1 Tbsp. grated fresh ginger, 3 Tbsp.** *shoyu,* and **2 Tbsp.** *sake.* Marinate for 10 minutes.

    B. Oven broiler method: Preheat oven broiler. Place octopus in grilling net and broil 3 to 4 inches from the heat for 3 to 4 minutes on each side.

    C. Brush A's leftover marinade onto octopus while still in the net and continue to broil 2 to 3 minutes on each side. Cut each piece in half lengthwise and score the outside. Serve on individual plates.

Yasai — Vegetables

■ Yakinasu — Broiled eggplant

    A. Broil **4 Japanese eggplants** (approximately 10 inches in length) 3 to 4 inches from heat, turning occasionally until the skin is blistered all over and steam is released.

    B. Immerse in ice water, and quickly remove skin and stem. Tear into sections lengthwise. Place on individual plates.

    C. Garnish with **1/2 tsp. grated ginger, 2 tsp. shaved bonito, 2 tsp.** *shoyu,* **1/2 tsp.** *mirin,* and if you wish, **1 tsp. vinegar** per serving.

■ Yakinasu no dengaku — Broiled eggplant flavored with walnut miso

    A. Broil **4 Japanese eggplants** (approximately 10 inches in length) 3 to 4 inches from heat, turning occasionally until the skin is blistered all over and steam is released.

    B. Immerse in ice water, and quickly remove skin and stem. Tear into sections lengthwise. In a cooking pot mix **3 oz. red** *miso,* **1 1/2 Tbsp. sugar, 1 Tbsp.** *mirin,* and **1 Tbsp.** *sake.*

    Cook over low heat and stir gently for 7 to 10 minutes. Be careful not to burn. Crush **4 whole shelled walnuts** with mortar and pestle and fold in.

    C. Place eggplant on individual plates and spoon *miso* sauce in a line across the center. Garnish with **roasted white sesame seeds.**

■ Tofu no miso zuke yaki — Broiled tofu pickled in miso

A. Cut **1 block hard *tofu*** in half and place on a mesh drainer. Press out water with a weight the same as the *tofu*. Drain for 15 to 20 minutes.

B. In a bowl, combine **3/4 lb. *akamiso*, 1 Tbsp. sugar, 4 Tbsp. *mirin*,** and **2 Tbsp. *sake*** to make the marinade. Wrap *tofu* in gauze and place in marinade overnight.

C. Remove *tofu* and rinse lightly. Cut into bite-sized cubes and serve or cut into 1/2-inch slices and saute in a heated skillet lightly greased with **sesame oil** for 1 to 2 minutes.

■ Tofu no dengaku — Sauteed tofu with a variety of miso sauces

Tofu no dengaku.

A. Cut **1 block hard *tofu*** in half and place on a mesh drainer. Press out water with a weight the same as the *tofu*. Drain for 15 to 20 minutes.

B. Four varieties of *neri miso* (*miso* sauces)

1) White *neri miso* — In a small cooking pot combine **8 Tbsp. white miso, 2 Tbsp. *mirin*, 2 Tbsp. *dashijiru*, 2 Tbsp. sugar,** and **1 egg yolk.** Cook over low heat, stirring frequently, for 7 to 10 minutes.

2) Green *neri miso* — Combine 1/2 of the **white *miso* sauce** with 3 or 4 quickly boiled **spinach leaves.** Grind with mortar and pestle.

3) Red *neri miso* — In a small cooking pot combine **4 Tbsp. red *miso*, 4 Tbsp. sugar, 2 Tbsp. *mirin*, 2 Tbsp. *dashijiru*,** and **1 egg yolk.**

Cook over low heat, stirring frequently, for 7 to 10 minutes.

4) Plum *neri miso* — Combine 1/2 of the **red *miso* sauce** with **2 pitted umezuke** and grind with mortar and pestle.

C. In a heated skillet lightly greased with **sesame oil,** saute *tofu* over high heat on both sides until golden brown.

Serve on individual plates and top with the sauce of your choice. If you wish to barbeque, saute the *tofu* first in a pan on both sides. Then place them on skewers. (This way the pieces won't fall apart as easily on the grill.)

■ Gisei dofu — Tofu omelette

A. Separate **1 block hard *tofu*** into 5 or 6 pieces with your hands and add to boiling water. Boil for 5 to 6 minutes.

Drain by wrapping in cloth, twisting tight, and pushing out excess water with a wooden spoon. Grind **1 egg, 1/4 tsp. salt, 1 Tbsp. sugar,** and **2 tsp. *shoyu*** with a mortar and pestle.

B. Peel and dice **1 oz. carrots.** Soak **3 *shiitake* mushrooms,** and cut into slivers. Soak and rough chop **1/2 oz. *wakame.*** In a small cooking pot, combine carrots, mushrooms, and *wakame* with **5 Tbsp. *dashijiru*, 1 tsp. sugar,** and **2 pinches salt.** Bring to a boil, reduce the heat to low, and simmer until liquid is absorbed.

C. Soak **1/2 oz. *sukikombu*** and **1/2 oz. *funori*** until soft and mix into B. Mix B with A. In a heated skillet put **2 Tbsp. vegetable oil** to coat the bottom. Add all ingredients and flatten evenly with a spatula. Cover and cook for 15 minutes over extremely low heat. Pick up the pan (holding down the lid) and turn it completely over so the ingredients are in the lid. Put the pan down and slide the "omelette" back into it such that the "omelette" is upside down. Cover and continue to cook for 5 to 6 minutes. (Before you turn the omelette, grease the lid with a small amount of vegetable oil so it won't stick.) Turn off heat and let it cool. Cut into bite-sized pieces while it is still in the pan.

■ Yaki dofu — Fried tofu

A. Cut **1 block hard *tofu*** into 1/2-inch slices.

B. Choose one of the following to create a variety of dip sauces:

1) **3 Tbsp. grated *daikon*** and/or **1 Tbsp. grated ginger** and 2 **Tbsp. *shoyu***

2) **1 Tbsp. lime juice** and **1 Tbsp. *shoyu***

3) **1/3 tsp. Japanese hot mustard** (premixed) and **1 Tbsp. *shoyu***

4) **1 Tbsp. *miso*, 1 tsp. sesame seeds,** and **1 tsp. sugar** ground with mortar and pestle

C. Roll *tofu* slices in cornstarch and pat off excess. In a heated skillet, saute *tofu* in **1 Tbsp. vegetable oil** until golden brown on both sides. Serve hot with one of the above dip sauces. Garnish with **chopped scallion** or **shredded *nori*** to taste.

■ Age no hasamiyaki — Grilled soybean puffs

A. Dip **4 *age* puffs** in boiling water for 30 seconds to remove excess oil. Completely squeeze out the excess water. Cut in half and gently open. Mix **1 Tbsp. *miso*** with **2 chopped scallions** and spread equal amounts inside each 1/2 puff.

B. Preheat broiler. Place *age* in a grilling net and broil 3 to 4 inches from the heat until crunchy (be careful not to burn).

C. Garnish with **1 Tbsp. grated, squeezed *daikon*, 1 tsp. *shoyu*,** and a **fresh squeeze of lemon.**

How to prepare hasamiyaki.

■ Negi no dengaku — Grilled leek with miso paste

A. Use **1/2 lb. leek** (white part only); if it's tough, peel the outside layer. Cut into 1-inch pieces. Wash well, drain.

B. In a small cooking pot combine **3 Tbsp. white *miso*, 3 Tbsp. sugar,** and **1 Tbsp. *dashijiru*.** Heat slowly to make a paste. Mix in **1 Tbsp. lemon juice** and turn off heat.

C. Preheat broiler. Place leeks in grilling net and broil 3 to 4 inches from the heat on both sides until the skin starts to blister. This indicates the inside is sweet and ready to eat. Serve on individual plates. Top with ***miso* paste. Celery, bell pepper, zucchini,** and **eggplant** will also work with this recipe.

■ Serori no yaki bitashi — Grilled celery flavored with red chili and soy sauce

A. Separate **1 bunch celery hearts,** rinse and drain. In a separate bowl, mix **2 Tbsp. *shoyu*, 2 Tbsp. *sake*,** and **1 crushed dried red pepper** (seeds removed).

B. Preheat broiler. Place celery in grilling net and broil 3 to 4 inches from the heat on both sides until the skin begins to blister. While still hot, soak in A's sauce for 5 minutes.

C. Serve on individual plates. Spoon over with A's sauce.

Leeks and **bell peppers** will also work for this recipe.

Agemono and Itamemono — Deep-Fried and Sauteed Dishes

Dishes using oil for deep-frying or sauteeing are called *agemono* and *itamemono*. The most popular fried Japanese dish is, of course, *tempura*. Fried foods were only fairly recently introduced into the Japanese diet. A book written during the middle of the Edo period called *Yo Jo Kun* by Ikken Kaibara states that oily foods are not recommended for the Japanese digestive system. Fried or sauteed foods were introduced from China, but instead of using the large quantities of oil the Chinese recipes called for, the Japanese adapted the recipes, using only a small amount of oil, and then continued to prepare the dishes by traditional Japanese methods.

Even today, Japanese traditional country cooking does not incorporate deep-frying techniques. In this book I will introduce a few deep-fried recipes. While they do not have traditional roots, they are popular and delicious.

Deep-fried Foods

The most important consideration when deep-frying is the temperature of the oil. The amount of oil should be 3 times the volume of the foods being fried. Using a heavy cast-iron pan is recommended. Increase the temperature of the oil slowly over a low heat. To determine if the oil is ready, add one piece of the intended food to be fried. Watch to see if it sinks to the bottom and soon rises to the surface. This indicates the correct temperature for making *tempura*.

The temperature should be 220° to 230° Fahrenheit. Remember that when foods are added the temperature of the oil decreases, so it is important to control the temperature manually by adjusting the heat. Fry the ingredients for 1 to 2 minutes until crunchy then slowly remove from the oil and place gently on paper towels to drain. If you are deep-frying fish, place the fish meat side down on the paper towel to drain for about 30 seconds and serve while hot.

You may have experienced shrimp *tempura* at a Japanese restaurant in which small shrimp are breaded so heavily they appear twice their size. Sometimes I have found the batter to be raw on the inside, or the opposite where the batter is so crispy and dark it cuts your mouth. As a former restaurant owner I understand food costs, but I have noticed a few tricks that I cannot condone, such as pinching the joints of the shrimp to "stretch" it to look longer, or slicing a shrimp in half lengthwise and placing the pieces end-to-end before adding batter.

Very little batter is used at really good Japanese restaurants. The *tempura* is almost transparent, allowing you to visually appreciate the colors and shapes of the foods inside, as well as their delicious tastes.

If eating *tempura* has upset your stomach, the *tempura* was too oily. *Tempura* should be served correctly with a sauce and grated *daikon* and ginger to aid in digestion. Japanese gourmet diners enjoy *tempura* with salt and no sauce, but I don't think this is very good for your health.

Today in the United States there are many nice restaurants with mixed menus, such as American and Italian, or American and Mexican. More recently American and *tempura-teriyaki* restaurants have been introduced.

Basically, *tempura* is a dish that is battered and deep-fried, and *teriyaki* is a dish that is broiled and accompanied by a sauce. It sounds easy, but in Japan, a *tempura* chef needs more experience and training than even a *sushi* chef. It is a very difficult art. Anyone who has experienced real *tempura* knows there is a big difference between true *tempura* and a deep-fried imposter.

Foods that are sauteed in oil are called *itamemono*. The Japanese method for sauteing is completely different from the Chinese, which uses a great deal of oil and cornstarch as a thickener. The Japanese sauteing method requires very little oil, and the ingredients are cooked very quickly.

Agemono Recipes
(Each recipe serves 4 people.)

■ Wakasagi no karaage — Deep-fried smelt

A. Remove the heads and clean **12 smelt** about 6 inches long (please read basic fish preparation, Chapter 4). If the smelt are not firm, they are not fresh. Use only fresh smelt. Rinse and drain on *zaru* (or any flat drainer or paper towel). Add **salt** and **pepper** and let sit for 20 minutes.

B. In a deep skillet, heat **vegetable oil** slowly over low heat until it reaches 220° to 230° Fahrenheit. Stir occasionally with chopsticks. Roll the smelt in **flour** and tap off excess. Add only enough smelt at one time to cover 1/3 of the surface area of the pan so the temperature of the oil will not decrease.

C. Deep-fry until golden brown. Remove slowly and drain on paper towel, meat side down. Pit **4 or 5 *umezuke*** and grind with a mortar and pestle to make a dip sauce. Or, serve with a small dish of ***tentsuyu*** (*tempura* sauce) which will be explained in the next recipe, or **grated squeezed *daikon*** flavored with *shoyu*.

■ Karei no karaage — Deep-fried flounder

A. Select a **2-lb. whole, cleaned flounder** (1/2-lb. per serving). (Please see basic fish preparations in Chapter 4.) Make an incision in the center of the side of the fish lengthwise. Blot excess water with a paper towel, roll in flour, tap off excess, and let sit for one minute.

Slice flounder down the side.

B. In a small cooking pot, boil **1 cup *dashijiru*, 1/4 cup *mirin*, 1/4 cup *shoyu*,** and **1/2 cup shaved bonito** and turn off heat. Pour through strainer to remove bonito. This makes a *tempura* sauce called *tentsuyu*.

C. In a deep skillet, heat oil to 220° to 230° Fahrenheit. Holding the fish by the head, slide it in gently from the side. After the initial frying activity, turn the fish 2 to 3 times and fry until golden brown. Gently remove and drain on layers of paper towel. Serve on individual plates and with a small dish of B's *tempura* sauce. Garnish with **grated squeezed *daikon*** and **ginger** to taste.

■ Tori no tatsutaage — Deep-fried chicken flavored with soy sauce

    A. Skin, debone, and cut **1/2 lb. chicken** into bite-sized pieces. In a bowl, combine **1/2 cup** *shoyu,* **1/2 cup** *sake,* and **1 Tbsp. grated ginger** to make a marinade. Marinate chicken 15 to 20 minutes.

    B. Remove chicken from marinade and shake off excess. Just before frying roll in **cornstarch** and tap off excess. Gently add to oil 220° to 230° Fahrenheit. Fry until golden brown.

    C. Drain on paper towel and serve hot with premixed **Japanese hot mustard** as a dip. If the chicken cools it can be used for picnics or box lunches. **Turbot** or **halibut** can be substituted for this recipe.

■ Age dofu — Deep-fried tofu

    A. Cut **1 block soft** *tofu* into 1/2-inch squares and drain between layers of paper towels. Press to excellerate draining.

    B. Roll the *tofu* in **kuzuko (arrowroot starch).** If you do not have arrowroot starch, cornstarch will do. Tap off excess just before frying.

    C. Place in skillet of oil 230° to 240° Fahrenheit. Add the *tofu* individually, allowing it to sink to the bottom. When it returns to the surface turn the pieces over and continue frying 1 to 2 minutes on the other side. Remember to add only enough *tofu* at one time to cover 1/3 of the surface area of the pan or the temperature of the oil will decrease. Drain on paper towel.

    Serve in individual bowls. Spoon over with *tempura* **sauce** and place as garnishes next to the *tofu* **1 Tbsp. grated squeezed** *daikon* **and 1 Tbsp. grated ginger.**

■ Ebi to yasai no tempura — Shrimp and vegetable tempura

A. Peel, shell, and de-vein **12 jumbo shrimp** (1/2 lb.) leaving tails intact. Cut off the tips of the tails so they will not explode while frying (sometimes the tails fill with water). Score the inside of the shrimp, then turn the shrimp over and press down on each joint of the back side until it "pops." (This keeps the shrimp from curling as they are cooked.)

B. Slant cut **4 zucchini** into 1/2-inch sections. Separate **4 broccoli florets** into bite-sized pieces, stem area included.

Snap the tips off **4 green beans** and slant cut into 12 pieces. Slant cut **4 asparagus spears** into 12 2- to 3-inch pieces. Cut **3 oz. carrots** into long slivers with a grater. Rinse **8 mushrooms** — *shiitake, shimeji, enoki, or oyster* (whichever is fresh) — and cut away stem area that is hard or dirty. Towel dry.

C. Chill a flat-bottom dish in the refrigerator. Place **3 cups flour** on one side of the dish. On the other side slowly add **3 egg yolks** mixed with **3 cups cold water.** Do not mix the two sides together. A natural "dam" will form in the middle between them.

D. In a deep skillet, heat oil to 220° to 230° Fahrenheit. Start with the vegetables first. The broccoli and zucchini have already been cut into bite-sized pieces. Individually dip each one in the egg-water mixture. Then lightly touch the flour, back to the egg water, and then back to the flour again, turning until about 2/3 of the vegetable is covered with batter. For broccoli especially you do not need to coat the entire piece — leave the stem area uncovered. Place in the oil for about 30 seconds, turn, and continue to fry an additional 20 to 30 seconds. Use chopsticks to hold the rest of the vegetables a few at a time while you brush them in the egg-water solution and flour, and place them in the oil to fry. (Don't try to line them up in a row; a random order is more beautiful when finished and allows for more even cooking.) If you do not feel comfortable using chopsticks, use *yakitori* bamboo sticks to skewer the vegetables a few at a time.

E. Heat oil to 220° to 230° Fahrenheit. Hold each shrimp individually by the tail and cover with batter head first in the same manner as the vegetables. Dip the battered shrimp into the oil half-way and hold for 10 to 20 seconds then gently drop them all the way in. This keeps the shrimp from curling. Deep-fry until golden brown. Remove carefully and drain on paper towel.

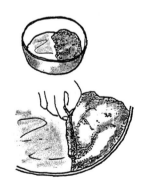

How to batter shrimp.

Snapper, butterfish, salmon, large deboned flounder, shark, orange roughy, grouper, sole, snapper, or **scallops** can be substituted for the shrimp or vegetables.

F. Place the *tempura* on decorative paper on top of individual plates. Add a spoonful of **grated squeezed *daikon*** and **ginger** and serve with ***tempura* sauce.**

Itamemono Recipes
(Each recipe serves 4 people.)

■ Takenoko, sukikombu, ninjin no itamemono — Sauteed bamboo shoots with sliced kelp and carrots

A. Cut **7 oz. slender bamboo shoots** into 1-inch-long matchstick slivers. Peel **4 oz. carrots** and grate into long slivers. Soak and slice **1 oz. *sukikombu.***

B. In a heated skillet saute **1 crushed dried red chili** (seeds removed) in **2 Tbsp. sesame oil** over high heat for 10 seconds. Add A, completely drained of excess water, and saute for 3 to 4 minutes. Add **2 Tbsp. *shoyu,* 2 Tbsp. *mirin,* 3 Tbsp. *dashijiru,*** and **a few pinches of salt.** Continue to saute for another 2 to 3 minutes. Turn off heat and let sit for 1 hour to allow the vegetables to absorb the marinade. This dish will store in the refrigerator for a few days.

Green beans and **asparagus** can be substituted in this recipe, and you can add **2 oz. diced chicken** if you wish.

■ Butaniku no shichimiitame — Sauteed pork flavored with seven-taste pepper and soy sauce

A. Dice **1/2 lb. pork roast** and marinate in **2 Tbsp. *sake*** for 15 minutes. Cut **1 rib celery** into 2-inch-long matchstick slivers. (**Carrots, bell pepper, green beans,** or **asparagus** can be substituted for this recipe.)

B. In a heated skillet saute pork in **2 tsp. sesame oil** over high heat for 3 to 4 minutes. Add celery and continue to saute for an additional 2 minutes.

C. Add **1 Tbsp. *sake,* 3 Tbsp. *shoyu,*** and **seven-taste pepper** to suit your taste. Turn off heat and serve. Garnish with **1 pitted *umezuke.***

■ Yasaiitame — Sauteed vegetables

In a heated skillet saute a combination of vegetables chosen from the chart below in **2 to 3 Tbsp. sesame oil** over high heat for 2 to 3 minutes. For a change of pace use **1/5 of a stick of butter** or **2 to 3 Tbsp. of olive oil.** While sauteing, season with **salt and pepper** or **1 to 2 Tbsp.** *shoyu* and **1 tsp. of** *mirin.* If you wish you may add **diced chicken.**

EXAMPLES OF VEGETABLES THAT COMPLEMENT ONE ANOTHER FOR ITAMEMONO RECIPES:

Bean sprouts and sliver cut asparagus — *moyashi to asuparagasu*

Sliced cabbage, bean sprouts, and slivered carrots — *kyabetsu, moyashi, ninjin*

Sliced onion and soaked *wakame* — *tamanegi to wakame*

Spinach and slivered carrots — *horenso to ninjin*

Mushrooms and soaked sliced kelp — *mashurumu to sukikombu*

Sliced bell pepper or green beans and shaved carrots — *piman or sayaingen to ninjin*

Chopped scallion and bean sprouts — *negi to moyashi*

Rapeseed flower or spinach and bean sprouts — *nanohana or horenso to moyashi*

Sliced zucchini and soaked sliced kelp — *zukini to sukikombu*

This concludes the section on basic dinner recipes. There is quite a variety to choose from. Select one dish as the main entree and two or three additional dishes as side dishes. For a regular everyday dinner at home, select one of the meat or fish recipes as the main dish and balance with one or two side dishes.

If the dinner meal is planned to be a *nabe* dinner (one pot cooking), the side dishes are selected to balance and offset the center pot. The *nabe* dishes detailed in the next *section are all* favorites with our hungry Nippon Kan students.

Nabemono — One-Pot Cooking

One of the most popular dinner dishes in Japan is called *nabemono.* Traditionally *nabemono* is eaten as the dinner meal except on *hare no hi,* when it can be eaten anytime.

Nabe ryori (one-pot cooking) is done in a large cast-iron or porcelain pot. This large pot is filled with different meats or fish and/or shellfish as the main ingredients, accompanied by *tofu,* yam cake, and a variety of vegetables to create a balance of taste, shape, and color.

The ingredients are stewed in broth seasoned with various combinations of *shoyu, miso, sakekasu* (rice wine lees), and salt. For the traditional farmer, life revolved around the *irori* (sunken hearth). A large cast-iron pot hung from the hook over the fire. A large plate filled with prepared meats and vegetables would be set beside the *irori.* As everyone sat down to eat, the meats and vegetables would be added to the pot, cooked, eaten, and the pot refilled until everyone had had their fill.

In my home town, if you were invited to eat at someone's home, the host would begin the meal by asking you to be the first to take from the pot. The phrase used was *"dozo agenasai,"* which directly translates to mean pick up or lift (in the command form). The more polite form in Japanese is *"O Agari kudasai."* This phrase originated from eating *nabe ryori,* but it has become a general request for a guest to begin eating.

Each locality has its own varieties of *nabe ryori*. *Nabe ryori* can be divided into basic categories according to the taste or flavoring of the soup stock. There are then various combinations of *gu* (solid ingredients). *Nabe ryori* dishes falling into the same general category will have slightly different flavors as they are influenced by what *gu* are added.

On the Japanese island of Honshu, in the northern part of Japan, on the border of Akita and Aomori Prefectures in the Hakkoda mountain range, lies Lake Towada National Park. This is the home of the Lake Towada National Science Museum. This is a sister museum to the Lake Ogawara Folk Art Museum. Both are owned by Mr. Yukio Sugimoto.

Occasionally I worked at this sister museum as well. I helped assemble the reptile, aquatic, and botanical displays still showing today. In the Lake Ogawara area, special hunting permits were issued to the local villagers just before winter to control certain wild game animals in the national park area. This was the season for giant flying squirrel, rabbit, pheasant, turtledove, and bear. Only at this particular time can game-meat *nabe* be found.

Just outside of Lake Ogawara lies the town of Gonohe. This town is famous for dishes made with horsemeat. Horsemeat *nabe* served with hot *sake* on a cold winter night warms the body. The town is also famous for its horsemeat *sashimi* (served raw, sliced thin with grated ginger, garlic, and *shoyu*). If this surprises you, I can also remember eating grasshoppers, sparrows, and whale meat. It was not because we didn't have enough to eat; these foods were part of a long Japanese tradition.

Nabe ryori are simple dishes that look impressive when served and are a good way to feed a lot of hungry mouths at one time. *Nabe ryori* is nutritionally well-balanced, with each ingredient supplying a different assortment of vitamins and minerals. Clean-up is also easy: only one pot and

the small dishes used to serve each individual.

Today this tradition may not be observed as much, but when I was a child, school groups — elementary through high school — companies, and neighborhood associations held outdoor cooking parties called *nabekko*. The root of this word is *nabe*, which, as we have been discussing, means cooking pot.

These *nabekko* or cooking parties were usually held in autumn. Everyone would gather by the riverside and make *kamado* (stone fireplaces) out of large river rocks. After the fires were started, fresh mushrooms were added to the pot along with fresh fish or meat and vegetables brought from home.

In Japan this type of fall day is called *akibare*, which translates to mean a beautiful autumn day under a clear blue sky. These *nabekko* were held after harvest so there were plenty of fresh foods and everyone had the time to enjoy them. The river supplied fresh water and a nice backdrop, but looking deeper the river had a meaning found in the roots of folk religion.

Traditionally, the young gathered by the river in a religious celebration and ate together from one pot to symbolize their appreciation of one another, the beauty of the river, and the fruits of the harvest. The river was used to wash the meats, fish, and vegetables — washing away the bad *ke* and preparing them for the feast.

I was in elementary school during the "baby boom" after WWII. My grade was divided into five classes of 50 students each. There was the plum class, cherry class, peach class, pinetree class, and bamboo class. There were other schools within 20 minutes' walking distance of mine that also had five classes of 50 students. There were a lot of children in Japan during that era! For an entire grade of 250 people to go on a hiking trip to the riverside was quite a production. Each class was divided into five or six smaller groups, with kids from the same neighborhoods put into the same groups. Each group would choose a leader. That leader was not necessarily chosen for his scholastic achievements; he was usually more of the "underground" type. I don't know why, but I was always picked to be group leader. I would plan the group's menu for the day and assign each kid ingredients to bring from home. At that time the river was clean enough to swim in and drink from, so the foods could be washed at the cooking sites, and the river water used for cooking.

The biggest test for the leader was to build the *kamado* out of river rocks and get the fire going. The leader's value was determined by how quickly he got the fire started. If the next group had already started cooking before your group got its fire started, it looked very bad. It was quite a nervous time for the leader!

As a reward for getting the fire started the leader was not responsible for cleaning the soot from the pot after it was used. All the kids learned to cook together, bringing ideas from home, ingrained from watching their mothers on a daily basis. These outings were educational as well as fun.

We were supervised by teachers and PTA staff, but they stayed a fair distance away, eating their own *nabe* dishes, drinking *sake,* and reminiscing about when they were down by the river trying to get a fire started. What? Teachers drinking *sake* in front of the students!? At that time it was a common and acceptable practice, not strange in the least.

In Japan the students were expected to stay after school to clean the classrooms. After we had finished we were required to let the teacher know. One day I went to the teacher's office to let him know we were done. Finding no one in the office, my natural assumption was that he was visiting the boarding quarters of the custodian couple who lived on the premises. When I arrived, the *shichirin* (clay *hibachi* grill) was ready for cooking. The *nabe* placed on top was

sending out delicious odors. The teachers were enjoying each other's company over a cup of *sake.* I can still remember the wonderful smells that permeated the room.

In those days two male teachers were required to stay at the school during the night along with the custodial couple. They were to guard the building and to be prepared in case of any student emergency. They were called *tochoku.* The custodial couple's boarding room was where the teachers met to relax. If I went to inform a teacher we had finished our duties, one of the teachers might say, "Oh, it's Gaku. Will you go buy some cigarettes for me?" Today this kind of request would cause big problems, but in those days there were no laws against it, and there was not a problem with juvenile smoking or drinking. The teachers commanded respect from the students and put a lot of effort into communicating and educating not only scholastically but morally. The students respected the teachers and considered tobacco and alcohol as something that adults did. We were well aware of the differences in our positions and never dreamed of partaking ourselves.

The riverside cooking parties were meant to be training in teamwork. Another test for the leader on the return hike home was to see how many bags one could carry, helping the girls that were too tired to carry them.

As a young adult I returned to that river with a good friend. Remembering my times as a child, we drank *sake* and rested and enjoyed the beauty of the area. What a feeling of freedom. From the mountains we gathered plenty of mountain vegetables and mushrooms. From the river we easily caught fish and eel with spears. Everything has changed over the last twenty years, but I still have my good memories from these times.

Nabe ryori is a source for happy times, smelling nice aromas, watching steam rise on a cold day, and blowing on the soup to cool it. These are memories I never want to let go of. Therefore I do a lot of *nabe* cooking at Nippon Kan.

> *The farther away*
> *your home town is,*
> *the more your thoughts*
> *return there.*

I feel this poem, written by a famous Japanese poet, is absolutely true.

This section will introduce the basics of *nabe ryori*. The standard amount of *dashijiru* or water used for these recipes is 5 cups. The amount of each flavoring depends on your individual tastes. Start with about 80% of the amounts given and taste. If it is not strong enough, add more. If it is too strong, dilute with more *dashijiru* or water.

It is traditional to cook and eat *nabe ryori* at the same time. If you have an electric burner or hot plate, place it on the dining table so you can cook and serve at the same time. An electric wok will not work for *nabe ryori;* it doesn't reach a high enough temperature.

We can separate *nabe ryori* into categories by how it is eaten and what base flavoring is used:

1. The *nabe* dish itself is not flavored (a dip sauce accompanies the dish)
2. *Shoyu* flavor base
3. *Miso* flavor base
4. Rice wine lees flavor base
5. *Sukiyaki nabe*

Traditionally, *nabe ryori* is cooked in a clay pot called a *donabe.* If you do not have a *donabe* a heavy pot will do. For the following recipes, the *nabe* pot is 8 to 10 inches in diameter and 3 to 4 inches deep.

It is customary for *nabemono* dishes to be cooked at the table. When you arrange the ingredients on the serving platter to bring to the table to be cooked, it looks like a great deal of food. After all the ingredients are cooked, however, there isn't as much as you might have thought. It is better to prepare a little extra. If you do have leftovers, they can easily be stored in plastic bags, refrigerated, and saved for other recipes.

Do not cook everything at once; add some of each a little at a time to ensure that the ingredients do not become overcooked. The actual cooking time is very short. If you use hard vegetables such as burdock, carrots, and potatoes, add them first because they need to be cooked longer. Greens such as chrysanthemum leaves are saved for last. Make sure you do not stir like a stew or soup. The ingredients should be arranged in sections.

Nabemono Recipes
(Each recipe serves 4 people.)

Nabemono with a dip sauce

- Yudofu — Tofu in hot water

How to cook yudofu.

A. In a *donabe* (if you do not have one, a flat pan at least 2 inches deep will do) soak **1 5-inch square piece of** *dashikombu* in **5 cups water** and **1/2 tsp. salt** for 1 hour.

B. In a bowl, mix **1/2 cup** *shoyu,* **1 1/2 cups** *dashijiru,* **2 tsp.** *mirin,* and **1/3 cup shaved bonito.** Place large cup and all into the center of the pan. Make sure the cup is tall enough that the rim will still be above the water level after the *gu* is added.

C. Boil A and add **1 block soft** *tofu,* cut into 1-inch cubes. (Add as much as will fit in the pan, but not the entire amount.) When the *tofu* starts to rise up it is ready to eat.

Individuals serve themselves from the *nabe,* picking up the *tofu* and dipping it in the center sauce. Garnish the sauce with **grated ginger, chopped** *nori,* and **chopped scallion** to suit your taste. Be careful not to overcook the *tofu;* it will harden. Reduce heat to very low to keep warm.

- Kaisen yudofu — Tofu and seafood casserole

A. Cut **1 block soft** *tofu* into 1-inch squares. Thoroughly wash **8 jumbo shrimp** (do not peel) and skewer them lengthwise on small skewers (*yakitori* sticks). Lightly rinse **8 jumbo scallops.** Soak and rough chop **1 oz.** *wakame.*

B. In a *donabe* boil **6 cups** *shiitake dashijiru* and add **shrimp, scallops,** and *wakame.* Remove *aku.* Add *tofu.* When the *tofu* begins to rise it is ready to eat. Reduce heat to very low to keep warm.

C. Combine in each individual serving bowl **2 Tbsp.** *shoyu,* **1 tsp.** *mirin,* and **1/2 tsp. lemon** or **lime juice** to make a dip sauce. Garnish with **chopped scallion, chopped** *nori,* and **grated ginger** or **grated squeezed** *daikon.* Individuals serve themselves from the *nabe.*

■ Niku yudofu — Tofu and meat casserole

A. Choose one or two of the following meats: Thinly slice **1/4 lb. beef** or **1/4 lb. pork;** or skin, debone, and thinly slice **1/4 lb. chicken.** (Freeze slightly so it is easier to cut into thin slices.) Cut **1 block soft *tofu*** into 1-inch squares. **Cut 1/4 lb. leeks** (white part only) into 1-inch match-stick slivers. Tear **6 Chinese cabbage leaves** into bite-size pieces.

B. In a *donabe,* boil **6 cups water.** Add meat(s) and cook for a few minutes until they change color. Remove *aku.* Add **1 large, pitted *umezuke,*** cabbage, and leeks. Then add *tofu.* Add as many pieces of *tofu* as can fit in the pan. As the ingredients cook down, add more.

Turn the heat down to very low to keep warm. Combine in individual small serving bowls, **2 Tbsp. *shoyu,* 1 tsp. *mirin,*** and **1/2 tsp. lemon** or **lime juice** to make a dip sauce.

Garnish with **chopped *nori,* chopped scallion,** and **grated ginger** or **grated squeezed *daikon. Umezuke,*** pitted and ground, can also be used as a garnish. Individuals serve themselves from the *nabe.*

■ Sankai yudofu — "Surf and turf" with tofu

A. **This recipe uses the same preparation as seafood and meat yudofu recipes, only halve the amounts of each.** In a *donabe* boil **7 cups of water.** Add your choice of meats and seafoods, *tofu,* and vegetables, **1 oz. soaked *sukikombu,* 1 oz. soaked *funori,*** and cook until *tofu* rises, then reduce heat to very low to keep warm. Be careful not to over-cook the *tofu.* **Snapper, cod,** or **salmon** cut into bite-sized pieces can be substituted for shrimp.

B. In individual small serving bowls, add to each **2 Tbsp. *shoyu,* 1 tsp. *mirin,*** and **1/2 tsp. lemon or lime juice** to make a dip sauce. Garnish with **chopped *nori,* chopped scallion,** and **grated ginger** or **grated squeezed *daikon.***

Umezuke, pitted and ground, can also be used as a garnish.

Individuals serve themselves from the *nabe.*

Nabemono with shoyu flavor base

■ Tori nabe — Chicken and vegetable casserole flavored with soy sauce

A. Skin and debone **1 lb. chicken** and cut into bite-size pieces. Slant cut **1/2 oz. ginger.** Fill a *donabe* 1/2 full with water and add chicken bones and ginger. Bring to a boil over high heat, reduce to medium heat, and simmer for 20 minutes. Remove *aku.* Turn off heat. This makes your soup stock.

B. Break **1/2 block hard *tofu*** into bite-size pieces with chopsticks. Salt your hands and rub over **1 package of yam cake noodles.** Rinse thoroughly and shake off excess water. Slice **1/2 lb. Chinese cabbage** into 2-inch sections.

Peel **2 oz. potato** and cut into bite-size pieces. Peel and slant cut **2 oz. carrots.** Remove the stems from **one handful of *enoki*** or ***shimeji* mushrooms** and tear into pieces with your fingers. Wash **1/4 lb. chrysanthemum leaves** or **spinach** and cut into 2-inch pieces. Peel and shave **1/4 lb. burdock.** Soak burdock shavings 15 minutes and remove *aku.* Arrange all ingredients decoratively on a large platter.

C. If you have a hot plate, set it up at the dinner table.

Place a *donabe* on the hot plate turned to high. Add A's soup stock plus burdock, potatoes, and carrots. Cook covered until potatoes are soft. Add chicken, yam cake noodles, *tofu,* and remaining vegetables. Arrange them beautifully in the pan by sections. (Save a portion of each item, so when the first batch is eaten you can replace it with more of the same.) Do not stir. Remove any *aku* and add **1/2 cup *shoyu*, 4 Tbsp. *sake*,** and **4 Tbsp. *mirin*.** Bring again to a boil then lower the heat to very low to keep warm. Individuals serve themselves from the *nabe.*

■ Buta nabe — Sliced pork and vegetable casserole flavored with soy sauce

A. Thinly slice **1 lb. pork roast** (slightly frozen is easier to slice) as thin as possible. Salt your hands and rub over **1 package of yam cake noodles.** Rinse thoroughly and shake off excess water. Slice **1/2 lb. Chinese cabbage** into 2-inch-long sections. Wash **1/4 lb. chrysanthemum leaves** or **spinach** cut into 2-inch-long pieces. Peel and shave **1/4 lb. burdock.**

Soak 15 minutes and remove *aku.* Break **1 block hard *tofu*** into bite-size pieces with chopsticks.

B. In a *donabe,* saute pork in **2 Tbsp. sesame oil** over high heat until color changes to white. Fill *nabe* 1/2 full with water and bring to a boil. Remove *aku*. Push the pork to the side of the *donabe* and add yam cake noodles, burdock, and *tofu*.

C. Add **1/2 cup *shoyu,* 3 Tbsp. *sake,* 3 Tbsp. *mirin,*** and bring to a second boil. Add cabbage and chrysanthemum leaves or spinach and reduce heat to very low to keep warm.

Individuals serve themselves.

Important tips: Do not add all of the *gu* ingredients at the same time; save some for second or third servings. The amounts of each *gu* ingredient can be adjusted to suit your taste. Once you have added the flavorings do not continue cooking for a long period; reduce heat to very low just to keep warm. Remember the flavorings can be adjusted to suit your taste.

■ Hikiniku dango nabe — Meatball and vegetable casserole flavored with soy sauce

A. In a mixing bowl, combine **3/4 lb. sliced, minced, or ground chicken or beef, 5 chopped scallions, 1/2 oz. minced ginger, 1/4 tsp. salt, 1/4 tsp. pepper,** and **1 egg.** Roll into bite-size balls.

B. Cut **3/4 lb. Chinese cabbage** into 2-inch sections, cut **1/2 lb. leeks** (white part only) into 2-inch matchstick slivers, thoroughly wash **1/4 lb. chrysanthemum** or **spinach leaves** and cut into 2-inch-long pieces, and soak and rough chop **1 oz. *wakame.*** You can also add **1/2 block** *tofu* and **1/2 package yam cake noodles.**

Fill a *donabe* 1/2 full with water and bring to a boil. Add the chicken or beef balls. Boil until *aku* appears. Remove *aku*. Add **1/2 cup *shoyu,* 4 Tbsp. *mirin,*** and **4 Tbsp. *sake.***

Just before second boil, add vegetables, *tofu,* and yam cake noodles and bring to a boil. Lower heat to very low to keep warm. Individuals serve themselves.

■ Tsumire nabe — Fish ball and vegetable casserole flavored with soy sauce

A. Mince **3/4 lb. of any boneless white fish** and grind into a paste using a mortar and pestle. In a separate bowl, mix with **1 Tbsp. *miso*, 1 Tbsp. *shoyu*, 1 Tbsp. flour,** and **1/2 oz. finely chopped ginger.** Roll into bite-size balls.

B. Cut **3/4 lb. Chinese cabbage** into 2-inch sections, cut **1/2 lb. leeks** (white part only) into 2-inch matchstick slivers, thoroughly wash **1/4 lb. chrysanthemum** or **spinach leaves** and cut into 2-inch-long pieces. Soak and rough chop **1 oz. *wakame*.** You can also add **1/2 block *tofu*** and **1/2 package yam cake noodles.**

Fill a *donabe* 1/2 full with water and bring to a boil. Add the fish balls. Boil until *aku* appears. Remove *aku*. Add **1/2 cup *shoyu*, 4 Tbsp. *mirin*,** and **4 Tbsp. *sake*.** Just before second boil, add vegetables, *tofu*, and yam cake noodles and bring to a boil. Lower heat to very low to keep warm.

Individuals serve themselves.

■ Kaisen nabe — Seafood casserole flavored with soy sauce

A. Peel, de-vein, and remove the tails from **12 jumbo shrimp,** combine with **2 oz. shelled crab meat,** cut **1 medium salmon fillet** into bite sized pieces (with skin), rinse and drain **8 jumbo scallops,** separate **1 block hard *tofu*** into bite-size pieces with chopsticks. Rub **1 package of yam cake** noodles with salted hands, rinse, and drain. Cut **12 slender bamboo shoots** (canned is fine) into 2-inch-long sections and then into matchstick slivers. Remove the stems from **one handful of mushrooms,** any kind, and tear into bite-size pieces with your fingers. Cut **1/2 lb. leeks** (white part only) into 2-inch-long sections and then into matchstick slivers lengthwise. Wash **1/4 lb. chrysanthemum leaves** and cut into 2-inch-long sections.

B. Fill a *donabe* 1/2 full with water and bring to a boil.

Add seafood and bring to a second boil. Remove *aku*. Add **1/2 cup *shoyu*, 4 Tbsp. *mirin*, 4 Tbsp. *sake*,** and again bring to a boil. Add vegetables, *tofu*, and yam cake. As you add each ingredient, place it in the front of the pot and gently push to the back and add more to create an attractive arrangement. Do not add all of each ingredient.

C. Bring again to a boil, then reduce heat to low to keep warm. Individuals serve themselves. When an ingredient is eaten, replace it with more of the same. The amounts given for each ingredient are general guidelines; adjust to suit your own tastes.

Nabemono with a miso flavor base

■ Butaniku or toriniku nabe — Pork or chicken and vegetable casserole flavored with miso

A. Thinly slice **3/4 lb. pork** or **3/4 lb. chicken,** skinned and deboned. Peel and shave **1/4 lb. burdock.** Soak for 15 minutes and remove *aku.* Tear **1/2 block yam cake** into bite-size pieces with your fingers. Rub with salted hands and rinse thoroughly. Peel **1/2 lb. potato** and **3 oz. carrots,** cut both into bite-size pieces and trim with a rolling cut. Peel **1/4 lb.** *daikon,* shave into large shavings. Cut **one medium onion** in half, and each half into bite-size pieces.

B. In a *donabe,* saute pork or chicken and drained burdock in **5 Tbsp. sesame oil** over high heat until the meat changes color. Gently push the meat and burdock to the side and add **1/2 block hard** *tofu,* separated into bite-size pieces with chopsticks. Be careful not to crumble it. Saute 3 to 4 minutes. Add water to fill pot 1/2 full and continue cooking until *aku* rises. Remove *aku.* When it boils again, add other *gu* ingredients in sections.

C. In a separate bowl, combine **4 Tbsp.** *sake,* **4 Tbsp.** *mirin,* **1 Tbsp. sugar, 1/3 cup** *miso,* and **a little juice from the** *donabe.* When the potatoes are soft add the mixture to the *donabe* a little at a time to taste. Reduce heat to low to keep warm. Individuals serve themselves.

■ Gyuniku nabe — Beef and vegetable casserole flavored with miso

A. Thin slice **1 lb. beef.** Peel and shave **1/4 lb. burdock** then soak for 15 minutes and remove *aku.* Tear **1/2 block yam cake** into bite-size pieces with your fingers. Rub with salted hands and rinse thoroughly. Peel **1/2 lb. potato** and **3 oz. carrots** and cut both into bite-size pieces and trim with a rolling cut. Peel and shave **1/4 lb.** *daikon* into large shavings. Halve **one medium onion** and cut each half into bite-size pieces.

B. In *donabe,* saute beef in **3 Tbsp. sesame oil** over high heat for 2 to 3 minutes. Fill the pot half full with water and bring to a boil. Remove *aku.* In a separate bowl, combine **4 Tbsp.** *sake,* **4 Tbsp.** *mirin,* **1 Tbsp. sugar, 1/2 cup** *miso* and **a little juice from the** *donabe.* Add to the *donabe* a little at a time to suit your taste.

C. Just before reaching second boil, add *tofu,* yam cake, and vegetables. Reduce heat to low to keep warm. Individuals serve themselves. Garnish with **seven-taste pepper** to taste.

- Kaisen nabe — Seafood casserole flavored with miso

  A. Cut **1 salmon fillet** with skin (scales removed) into bite-size pieces. Remove the shells from **16 jumbo shrimp,** leaving the tails intact. Lightly rinse **8 jumbo scallops** and drain. Soak **1/2 oz. dried black mushrooms, 1/2 oz. *wakame*,** and **1/2 oz. *sukikombu*** until soft. Peel and shave **1/4 lb. burdock** then soak for 15 minutes and remove aku. Tear **1/2 block yam cake** into bite-size pieces with your fingers. Rub with salted hands and rinse thoroughly. Peel **1/2 lb. potato** and **3 oz. carrots,** cut both into bite-size pieces and trim with a rolling cut. Peel **1/4 lb. *daikon*** and shave into large shavings. Halve **one medium onion,** and cut each half into bite-size pieces.

  B. Fill a *donabe* 1/2 full with **kombu *dashijiru*.** (See *dashijiru* section in Chapter 3) and bring to a boil. In a separate bowl, mix **1/2 cup *sake*, 1 Tbsp. sugar,** and **1/2 cup *miso*** (premix with a small amount of juice from the pot to dissolve). Add to *donabe* to taste.

  C. Just before reaching a second boil, add salmon, shrimp, and scallops. Remove *aku* and add *tofu*, yam cake, and other vegetables. Add the sea vegetables last, and reduce heat to low to keep warm. Be careful not to overcook.

Nabemono with a rice wine lees flavor base

- Sake nabe — Salmon and vegetable casserole flavored with rice wine lees

  A. Cut **2 salmon fillets** with skin (scales removed) into bite-size pieces. Peel **2/3 lb. *daikon*** and cut horizontally into 1/2-inch slices (if large, halve and make half-moon cuts). In a separate pot, using the **water left from washing rice,** boil *daikon* for 10 minutes, drain, replace with fresh water and let soak until it is time to add to the *donabe,* then drain. Peel **3 oz. carrots** and slant cut into 2-inch sections. **Rub 1/2 package yam cake noodles** with salted hands, rinse thoroughly, drain, and rough chop. Remove the stems (and hard or dirty areas) from a **handful of *shimeji*** **mushrooms** and tear into bite-size sections. Wash **1/4 lb. chrysanthemum leaves** and cut into 2-inch-long pieces.

  B. In a *donabe* thoroughly mix **5 cups kombu *dashijiru*, 4 oz. rice wine lees,** and **3 oz. *miso*.** Add A, and bring to boil.

  Remove *aku* and reduce heat to low to keep warm. Individuals serve themselves.

■ Kaki nabe — Oyster and vegetable casserole flavored with rice wine lees

How to rinse oysters.

A. Grate **2 oz. *daikon*** and add to **1/2 gallon water.** Gently wash **1 lb. shelled oysters** in a strainer and drain. Peel **2/3 lb. *daikon*** and cut horizontally into 1/2-inch slices. (If large, cut into half-moon sections.) In a separate pot, using the **water left from washing rice,** boil *daikon* for 10 minutes. Drain and replace with fresh water. Let soak until it is time to add to the *donabe,* then drain.

Peel **3 oz. carrots,** cut into 2-inch sections, and slant-cut slice and boil separately until soft. Rub **1/2 package yam cake noodles** with salted hands, rinse thoroughly, drain, and rough chop. Remove the stems (and hard or dirty areas) from **a handful of *shimeji* mushrooms** and tear into bite-size sections. Wash **1/4 lb. chrysanthemum leaves** and cut into 2-inch-long pieces.

B. In a *donabe,* combine and mix **5 cups *kombu dashijiru,* 4 oz. rice wine lees,** and **3 oz. *miso.*** Heat on high to just before boiling. Add oysters, **1/2 block soft *tofu*** separated into bite-size pieces with chopsticks, and other *gu* ingredients. Bring to boil and remove *aku.* Reduce heat to low to keep warm. Individuals serve themselves.

Rice balls for nabemono.

Sukiyaki nabe — Casseroles cooked with little liquid

■ Gyuniku sukiyaki — Beef sukiyaki

A. Thinly slice **1 lb. beef pot roast.** Marinate in **2 Tbsp.** *sake* to tenderize for 15 minutes. Arrange decoratively on large platter **1/2 lb. slant-cut Japanese scallions** or **1/2 lb. leeks** (white part only), **1/4 lb. washed chrysanthemum leaves** cut into 2-inch-long pieces, **8** *shiitake* **mushrooms** soaked until soft and cut in half diagonally (save the water to use for cooking), **5 oz. yam cake noodles** rubbed with salted hands, rinsed thoroughly and drained, and **1/2 block** *yakidofu* (pan-fried *tofu*) or **1/2 block regular** *tofu,* cut into 1-inch cubes. Make sure all ingredients are drained completely.

B. In a small cooking pot, boil **1/2 cup** *shoyu,* **1/2 cup** *mirin,* and **3 Tbsp. sugar** over high heat. Turn off heat and let sit. This makes the *warishita* (cooking sauce).

C. Grease a 10-inch *sukiyaki* pan (or regular, flat cast-iron skillet) with fat from the beef. Add 1/2 of B's cooking sauce and bring to a boil. When boiling reduce heat to medium and cook 1/2 of the beef, laying each piece flat separately and cooking on both sides for 30 seconds. Be careful not to overcook. Remove each piece and place on a plate temporarily. Add the other half of the cooking sauce and return heat to high. Add yam cake noodles, *tofu,* and *shiitake* mushrooms and cook about 2 to 3 minutes until done.

Reduce heat to low to keep warm. Make a space in the pan and return the cooked beef. Just before serving, add chrysanthemum leaves for color.

Individuals serve themselves a little at a time. As they are enjoying the meal, the cooking liquids will be depleted or get too salty. Use the water from soaking the *shiitake* mushrooms in A to keep the *sukiyaki* moist and to control saltiness. As the meat is eaten, turn up the heat, add more and cook in the same way, and then reduce heat again to keep warm.

Traditionally, each individual is given a small bowl with **a beaten raw egg.** Dip a bite of the *sukiyaki* in the egg before eating. (This is optional.)

■ Butaniku sukiyaki — Pork sukiyaki

A. Thinly slice **1 lb. pork roast** as thin as possible. Marinate in **3 Tbsp. *sake*** for 10 minutes. Wash **4 or 5 cabbage leaves** and cut into 1-inch squares. Wash **1 handful *shimeji* mushrooms,** remove any stem section that is hard or dirty, and tear into bite-size pieces. Slant cut **1/2 lb. Japanese scallions** or **1/2 lb. leeks** (white parts only) lengthwise.

Rub **1/2 package yam cake noodles** with salted hands, rinse, and drain. Cut **1/2 block *yakidofu*** (pan-fried *tofu*) or regular *tofu* into 1-inch cubes. Wash **1/4 lb. chrysanthemum leaves** and cut into 2-inch-long pieces. Slant cut **1 rib celery** into 1/2-inch sections.

B. In a small cooking pot, quickly boil **1/2 cup *shoyu*, 3 Tbsp. *mirin*, 1 Tbsp. sugar, 2 Tbsp. *sake*** and turn off heat.

This makes the *warishita* (cooking sauce). Let sit.

C. Grease a 10-inch *sukiyaki* pan (or regular flat cast-iron skillet) with **vegetable oil** (spread evenly with a paper towel). Combine pork, *tofu*, yam cake noodles, and 1/2 of the *warishita* and bring to a boil. Remove *aku* and add vegetables. When it returns to a second boil, reduce heat to low to keep warm. In individual serving bowls, add **grated squeezed *daikon*** and a **squeeze of lemon.** Use this as a dip sauce for the *sukiyaki.*

D. The *sukiyaki* pan will not hold all of the ingredients at one time. As portions are eaten add more of the cooking sauce, meat, and vegetables and repeat heating instructions.

Make sure the pork is cooked thoroughly. **Umezuke** (pitted, pickled plum) can be ground and added to the *daikon* for a different-tasting dip sauce.

■ Hikiniku sukiyaki — Ground meat sukiyaki

A. Combine **1 lb. ground chicken, beef,** or **pork, 1 egg,** and a **few pinches of salt and pepper.** Shape into 4 patties.

B. Slant cut **1/2 lb. Japanese scallions** or **1/2 lb. leeks** (white part only). Wash **1/4 lb. chrysanthemum leaves** and cut into 2-inch-long pieces. Soak **8 *shiitake* mushrooms** until soft and cut in half diagonally (save the water to use for cooking). Rub **5 oz. yam cake noodles** with salted hands, rinse thoroughly, and drain. Cut **1/2 block *yakidofu* (pan-fried *tofu*)** or **regular *tofu*** into 1-inch cubes. Make sure all ingredients are drained completely. On a large platter, arrange decoratively in sections.

B. In a small cooking pot, quickly bring to a boil **1/2 cup *shoyu,* 1/2 cup *mirin,*** and **3 Tbsp. sugar.** Turn off heat and let sit.

This makes the *warishita* (cooking sauce).

C. Grease a 10-inch *sukiyaki* pan (or regular flat cast-iron skillet) with **vegetable oil.** (Spread evenly with a paper towel.) Add 1/2 of the *warishita* and bring to a boil. When boiling reduce heat to medium and cook the meat patties, remove *aku.* Add the other half of the *warishita* and return heat to high. Add yam cake noodles, *tofu, shiitake* mushrooms, scallions and cook 2 to 3 minutes until done. Reduce heat to low to keep warm. Just before serving, add chrysanthemum leaves for color.

Individuals serve themselves a little at a time. As they are eating, the cooking liquids will be depleted or get too salty. Use the water from soaking the *shiitake* mushrooms in A to keep the *sukiyaki* moist and to control saltiness.

This concludes the section on *nabemono* recipes. There are countless variations on these recipes depending on the location or season. I can tell what part of Japan a particular *nabemono* originated from and the season by simply looking at it. The amounts given for these recipes are generally for four people. Since individuals serve themselves, it is difficult to calculate how much someone might eat. If you prepare extra *gu* ingredients you might be prepared for an extra guest, or a guest with a large appetite. Garnishes are important to vary the tastes. Use your own creativity to make unusual and delicious varieties.

It is customary to serve *nabemono* with *sake.* The two go hand in hand. If you do not drink, this might not interest you, but *sake* deserves a few pages of explanation. I have been fairly well acquainted with the *sake* of Japan over my lifetime.

When I was 16, I was a live-in student at a *dojo* (school, in this case a school of the martial art, Aikido). My first experiences with alcoholic beverages came during this time. My mid-twenties was when I "indulged" the most. I look back now and, like most people my age, I am amazed that I could consume that much *sake.*

Those days were long ago. Today if I try my best, two or three beers or 1 or 2 small *sake* pots is all I am able to drink. My body has already "graduated" from alcoholic beverages.

There is a great deal of media attention focused on the problems related to alcohol consumption. Twice every year for two or three months I take a "*sake* vacation." I drink no alcohol at all. For a special occasion I can still enjoy *sake* without feeling guilty, however. It is important to me that I control alcohol rather than the reverse. When I do drink I eat foods high in protein. I enjoy *sake* brought to me as gifts from friends and businessmen visiting from Japan. In Japan, *sake* is ranked and tested stringently. *Sake* is ranked by quality: labeled *ikkyu*, *nikkyu*, *tokkyu*, or *chotokkyu*, meaning 2nd, 1st, top, and special blend.

All *sake* is tested for percentage of alcohol content in the laboratory and then graded by *sake* tasters for smell, taste, and color. A Japanese "*sake* testing" is called a *kikizake*, where a panel of judges rates *sake*, taking only one sip to analyze. Maybe you have seen white *sake* cups with two rings lining the bottom of the inside of the cup. These are called *janome*. With these cups the judges tasting the *sake* can test the color and viscosity by noting the effect the *sake* has on the movement of the lines in the bottom of the cup.

In Japanese restaurants in the United States, it is very popular to serve hot *sake*. If heated slowly, hot *sake* is delicious. Heating the *sake* indiscriminately can have adverse effects.

I have noticed that many restaurants use hot *sake* machines to heat the *sake*. It reminds me of an office hot-and-cold water dispenser! A large bottle of *sake* is turned upside down and poured into the dispenser to be heated. One must remember that *sake* is a very delicate creation that requires 45 to 60 days to develop. The usual alcohol percentage is 7 to 9%. If you are going to heat *sake*, it is better to fill a small *sake* pot or

tokkuri (serving container) and place the pot gently into a sauce pan or kettle of boiling water. When you place the *sake* pot in the pan of boiling water you will hear a sound because the pot is hollowed out underneath.

When *sake* is heated it boils up quickly, so fill the *sake* pot to a inch below the rim, so it will not boil over. Once the *sake* is hot, if you have filled it too full it will be too hot to pick up and pour. The best temperature to serve *sake* is about the same temperature as the human body temperature. This is called *hitohada*. If the *sake* is served cooler than this temperature it is called *nurukan*.

A standard small *sake* pot contains about 6 oz., which is counted in Japanese as one "*go*" or *ichigo*. Ten *go* equals 1.8 liters, which is called *issho*. This is the standard large-sized bottle available at the liquor store. To heat, bring water to a boil in a sauce pan over high heat and place the *sake* pot into the sauce pan just before it reaches a boil. As the *sake* is heating, the air trapped underneath the raised bottom of the container will escape in a bubble. After the bubble escapes, boil for 1 minute. This should result in the *sake* being heated to the correct *hitohada* temperature.

To heat the *sake* to a temperature higher than *hitohada* is called *atsukan* or very hot *sake*. Some people do prefer to drink their *sake* very hot. When *sake* is heated this hot it is difficult to hold the cup in your hand. In my opinion you can lose a lot of the *sake* taste as well. You can heat *sake* in the microwave but sometimes it heats unevenly, where the neck of the *sake* pot is too hot to touch while the bottom is still cold.

If you are having a large party you can place the entire 1.8-litre bottle open into a larger pot of boiling water to heat. As long as all of the *sake* is served within 30 minutes, this will work. Once *sake* has been heated and cooled it is called *kanzamashi*. In this state the alcohol has dissipated and is no longer suited for drinking. It can be used for a few days for cooking.

Japanese Country Cooking   233

When ordering *sake* at a restaurant, check to make sure the *sake* pot has been filled to almost full, and make sure water has not been added. When the waitress removes the *sake* pot from your table, make sure it is empty. When enjoying *sake,* the elders' advice is to always accompany *sake* with food or it will "poison" you. Japanese *sake* bars always offer a wide variety of appetizers.

There are special brands of *sake* brewed to drink chilled. Most brands are usually designed to drink warm although they are sometimes drunk cold or at room temperature during festivals or special events. During an exciting event, match, or festival many of the Japanese young people have found unheated *sake* to be a smooth refreshment, only to be overcome by the effects of too much consumption. The Japanese elders have a saying, "Cold *sake* and parents' lectures work as lessons only after partaking." Good quality *sake*, enjoyed while communicating with friends, and accompanied by delicious foods of the season, is a most happy way to enjoy both company and the fruits of the earth.

Donburimono

The word *donburi* translates as a large dish or bowl shaped like, only larger than, a rice bowl. *Donburimono* are dishes served in a *donburi* bowl filled with rice and covered with a mixture of cooked ingredients. If you have all the ingredients, *donburimono* can be made in 10 minutes. One *donburi* dish and a bowl of soup makes up a healthy meal. At Nippon Kan *donburimono* is popular among our students after a hard practice.

Donburimono are prevalent on the menus in Japanese *shokudo* (neighborhood restaurants). There are fast-food chains in Japan that specialize in *donburimono*. Some of these restaurants concentrate on quality while others focus on speed and price. When I was a student, we referred to the latter's beef *donburi* as rubber *donburi*. I have been saddened to see some of these fast-food chains make their way to the United States. This is not a good representation of Japanese fast-but-healthful *donburimono*. *Donburi*-style cooking is very simple, but if good quality ingredients are used and care is taken, one can prepare a delicious meal.

A *donburi* bowl is deeper and larger in shape than a Japanese rice or soup bowl. If you do not have any *donburi* bowls you can serve *donburimono* on a plate. If you use a plate, one suggestion might be to fill one side of the plate with rice and lay the topping on the other side. Serve with a salad on the side.

To make *donburimono* it is important to understand the ratio between topping and rice, and how to control the temperature while cooking the topping. With this in mind, *donburimono* is easy to prepare.

In Japanese restaurants in the United States, I have seen *donburimono* priced from $2.50 to $7 to $10. Something is amiss. For the recipies in this book, the price-per-person for *donburi* ingredients is between 50 and 75 cents. I also feel the ingredients described in this book are of better quality than the ones used in some overpriced Japanese restaurants.

Donburimono Recipes
(Each recipe serves 4 people.)

(Note that plates can be substituted for *donburi* bowls in all of these recipes.)

■ Tomago don — Rice bowl with egg and onion topping

    A. Peel **1/2 lb. onion,** halve, and slice thin. In a separate bowl beat **4 eggs** thoroughly.

    B. In a 10- to 12-inch flat-bottomed skillet combine **3/4 cup *dashijiru*, 4 Tbsp. *mirin*, 4 Tbsp. *shoyu*** and heat over high heat. Just before boiling, add onion and cook for 3 minutes.

    Reduce heat to low and pour in beaten eggs. Cover and cook until egg is half cooked. Turn off heat and let sit covered for 1 to 2 minutes.

    C. In 4 *donburi* bowls, add 1 serving of rice to each. Divide the topping into 4 sections and place one portion on each rice bowl. Garnish with **chopped *nori*.**

■ Oyako don — Rice bowl with chicken and egg topping

    A. Skin and debone **3/4 lb. chicken** and cut into bite-size pieces. Peel **1/2 lb. onion,** halve, and slice thin. Peel **1/2 cup carrots** and sliver with a grater. Choose a small amount of any green vegetable, such as broccoli, zucchini, snow peas, or green beans for color balance. Cut into bite-size pieces.

    B. In a 10- to 12-inch flat-bottomed skillet combine **3/4 cup *dashijiru*, 4 Tbsp. *mirin*, 4 Tbsp. *shoyu*** and heat over high heat until just before boiling. Add chicken and cook until *aku* rises. Remove *aku*. Add onions and continue to cook.

    When chicken is done, reduce heat to low and pour in **4 beaten eggs.** Sprinkle with carrots and green vegetables and cover. When the egg is half cooked, turn off heat and let sit covered for 1 to 2 minutes.

    C. In 4 *donburi* bowls, add 1 serving of rice to each. Divide the topping into 4 sections and place one portion on each rice bowl. Garnish with **chopped *nori*.**

■ Niku don — Rice bowl with sliced meat topping

A. Thinly slice **3/4 lb. pork roast** or **beef roast**. Peel **1/2 lb. onion** and slice thin. Peel **1/2 cup carrots** and sliver with a grater. Choose a small amount of any green vegetable such as **broccoli, zucchini, snow peas,** or **green beans** for color balance. Cut into bite-sized pieces. Cut **1/2 oz. ginger** into matchstick slivers.

B. In a heated 10- to 12-inch flat-bottomed skillet, saute ginger in **1 Tbsp. sesame oil** for 1 to 2 minutes. Add meat and continue to saute.

C. When meat changes color, add **1/2 cup** *dashijiru,* **4 Tbsp.** *mirin,* **1 tsp. sugar, 4 Tbsp.** *shoyu,* carrots, and green vegetables. If you wish, you can also add **1/3 block** *tofu.*

Cook 3 to 4 minutes over low heat.

Divide and serve over individual bowls of rice. This is called *sukiyaki donburi.* If you wish add **4 beaten eggs.** This is called *tanin don.* Garnish with **chopped** *nori* to taste.

■ Ten don — Rice bowl with tempura topping

A. **See** *Agemono* **section for** *tempura* **recipes, or use leftover** *tempura* (remember to store leftover *tempura* by wrapping in paper towel and then plastic wrap, before placing in the refrigerator). **A few pieces per serving will do.**

B. In a 10- to 12-inch flat-bottomed skillet boil **1/2 cup** *shiitake dashijiru,* **4 Tbsp.** *mirin,* **3 Tbsp.** *shoyu,* and **1 tsp. sugar** over high heat. Separate the *tempura* into 4 equal portions. Add the *tempura.*

C. Bring to a second boil. Beat **4 eggs** and pour over mixture. Turn heat to low, cover and cook until egg is half cooked. Turn off heat. Let sit covered for 1 to 2 minutes.

Divide into equal portions and serve over 4 individual bowls of rice. Garnish with **seven-taste pepper, grated squeezed** *daikon,* and/or **chopped** *nori* to taste.

■ Katsu don — Rice bowl with a deep-fried pork cutlet topping

A. Debone and score the tendons of **4 medium-sized pork chops.**

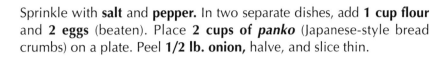

Sprinkle with **salt** and **pepper.** In two separate dishes, add **1 cup flour** and **2 eggs** (beaten). Place **2 cups of *panko*** (Japanese-style bread crumbs) on a plate. Peel **1/2 lb. onion,** halve, and slice thin.

Salt and pepper...

B. In a heavy, deep skillet heat **2 inches of vegetable oil** over high heat to 230° Fahrenheit. Roll pork chops individually in flour and tap off excess. Then dip in egg, press firmly in *panko* and shake off excess. Carefully place into oil and fry until golden brown on both sides. Check to see if the inside is done by making a small slice with a knife. Drain on paper towel.

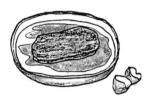

...dip in beaten egg...

C. In a 10- to 12-inch flat-bottomed skillet, bring **1 cup *dashijiru*** and onion to a boil and continue to cook for 2 to 3 minutes. Add **4 Tbsp. *shoyu,* 4 Tbsp. *mirin,*** and bring to a second boil. Slant-cut slice the pork cutlets into 1/2-inch-wide sections and gently place in the pan. Pour **4 beaten eggs** over the pork. Reduce heat. Cover and cook until the egg is half cooked. Turn off heat and let sit covered for 1 to 2 minutes. Divide into equal portions and serve over 4 individual bowls of rice. Garnish with **chopped *nori*** to taste.

...coat in flour...

...press into breadcrumbs...

...deep fry.

Closing

I have tried to make this book interesting for anyone to read, not only those whose lifestyles and interests revolve around the culinary arts.

The Japanese food boom in the United States has caused lots of Japanese restaurants to spring up. To enjoy the foods served in these restaurants it is important to understand the long history behind each recipe. It is important to understand the significance food has from the Japanese way of thinking.

My goal has been to help you obtain a deeper understanding of the Japanese heart and soul. The vehicle for understanding has been an examination of the relationship between the people and their original native cuisine.

Cookbooks are usually filled with beautiful color photographs and recipes. I realize everyone is more familiar with cookbooks that follow this form. This book is made of my memories, my tastes, and the Japanese spirit of cooking.

It has been important for me to have shared what I have learned and experienced about the deep-rooted culture of the people of Japan.

It was difficult to accomplish this and retain a standard cookbook format.

It was only 45 years ago when Japan had no food and people survived by eating potato vines. As a child, I can remember the government rationing fish and vegetables. These are personal memories of times that were not so long ago.

Japan's economy has, of course, developed dramatically. You can read something about Japan in the papers or see something on television every day. The story behind this economic and technological growth lies with the common people, especially the farmers, fishermen, and mountain people. We cannot forget the power and creativity of these people who have built the foundation.

There are many beautifully done, colorfully illustrated books on Japan that depict a world filled with awe-inspiring temples, shrines, castles, and gardens. Museums display wonderful artifacts, beautiful swords, furniture, art, and *kimonos.* These artifacts are the products of the ingenuity and diligence of the craftsmen.

Modern Tokyo is a mega-metropolis that stands in part as a monument to the work of the rural children who came to build a new life in the city. Most businesses are staffed by people from outlying areas.

The daily foods of these farmers, craftsmen, and urban pioneers is the subject of this book. If we delve into the culture of their foods we have a chance to understand them in a new way. I have written this book as a vehicle for understanding. The businessman from Japan sitting across from you at the conference table might not seem so different if you understand what he likes for breakfast.

I am not a professional nutritionist or a famous chef. I never use measuring cups when I cook. I create tastes by feel and instinct. The recipe section was certainly a challenge! Tastes can vary widely depending on subtle changes in the ingredients and brands you use. You need to use your own taste as the final guide.

In order to publish this book, it first had to be translated into English. Aikido Nippon Kan staff member, Emily Busch, a very busy jewelry designer and goldsmith, has donated a great deal of time to this project. She has had experience living in rural Japan and has traveled extensively throughout Southeast Asia. Her having lived a true native lifestyle has been very valuable in translating the heart of the concepts in this book. This book's completion is largely due to her efforts, and I wish to thank Emily from my heart.

After the initial draft left my hands, many people have helped to make this book a reality. I have a great deal of respect for the editorial and technical staff who have taken time from their busy professional careers to take on this major undertaking. I know it has not been an easy task to try to understand the products, techniques, and ideologies involved in traditional Japanese country cooking. Many thanks to all.

Special thanks to the editors John Cruise and Jeff Gregory, to the technical advisor Howard Rabinowitz, to assistants Paul Roebuck, Marvin Oderberg, Celeste Velasquez, Chris Endres, Matt Davis, Diane Burkhardt, Art Kaufmann, and to Nippon Kan's American and Japanese staff, especially Nobu Fukushima, Yutaka Kikuchi, and Takashi Baba.

More information about Japanese country cooking, its foods, utensils, and folklore is available through our Domo Products newsletter. Please write to: Domo Products, P.O. Box 4487, Denver, CO 80204.

About the Lake Ogawara Folk Art Museum and its founder Yukio Sugimoto

Name of museum: Ogawarako Minzoku Hakubutsukan

Founded by: Mr. Yukio Sugimoto

Officially opened: August 28, 1961

Location: Furumagi, Misawa City, Aomori Prefecture, Japan

Displays: Over 15,000 pieces of folk arts and crafts have been collected from the southern end of northeastern Japan, including 5,000 government-certified national cultural assets.

The Lake Ogawara Folk Art museum is a private foundation that has been authorized and approved by the Japanese Ministry of Education.

The founder, Mr. Yukio Sugimoto, was born in 1912 in the Shizuoka Prefecture. Mr. Sugimoto began his boyhood apprenticeship in 1927 under Mr. H. Eiichi Shibusawa, then a very prominent leader in finance and the founder of Japan's first national bank. After Mr. Shibusawa's, death, Mr. Sugimoto became the secretary of his former employer's grandson, Keizo Shibusawa who was the President of the Bank of Japan during World War II.

After the war Mr. Shibusawa became Japan's Minister of Finance. At Mr. Shibusawa's request, Mr. Sugimoto left for Aomori Prefecture in 1946 to take managerial control of the extensive Shibusawa ranch located there. Mr. Sugimoto was to maintain the extensive holdings while protecting and promoting the local culture. Early on he began to collect the artifacts which formed the foundation of the museum which was to follow some 15 years later.

Mr. Yukio Sugimoto finishing a scroll for Denver's Nippon Kan.

Today the museum covers a 50-acre area called Saigyo Park and the Komaki Hot Springs resort. The park is visited by more than 800,000 people each year, making it the largest historically preserved center in southern northeastern Japan. Mr. Sugimoto is also the owner of the Lake Towada National Park Science Museum and Youth Hostel.

I worked under Mr. Sugimoto for about four years. The inspiration for the operations and activities of Denver Nippon Kan came directly from experiences shared with Mr. Sugimoto.

I am very grateful to him and am glad to have this opportunity to thank him publicly.

Thank you!

Gaku Homma

Glossary/Index

Recipe Index